1440186

Co
11/7/07

D1566399

PERSONAL AUTONOMY IN SOCIETY

People are socially situated amid complex relations with other people and are bound by interpersonal frameworks having significant influence upon their lives. These facts have implications for their autonomy. Challenging many of the currently accepted conceptions of autonomy and of how autonomy is valued, Oshana develops a 'social-relational' account of autonomy, or self-governance, as a condition of persons that is largely constituted by a person's relations with other people and by the absence of certain social relations. She denies that command over one's motives and the freedom to realize one's will are sufficient to secure the kind of command over one's life that autonomy requires, and argues against psychological, procedural, and content neutral accounts of autonomy.

Oshana embraces the idea that her account is 'perfectionist' in a sense, and argues that ultimately our commitment to autonomy is defeasible, but she maintains that a social-relational account best captures what we value about autonomy and best serves the various ends for which the concept of autonomy is employed.

Personal Autonomy in Society

MARINA OSHANA
University of Florida, USA

ASHGATE

Published by
Ashgate Publishing Limited
Gower House
Croft Road
Aldershot
Hampshire GU11 3HR
England

Ashgate Publishing Company
Suite 420
101 Cherry Street
Burlington, VT 05401-4405
USA

Ashgate website: http://www.ashgate.com

British Library Cataloguing in Publication Data
Oshana, Marina
Personal autonomy in society
1.Autonomy (Psychology) 2.Autonomy (Philosophy)
I.Title
155.2'5

Library of Congress Cataloging-in-Publication Data
Oshana, Marina
Personal autonomy in society / Marina Oshana.
    p. cm.
  Includes bibliographical references and index.
  ISBN 0-7546-5670-5 (hardback : alk. paper)
    1. Autonomy (Philosophy) I. Title.

  B808.67.O84 2006
  126–dc22

2006008838

ISBN-13: 978-0-7546-5670-8
ISBN-10: 0-7546-5670-5

Printed and bound in Great Britain by MPG Books Ltd. Bodmin, Cornwall.

Contents

Preface

The concept of autonomy has occupied a principal place in moral, legal, and political debate for centuries, particularly in the west. The idea that competent adult persons are entitled to govern themselves is the ideal around which debate about the appropriate configuration of social, political, and legal institutions and practices occurs. As early as ancient Rome and reaching fevered pitch in the writings of persons such as Charles-Louis de Secondat (Baron de Montesquieu), John Locke, Thomas Paine, and Thomas Jefferson, the ideal of autonomy served as the compass by which political argument about the status of colonists in America and the rights of the propertyless was oriented. More generally and, perhaps, more centrally with respect to the task of this book, the concept of autonomy has figured importantly within philosophical discussions of agency.

An autonomous person is an agent—one who directs or determines the course of her own life and who is positioned to assume the costs and the benefits of her choices. Autonomy thus establishes the descriptive standard for what is assumed distinctive of human beings. But autonomy serves as a prescriptive standard as well, for it sets norms for the proper treatment of persons. One who is able to decide the direction of her life is to be respected for this ability. It is prima facie impermissible to interfere with an individual's right of autonomy where the individual is respectful of that right in others. Someone who is self-governing faces minimal interference in the formation and execution of her actions and choices, and it is proper that interferences be kept to a minimum.

The past twenty-five years have witnessed an increased interest in the concept of personal autonomy. Within the recognized categories of autonomy as a political, a moral, and a personal ideal attempts have been made to come to terms with the distinct ideas of autonomous agents, autonomous lives, autonomous action, autonomous desires, and autonomous choice. This, in turn, has spawned debate about various qualities claimed as central to an adequate understanding of autonomy—qualities such as rationality, self-control, authenticity, and identification—as well as a focused exploration of the skills required for living in step with one's authentic self. Given the multifaceted nature of the concept of autonomy and the difficulties this raises for analysis of the concept, no one has (to my knowledge, at any rate) attempted to produce a precise taxonomy of autonomy in its many guises. That task would be daunting, and probably futile. Certainly, I have no intention of embarking on such an enterprise in this book. I intend to follow other writers who have offered analyses of autonomy that acknowledge the complexity of the concept. Such efforts to shed light on the concept of autonomy have borne fruit.

The most recent conceptual analyses break new ground in a number of ways. Most obviously, recent interest does not limit focus to the conception of autonomy central to Kantian moral philosophy. Rather, the model of autonomy operating at the heart of current theoretical debate is for the most part broadly neo-Humean. The central idea of the neo-Humean approach is personal autonomy is a function of the relation a person stands in with respect to those of her desires or pro-attitudes that bear on how she wants to live. There is, of course, considerable debate about just what a neo-Humean model of autonomy requires and what it captures about the autonomous personality that Kantian models have overlooked. In Chapter 2 some of these disagreements will present themselves. But there is agreement, too. It is undeniable that, once detached from the narrowly tailored focus on rationality and morality proper to Kant's work, the concept of autonomy reveals a rich, multifaceted, if not perspicuous character. Arguably, too, autonomy loses its otherworldly character and takes on a more naturalistic cast once it is set free from its Kantian trappings.

The task of this book is to offer a decidedly worldly, naturalistic interpretation of personal autonomy. However, the approach I shall take will not follow the path of the neo-Humean. The theory of autonomy advanced in this book is significantly different from both neo-Humean and Kantian models. My interest is in the concept of autonomy as a practical ideal. By this I mean I am concerned to bring to light the nature and function of autonomy, and the conditions of its existence, within the daily lives of its subjects. I think neither neo-Humean nor Kantian models can do this, but I will not argue directly against these models. I will, however, argue that recent attempts to unveil autonomy—particularly attempts that are neo-Humean in character—are misguided in two important respects.

The first and most pressing problem of such accounts is that they too readily construe autonomy as a phenomenon predicated on the etiology and occurrent state of a person's affective and conative psychology. As a result, insufficient attention is paid to autonomy as a state constituted by social and relational phenomena. While there have been gestures in the direction of illuminating the role played by environmental factors in facilitating the psychology of potentially autonomous agents, the possibility that environmental factors—things external to the agent—play an essential compositional role in autonomous agency has not been taken seriously. The focus remains on personal psychology as the locus of philosophical concern about autonomous agency. The second error or, better, trend with which I take issue is that the concept of autonomy is too readily and, often, uncritically paired with the concept of responsible agency. Increasing attention has turned to the central role played by autonomy in compatibilist analyses of moral responsibility. The result is that questions in philosophy about agent responsibility—for example, can moral responsibility coexist with an absence of alternate possibilities?—are taken to inform us of what would be true of autonomous persons as well. While autonomy may well play a central role in explanations of free, responsible agency, the phenomena are distinct and the conditions for each differ. Chapters 6 and 7 pick up these issues.

Chapter 1 begins with a look at what we are aiming at: a proposal consisting of general, arguably non-controversial thoughts about what it means to be personally autonomous. I think these intuitions will be accepted by those who propose quite different accounts of autonomy from my own, and I will employ them throughout this paper. The working definition of autonomy supplied by these intuitions will be refined by examining the distinction between the capacity for personal autonomy and the condition of personal autonomy. The concept will be crystallized to a still greater degree by contrasting personal or agent autonomy with the phenomena of moral autonomy and political autonomy. The level of discussion will be quite general. The aim of Chapter 1 is to familiarize the reader with the idea of autonomy by briefly surveying the philosophical legacy of that idea.

The approach to autonomy at the forefront of recent discussion is largely neo-Humean, but to avoid association with a particular historical figure and ideology they are better called "psychological authenticity accounts," or "proceduralist" accounts. Variants of this view, which are examined in Chapter 2, share the conviction that autonomy is a state of persons that is preserved within, and in virtue of, what has been metaphorically described as the inner citadel. The metaphor of an inner fortress is intended to characterize a center of agency that is authentic of the individual, a center in virtue of which the individual's agency is manifest and by whose lights the individual's sovereignty and integrity are protected against assault by entities that oppose, endanger, or threaten to compromise it. At times the metaphor is intended to describe some aspect of the individual such as the "authentic self" in virtue of which this guarantee is forthcoming.

There is certainly disagreement among those who tout autonomy as a psychological phenomenon. Some, for example, claim autonomy to be an ahistorical concept while others locate the nucleus of autonomy in the psychic etiology of the individual. But there is more agreement. One organizing theme of such theories is that the sort of freedom or independence lies at the heart of autonomous agency is *procedural* rather than *substantive*. These terms are technical and will be explored in Chapter 2. Briefly, the idea is that autonomy is entirely a function of ensuring that the principles, preferences, and values by which a person's choices and actions are governed have been authenticated or adopted by the person under suitably reflective conditions as her own. According to psychological authenticity accounts, it is not necessary that the principles, preferences, and values, chosen social roles and experiences of a person originate within specific content-laden contexts rather than others if the person is to be self-governing. The alleged advantage of psychological authenticity accounts is their value-neutrality. By importing no requirements about the choices, desires, social roles and social arrangements suitable for autonomy, psychologistic accounts are said to be better equipped to comport with a multiplicity of life-styles. The exegetical portions of Chapter 2 will be familiar ground to those who have followed debates about autonomy, free agency, and responsible agency that have mushroomed in the wake of work by Harry Frankfurt and by Gerald Dworkin. Because their work has been so much the topic of discussion, sections of Chapter 2 will be familiar to many readers. However, I hope the critical comments I provide regarding their analyses of autonomy and the plethora of analyses spawned in their wake will be fresh enough to capture the interest of even the well-acquainted reader.

In Chapter 3 I offer an alternative to these approaches. My objective is to defend a social-relational conception of personal autonomy or self-governance. A social-relational conception construes autonomy as a condition of persons constituted by the social relations people find themselves in or the absence of certain social relations.[1] According to psychologistic theories, people who share the same psychology and same psychological history are, *ipso facto*, equally autonomous (or nonautonomous). By contrast, an social-relational theory such as I offer denies that personal autonomy is a condition that supervenes on occurrent dispositional states, psychological states, and pro-attitudes of the individual, or the history of these states, alone. The emphasis of the discussion is on what, generally, constitutes being an autonomous person and on what, generally, autonomous living calls for as opposed to what constitutes autonomous preference and choice. Chapter 3 introduces the social-relational account with a series of case studies. Chapter 4 fine-tunes the model by exploring in some detail the conditions the model mandates and by introducing the implications of these conditions for the philosophical debate and for social science.

The account I advance has not been met without challenge. The task of Chapter 5 is to consider, and answer, the more pressing objections. Among these is the concern that the account I advance is inappropriately perfectionist, with the effect of denying too many competent adults the prerogative of autonomous agency. Particular attention is paid to the charge that the social-relational account of autonomy readily invites paternalism. Critics charge that the requirements of social-relational accounts are excessive and that as a consequence autonomy is robbed of practical effect as well as of its claim to value neutrality. Moreover, it is alleged that the account limits the class of person we call autonomous and subsequently diminishes the equal moral and political standing of adult persons so essential to liberal ideology. I do not think these criticisms stand. To deny personal autonomy of an adult is not to deny a capacity for or a right to moral or political self-government, nor for fair moral and political representation. Not every constraint curtails autonomy, nor does every perfectionist project constitute an impermissible encroachment of autonomy. Moreover, autonomy is not the sole and overarching value. Our commitment to autonomy is at best a defeasible commitment.

Chapter 6 turns to a consideration of autonomy's value. I examine the kind of value autonomy is believed to have and how this value fares when confronted with the challenge of meeting competing and, on occasion, incompatible goods. I note that there are different ways of valuing autonomy—autonomy may be prized for its usefulness as a means to achieving other desired goods such as respect, or it may be

---

1   The fact that autonomy is a phenomenon that is best understood relationally does not mean that a person can only be autonomous in an interpersonal context. People can, of course, oversee their choices and direct their lives when distant from others; a Robinson Crusoe, for example, who has never interacted with others could be described as autonomous. But Crusoe's autonomy would still be a matter of his not being irremediably subservient, and the like. The unfortunate Friday, by contrast, lacks autonomy. See Daniel Defoe, *Robinson Crusoe* (New York, 2001).

valued because it is an elemental component of the developed human personality. Autonomy can have different value for different individuals or cultures. I deny that autonomy is of agent-relative value only, or even primarily, while conceding that the question of when autonomy should be defended and when its absence give us little cause for lament may be one that depends upon the value perspective of the agent, or one for which no decisive answer can be given.

Chapter 7 turns to metaphysics, and addresses the kind of freedom autonomy requires. A space is carved between autonomy and other "freedom" concepts such as negative and positive liberty, self-creation, and free will. I argue that autonomy is essentially agnostic with respect to the thorny issues of causal determinism and human free agency. Chapter 8 concludes with a summary of the discussion, focusing attention on the nexus between personal autonomy and moral responsibility.

My interest in this topic began with the PhD thesis I wrote, many moons ago, at the University of California at Davis. I owe my greatest intellectual debt to my dissertation supervisor, John Martin Fischer, whose critical eye and encouragement never flagged. John continues to influence my work, and I am grateful for his friendship and unabated intellectual generosity. James Stacey Taylor somehow found the time in his busy life to read carefully a first draft of the entire manuscript, and offered a wealth of helpful comments. I am much indebted to him. David Copp patiently read through the portions of the manuscript I found most dissatisfying and the editorial suggestions he made helped immeasurably. I have also benefited from discussion with him over the years on my concerns about autonomy. A number of people read chapters or sections of the book in their various incarnations. I thank Paul Benson, Michael Bratman, John Christman, Ishtiyaque Haji, Don Hubin, Ellen Frankel Paul, Tony Roy, Stephen Darwall, Kirk Ludwig, John Santiago, Michael Wedin, Gene Witmer, the late Richard Wollheim, Sara Worley, audiences at the conference on Reasonably Autonomous Persons: Rationality, Neutrality, and the Self, at the University of Missouri, St. Louis in March, 1999; at the conference on Autonomy sponsored by the Social Philosophy and Policy Center at Bowling Green State University in April, 2002; at the University of Minnesota, Morris; members of the Ohio Reading Group in Ethics; participants at the Third Conference on Moral Philosophy and Practical Reason, June 2003, Geneva, Switzerland (especially Stephen Darwall, who commented on a version of Chapter 6); and members of the University of Florida philosophy discussion group (Gator PhED). Needless to say, none bears responsibility for whatever problems persist herein.

On a personal level, I owe much to my cats (Négro and Anaximander of late, V.I. Warshawski, Levi Stubbs, and Bob of present) for their unfaltering companionship. They give me boundless joy and bring the importance of philosophical scholarship into perspective. I owe most to David Copp. He has helped make my life a rich and happy one, marked by ample autonomy and ample support.

M.O.
Gainesville, Florida, U.S.A.

Acknowledgments

Portions of this book are based on previously published journal or anthology articles. Chapter 1 includes discussion from "Autonomy Naturalized," *Midwest Studies in Philosophy*, 9 (Minneapolis: University of Minnesota, Winter 1994): 76–94. Chapters 3 and 4 draw on "Personal Autonomy and Society," *Journal of Social Philosophy*, 29/1 (Spring, 1998): 81–102. A section of Chapter 3 incorporates ideas from "Autonomy and Self-Identity" in *Autonomy and the Challenges to Liberalism*, ed. John Christman and Joel Anderson (Cambridge, U.K.: Cambridge University Press, 2005), pp. 77–97. Chapter 6 takes account of discussion from "How Much Should We Value Autonomy?" *Social Philosophy and Policy*, 20/2 (Cambridge, U.K.: Cambridge University Press, 2003): 99–126. Chapter 7 incorporates material from "Autonomy and Free Agency," in *Personal Autonomy*, ed. J.S. Taylor (Cambridge University Press, 2004), pp. 183–204. Chapter 8 is based on "The Misguided Marriage of Autonomy and Responsibility," *Journal of Ethics*, 6/3 (2002): 261–80. I would like to thank the editors and publishers for permitting me to reproduce this material here.

Chapter 1

The Concept of Autonomy

Introduction

The overarching task of this chapter is to assemble a set of considered intuitions about personal autonomy. By doing this, we will have at our disposal a yardstick of sorts against which the success or failure of this book in accomplishing its task can be measured. That task is one of providing an account of autonomy that best captures the concept the term is used to express. This concept is concerned with a status an individual can have—the status of being personally autonomous—that is crucial to anyone who is a member of or a participant in a social and political milieu having potentially significant coercive or manipulative influence upon her life. The concept of autonomy has been employed in a variety of other contexts, both theoretical and applied. I will not be addressing the very rich realm of applied usage. There is an abundance of literature, much of it new and quite engaging, on the subject of autonomy in the realms of medicine, consumer rights, privacy, law enforcement, and so forth.[1] But one central theoretical task is the conceptual task of providing an account of autonomy, where autonomy is a key status of persons, particularly adult persons, who are interpersonally bound by political, cultural, and moral frameworks. Such an account will be judged by its success in explaining autonomy in light of a realistic view of persons as socially situated. Of the many issues concerning autonomy, this is the one with which this book is concerned.

A Commonplace Notion of Personal Autonomy

The word "autonomy" derives from the Greek *auto* ("self") and *nomos* ("rule" or "law"). Taking etymology seriously, to be autonomous is to act within a framework of rules one sets for oneself; that is, it is to have a kind of authority over oneself as well as the power to act on that authority. While a person's behavior and motivations can be traced to a variety of factors, to describe a person as autonomous is to claim

---

1   For example, see Thomas May, *Bioethics in a Liberal Society: The Political Framework of Bioethics Decision Making* (Baltimore: Johns Hopkins University Press, 2002); Tom L. Beauchamp and James Childress, *Principles of Biomedical Ethics*, 5th edn (New York: Oxford University Press, 2001); John Kleinig, *The Ethics of Policing* (Cambridge, 1996); Allan Buchanan and Dan Brock, *Deciding for Others: The Ethics of Surrogate Decision Making* (Cambridge, 1989); Gerald Dworkin, "Autonomy and Informed Consent," reprinted in Dworkin, *The Theory and Practice of Autonomy* (Cambridge, 1988), pp. 100–120.

that the person is self-directed in this way. A theory of autonomy must explain what kind of authority and power is involved.

Personal autonomy might be construed in a local, or occurrent, sense as a property of a person's acts or desires or choices considered individually, and pertaining to the manner in which a person conducts herself in particular situations. This localized construal seems to be especially apparent in judgments of responsible agency, as when we say of the thief, "No one made her steal. She acted autonomously; she did it of her own free will." For the better part of this discussion, however, autonomy will be treated as a global or dispositional phenomenon, the property of a person having *de facto* power and authority over choices and actions significant to the direction of her life.[2] The account of autonomy developed in the pages that follow will be an account of what it means to be this kind of agent as opposed to an account of what is involved in making a certain kind of choice. Unless stated otherwise, let us understand global autonomy of this kind as the intended sense of the term "personal autonomy."

The difference between the local and global notions is evident in the fact that a person's degree of global autonomy is not fully determined by facts about how autonomous or nonautonomous the person is *vis à vis* particular choices. A person is autonomous in the global sense, the sense that is our concern here, only if she manages her life. We correctly attribute global autonomy to a person when we have evidence of a person with *de facto* power and authority to manage matters of fundamental importance to her life within a framework of rules (or values, principles, beliefs, pro-attitudes) that she has set for herself. These matters are general and commonplace. They concern, for example, intimate relationships, access to and control over information about oneself, and the phenomena—education, employment, health

---

2   A global or dispositional conception of autonomy is developed in my "Personal Autonomy and Society," *Journal of Social Philosophy* 29/1 (Spring, 1998): 81–102. Also see Robert Young in *Personal Autonomy: Beyond Negative and Positive Liberty* (New York, 1986); Gerald Dworkin, *The Theory and Practice of Autonomy*; Paul Benson, "Autonomy and Oppressive Socialization," *Social Theory and Practice* 17 (1991): 385–408; and Paul Benson, "Free Agency and Self-Worth," *Journal of Philosophy* 91/12 (1994): 650–68. Diana Meyers treats the distinction between local and global autonomy as one between episodic and programmatic autonomy: "Autonomous episodic self-direction occurs when a person confronts a situation, asks what he or she can do with respect to it … and what he or she really wants to do with respect to it, and then executes the decision this deliberation yields. Autonomous programmatic self-direction has a broad sweep. Instead of posing the question 'What do I really want to do now?' this form of autonomy addresses a question like 'How do I really want to live my life?' To answer this latter question, people must consider what qualities they want to have, what sorts of interpersonal relationships they want to be involved in, what talents they want to develop, what interests they want to pursue, what goals they want to achieve, and so forth. Their decisions about these matters together with their ideas about how to effect these results add up to a life plan." Diana T. Meyers, *Self, Society, and Personal Choice* (New York, 1989), p. 48.

care, and family life, for example—that impart a distinctive configuration to a person's life.

Now let us suppose that a person is locally autonomous with respect to given choices and actions when they proceed from springs of action that typify her deepest, critically rendered and freely held values. Assume that this person's motives for action have not been induced in the person by the undesirable or surreptitious machinations of others. As episodes of autonomous activity increase in number and in range in her life, does her degree of global autonomy increase accordingly? Not necessarily. One reason global or dispositional autonomy is not necessarily increased by an increasing sum of episodes of self-governance is that the latter can be highly localized and restrictive—they might concern only a very narrow range of matters—or they might concern matters of little consequence to a person. But even in the case where a person is self-directed over a generous range of matters that are of significance to her, the person's success might not be due to her own efforts. The person might be permitted to act in a self-directed fashion only because others who are in a position to exert a governing influence over her choose to stay their hand. Or the person's displays of will might be coincidental, contingent on the presence of certain idiosyncratic patterns in her social environment or her psychology that favor bursts of self-governed activity. In these instances episodes of autonomy transpire despite the person's inability to manage her environment or despite the fact that others have the ability to hijack capriciously the person's efforts at self-management. A person does not manage her life when she is subject to the arbitrary will of another or when her ability to realize her values is incumbent on good fortune rather than on her labors. In such cases, she does not have full global autonomy.

The following is a very brief sketch of intuitive ideas about the kind of power and authority required for autonomy. I think these ideas are not controversial and I will say more about them, with elaboration and adjustment, in Chapter 3.

1. Power: Autonomous persons are beings in *actual* control of their own choices, actions, and goals. By this I mean the person is in possession of the *de facto* power to govern herself. Here we find the familiar idea that a self-determining person faces minimal interference in her actions and choices. Interference can be brought about by social or psychological or physical means such as coercion and manipulation, neurosis, weakness of will, or bodily impulse. The autonomous individual is not forced to do the will of another. Of course the autonomous person might share goals with others and pursue these goals in concert with others, and she might rely on the advice and judgment of others regarding the merit of these goals. But in the end the reasons for which the autonomous agent acts are her own.

Implicit in the idea of actual control over one's life is the idea of self-control. Two things are true of self-controlled people. One is that they are significantly motivated "to conduct themselves as they judge best," not succumbing to impulsive behavior antithetical to their interests. Another is that they have "a robust capacity" to do this "in the face of (actual or anticipated) competing motivations."[3] Self-governing persons must generally be moved to control themselves in the face of temptation to do otherwise.

2. Authority: Autonomous persons are in a kind of *authoritative* control of their own choices, actions, and goals. To have authoritative control is to "own" the management of one's choices, actions, and goals.[4] Presumably, even nonautonomous people have a moral right to control their own choices, actions, and goals, and even nonautonomous people might exhibit episodes of activity over which they exert power or control. But since an autonomous person is "an independent source of activity in the world,"[5] in command of the overall direction of her life, autonomy must involve some further variety of control. That is, the autonomous person must not only have *de jure* control of her choices, actions, and goals but must enjoy a status against other persons or institutions that might attempt to deprive her of her authority to command these choices, actions, and goals. Having the relevant kind of authority guarantees that a person's life is free of the domination of others.

In short, personal autonomy is a property of a person who manages matters of fundamental consequence to her agency and to the direction of her life. Autonomy calls for agential power in the form of psychological freedom—mastery of one's will—as well as power and authority within certain fundamental social roles and arrangements. So described, global autonomy is intended to capture commonplace, pretheoretical ideas about self-governance. They are ideas held, at a more or less developed level, by laypersons and academic philosophers alike.

Autonomy Naturalized

To understand personal autonomy in this manner is to view personal autonomy as a naturalized phenomenon. What does this mean? A naturalized view of personal autonomy is a view according to which autonomy is a natural property of persons, possession of which can be established *a posteriori* on the basis of natural facts. Judgments about whether or not a person is autonomous are judgments about how that person is in the world, and the property of being autonomous is an empirical, natural property.

By contrast, a non-naturalized account will make at least some of the conditions for autonomy ones that a person cannot be known *a posteriori* to satisfy. Non-

---

3   Alfred Mele, *Autonomous Agents: From Self-Control to Autonomy* (New York, 1995), p. 6; Mele, "Autonomy, Self-Control, and Weakness of Will," in Robert Kane (ed.), *The Oxford Handbook of Free Will* (New York, 2002), pp. 529–48.

4   The language of ownership is borrowed from Paul Benson, who claims that autonomy requires the agent to recognize herself as one who takes or "seizes" ownership or as one who has the authority to answer for herself. See his "Taking Ownership: Authority and Voice in Autonomous Agency," in John Christman and Joel Anderson, eds, *Autonomy and the Challenges to Liberalism: New Essays* (Cambridge, 2005), pp. 101–26.

5   Robert Kane, *The Significance of Free Will* (New York, 1998), p. 206.

naturalized theories all require something to be true of autonomous persons that cannot be known empirically. Immanuel Kant's notion of autonomy is non-naturalistic in so far as it links autonomy with a state of metaphysical freedom unobtainable in the empirical world. A theory of autonomy which views persons as self-governing only if they have "freedom from the world" or "triumph over socialization" or "liberation from others" is arguably non-naturalistic. Even if we could figure out what would count as success in these respects, these do not appear to be empirical conditions. Equally non-naturalistic is a conception of autonomy that requires that a person's character be "self-made," such that the person fashions himself *ex nihilo* and alone bears responsibility for his personality.[6] Each of these conceptions is arguably non-naturalistic since each treats autonomy as a type of freedom the possession of which could not be verified empirically.

A naturalized conception of autonomy must satisfy two conditions, or so I think. The first condition is a consequence of the general account of naturalism that I have been explaining. This is that the properties which constitute autonomy must be natural properties, verifiable through the senses or by introspection (or must supervene on natural properties). But I believe "naturalism" has a broader meaning in light of the view that a naturalized theory is one that takes realistic account of general empirical facts. There is, I believe, a second condition for a naturalized conception of autonomy. It is an empirical fact that persons are socially situated amid complex relations with other people, and because of this individuals are not self-governing unless they have a status that guarantees them freedom from interferences that are "external" in nature and origin. Hence I would say that a completely naturalized account must treat autonomy as, in part, a function of a person's status and relations that are extrinsic to facts about her psychological history and occurrent psychological state.

A conception of autonomy is not a naturalized one because it lends itself to investigation from an external point of view—because it can be scrutinized from a point of view external to that of the agent whose autonomy is in question. Naturalism is not a theory about who has access to the objects of investigation; it is not a theory about the knower, but a theory about the thing known and about the conditions of its knowability. Nor does naturalism claim that every object of study be approached from a perspective of facts about the social environment. A theory of mind that reduces mental states to states of the brain is clearly naturalistic, but does not call for an analysis from a perspective of facts about the social environment. The point is that certain necessary conditions of autonomy are themselves external to and independent of the individual's internal character. As a result, we cannot adequately investigate claims to autonomy without evidence that these conditions have been met in the natural world. Few theories of autonomy are naturalistic in the sense that they satisfy this second condition. Of course, not every naturalistic theory of autonomy will be a good theory of autonomy. But a tenable account of autonomy—a tenable account of self-government as a

---

6   Among contemporary philosophers, Susan Wolf takes autonomy to mean that a person is undetermined and "self-creating," and she rejects autonomy as a plausible condition for moral responsibility on this basis. See Wolf, *Freedom Within Reason* (New York, 1992).

condition that would be undermined in coercive or interfering moral, social, and political settings—must satisfy the two conditions of naturalism.

The conception of autonomy discussed above is a pretheoretic ideal that provides a gauge against which the plausibility of models of autonomy is assessed. The critical and the constructive tasks to which this essay aspires are to evaluate competing models of autonomy against the pretheoretic ideal and to provide a naturalized model of the ideal.

The Capacity—Condition Distinction

The theory of autonomy developed in this book concerns the state or condition of being personally autonomous—the state I have called global autonomy. My argument is premised, in part, on the idea that the state of being autonomous is primarily a function of the external situation a person finds himself in rather than being predominately a function of a person's psychological state or practical skills. The argument requires that the condition of being autonomous be distinguished from the capacity for autonomy and from the exercise of that capacity. A capacity for autonomy consists of the minimum of qualities a person must possess in order to lead a self-directed life. The need for a distinction between capacity and condition is pressing in light of the fact that the more familiar approaches define autonomy as a (primarily) psychological capacity of persons to rule themselves: a person is autonomous if she has the ability to evaluate, endorse, and revise her motives for action, or they define autonomy as the successful exercise of this capacity, understood as an array of coordinated skills.[7]

Differentiating among the capacity for self-government, the exercise of the capacity, and the condition of self-government enables us to distinguish persons who are self-governing from, first, persons who lack the psychological equipment needed to be self-determining (victims of profound psychological manipulation, for example) and, second, from persons who are equipped with the psychological and practical skills essential to self-government but who nevertheless are not self-governing. The latter preserve a capacity for autonomy even when they are subject to circumstances that deprive them from ability to act on their choices and actively be autonomous. It is imperative to draw the capacity/condition distinction in order to make plain that one can have the readiness for autonomy while lacking the opportunity to exercise this readiness.

Joseph Raz, for example, maintains that the capacity for autonomy is "the condition of a person who has a certain ability" that may or may not translate

---

7   See, for example, Richard Arneson, "Autonomy and Preference Formation," in Jules Coleman and Allen Buchanan (eds), *In Harm's Way: Essays in Honor of Joel Feinberg*, (Cambridge, 1991), pp. 42–73; Gerald Dworkin, *The Theory and Practice of Autonomy*; John Christman, "Autonomy and Personal History," *Canadian Journal of Philosophy* 20/1 (March 1991): 1–24; Bernard Berofsky, *Liberation from Self: A Theory of Personal Autonomy* (New York, 1995); Diana Meyers, *Self, Society, and Personal Choice*.

successfully into action.[8] Joel Feinberg defines the capacity for self-government in terms of an individual's competence to make rational choices.[9] This capacity is necessary for both the actual or *de facto* condition of self-government, as well as the moral and legal right of self-government or *de jure* sovereignty.

Four points are worth making at this juncture. The first is that the capacity for autonomy can be a matter of degree, although there are thresholds that must be satisfied in order for a person to be deemed sufficiently competent to be considered an autonomous being. One must, say, have reasonably astute cognitive skills and a developed set of interests and values in order to be capable of *de facto* autonomy and *de jure* sovereignty. The cognitive skills required in order for a person to be capable of even a right to self-determination include a capacity for deliberation, self-evaluation, and planning agency. These skills must be sufficiently developed to enable a person to comprehend the circumstances in which she functions and to tailor her activity as the situation necessitates, or the person must have the robust potential to have these skills become so developed. The values and interests of the person must be sufficiently developed to supply the person with a sense of which activities are significant to the course of her life, or the person must have the robust potential to develop such values and interests.

The scope of this discussion does not allow a satisfactory discussion of these thresholds, although more will be said of them in Chapters 3 and 4 where I make a case for social autonomy. It is enough to note that as the possession of these qualities is a matter of degree, so the capacity for autonomy is a matter of degree and can be cultivated more or less successfully in persons. A sense of the relevant threshold can be gained by a glance at cases in which it is clear the threshold is not met. The very small child, the individual afflicted with Alzheimer's disease, and the insane person lack the rudimentary ability to be self-governing. Absent from all three is the characteristic of being a sufficiently good "local sociologist," of apprehending the complexities of their external environments and of comprehending the normative expectations of other persons and adapting their behaviors accordingly. Absent from all three is the power of reasonably accurate self-appraisal, and the ability to plan for the future realistically and with a view to their preferences, and to function in a deliberative way. All three are creatures for whom certain forms of safeguarding and supervision are appropriate. (Ideally, of course, children will acquire the necessary

---

8   Raz, *The Morality of Freedom* (Oxford, 1986), p. 371.

9   Feinberg, *Harm to Self*. Feinberg remarks that the condition of autonomy "refers to a congeries of virtues" (31) present in a person and taken to be "components of the autonomous ideal" (44). These virtues constitute the necessary conditions for the exercise of autonomy, and consist of the qualities of self-possession; individuality; authenticity of preferences, values, and opinions; contribution to one's own development (being "self-made"); being subject to one's free-will as rational will; authenticity of one's moral convictions; fidelity to these convictions; self-control (which calls for a Platonic balance of passion and reason); self-reliance; initiative; accountability for the consequences of one's action; and having minimal moral and social commitments. Of these, authenticity and self-reliance have been taken to be most important for autonomy.

characteristics for self-determination as they mature.) As a point of contrast, consider the incarcerated rational adult who retains a capacity for autonomy; his talents for deliberation, self-appraisal, and planning are intact as is his attunement to the environment in which he operates. The prisoner is incapacitated in some ways but is not disabled in the relevant respects. As a result, the prisoner enjoys the promise of autonomy.

The second of the four points I wish to make at this stage is that the capacity for autonomy can be—indeed, typically is—heteronomously induced. We develop the requisite skills in a variety of ways, few of which are the result of our conscious handiwork and fewer of which can be wrought by sheer effort of will alone. Of course, if the capacity does not actually develop but, instead, the person is mislead "by simulation and deceit … to believe that he controls his own destiny," then the person would not genuinely be capable of autonomy.[10] What matters is that the capacity actually be present, even if the cause is general socialization.

The third point to be made at this stage is that the general capacity for autonomy is not a bare, potential condition of the kind we expect may be realized at some future moment. Where capacity is understood in that looser sense, as bare potentiality, an infant, a comatose being and an intelligent computer would all be capable of self-government given the availability of advanced practices in human cognitive development, medical science, and artificial intelligence. Nor is the general capacity for autonomy the merely "hypothetical possible world's ability" to become autonomous that is had by any individual possessed of certain minimal traits of personality and circumstantial fortune (such as teachability). The capacity for autonomy is not merely hypothetical, since some of the characteristics necessary for autonomy must already be in place; one who has the capacity for autonomy is empowered to do certain things.

The fourth point to be made at this juncture bears on the relation between the capacity to lead an autonomous life (that is, the capacity for global autonomy), the capacity for local autonomy *vis à vis* some choice or preference considered individually, and the basis for having a moral right to autonomy. A robust, not-merely-hypothetical capacity for global self-government may suffice for having the right to autonomy (for *de jure* autonomy) as well as for having the capacity for locally autonomous choice. A person with this right and this capacity may have "relatively little personal autonomy in the sense of a *de facto* condition, but like a badly governed nation, he may retain his sovereign independence (and so his *de jure* autonomy) nonetheless."[11] A person who abdicates his choices is not fully autonomous, even if his choice-making capacity remains intact and even if he has

---

10 Raz, *The Morality of Freedom*, pp. 376–77.

11 Feinberg, *Harm to Self*, p. 28; p. 30. The distinction between *de facto* and *de jure* autonomy is an important one, and bears on the response I will make to some criticisms that have been levied against the social account I defend. Unfortunately, the distinction has received insufficient attention, an oversight I hope to remedy in Chapter 5.

the right to autonomy. The capacity must be exercised or actualized in order for a person to qualify as globally autonomous.[12]

Distinguishing between global autonomy as a condition and autonomy as a capacity also is useful when we consider that the actual state of global personal autonomy may not be necessary for responsible agency, though local autonomy may be necessary. As we shall discover in Chapter 8, responsible agency requires a person to be a *free agent*, that is, an agent who has certain capacities for psychological self-governance coupled with having actual control of some variety. But if, as seems plausible, a person can be responsible for failing to act autonomously, and if, as seems plausible, a person can be responsible despite acting in a situation of, say, confinement then a person can meet the conditions for responsibility without being globally autonomous.[13] As Raz remarks, a person who is not autonomous may still be "a moral agent, fully responsible for his actions," ostensibly because the person can make moral choices.[14] This suggests that if responsibility requires autonomy in some guise, it is likely a capacity for autonomous choice that is important, a capacity that includes, for example, the ability to choose in a rational and deliberate manner. Responsibility requires having the characteristics that prepare a person for being autonomous rather than the robust condition of being an autonomous person.

Moral Autonomy

The capacity/condition distinction is also of use in illuminating the relation between personal autonomy understood in the sense I have been explaining and what might be called "moral autonomy." A theory of moral autonomy is concerned with the relation a person bears to a system of moral norms; such a theory might investigate how a person conceives of and subscribes to a moral code or moral principles and how the person responds to moral demands. The agent who is morally autonomous reflects on these principles and will not accept, without critical and independent scrutiny, the judgments of others as to what is morally correct.[15] It is plausible that a person who has global personal autonomy is also morally autonomous in this sense.

The notion of personal autonomy is morally significant since, as I have suggested, it is reasonable to think there is a moral right to autonomy and since

---

12 On this I follow Robert Young who charges that "to be autonomous is not merely to have a capacity, nor the opportunity to exercise the capacity. Autonomy is an *exercise-concept*, to use Charles Taylor's phrase." Young, *Personal Autonomy*, p. 49.

13 One instance is the case of the consenting slave (Chapter 3). A detailed discussion follows in Chapter 8.

14 Raz, *The Morality of Freedom*, p. 379.

15 For a discussion of the autonomy of moral agents that treats moral autonomy as a species of personal autonomy, see Gerald Dworkin, *The Theory and Practice of Autonomy*, Chapters 3 and 4. See also Jeremy Waldron, "Moral Autonomy and Personal Autonomy" in John Christman and Joel Anderson (eds), *Autonomy and the Challenges to Liberalism: New Essays* (Cambridge, 2005), pp. 307–29.

a capacity for autonomy appears to be a requirement for moral responsibility. But a theory of personal autonomy need not settle the matter of what is involved in being morally autonomous and we can characterize personal autonomy in terms that are silent on the question of morality.[16] Moral autonomy and personal autonomy are distinct concepts—they address self-determination with respect to different phenomena. Clearly, moral autonomy is not sufficient for personal autonomy. For if a morally autonomous person is just one who assents to and follows a moral code independently of the will of others, then a person who fails to live as a self-governing agent can nevertheless be morally autonomous. This may be the situation of an individual imprisoned for his political and ethical convictions, when these are in opposition to those of the ruling regime. A textbook example of persons whose moral autonomy is intact while their personal autonomy is compromised is that of the Jehovah's Witnesses incarcerated in Nazi concentration camps during the Second World War.[17] Not all violations of personal autonomy, then, compromise a person's moral autonomy.

The idea that people can be morally autonomous has origins dating back at least to the development of natural law theory in early modern Europe, evidence of which appears in the works of Hugo Grotius, Samuel Pufendorf, and John Locke.[18] But nowhere is the shared philosophical history of morality and autonomy more evident than in the work of Kant, whose ethical theory makes the ideal of personal autonomy a moral ideal. As the paradigmatic attempt to unite morality with autonomy, it bears discussion.

Kantian Autonomy

Kant's view is that the autonomous person acts from and according to moral rules that she imposes upon herself—the autonomous individual settles on her own moral principles—yet the principles the individual selects will be ones that every

---

16 Raz notes, for example, that "Personal autonomy, which is a particular ideal of individual well-being, should not be confused with the only very indirectly related notion of moral autonomy. Moral autonomy ... is a doctrine about the nature of morality. Personal autonomy ... is essentially about the freedom of persons to choose their own lives." Raz, *The Morality of Freedom*, p. 370. Jeremy Waldron suggests that, despite this claim, Raz in fact infuses personal autonomy with a substantively moral character, effectively associating personal autonomy with the pursuit of a particular conception of the good. See Waldron, "Moral Autonomy and Personal Autonomy," pp. 320–21.

17 I owe this example to Robert Young, *Personal Autonomy: Beyond Negative and Positive Liberty*, p. 16 ff, and Bernard Berofsky, *Liberation from Self: A Theory of Personal Autonomy*.

18 Hugo Grotius, *The Rights of War and Peace*, Richard Tuck (ed.) (Liberty Fund, 2005); Samuel Pufendorf, *On the Duty of Man and Citizen according to Natural Law* (Cambridge, 1991); Thomas Hobbes, *On the Citizen*, Richard Tuck and Michael Silverthorne (eds), (Cambridge, 1998); John Locke, *Two Treatises on Government*, Peter Laslett (ed.) (Cambridge, 1988).

autonomous person would accept.[19] This union of personal autonomy with morality rests in Kant's famous (and famously complex) characterization of the rational will.[20] The will just is the power of a person to choose among courses of action. The rational will, or the will of a rational individual, however, is a will that selects only those acts which conform to the moral law. Because autonomous agents are rational, and are all the same to the extent that they are rational, they will not hold opposing views about what morality necessitates unless their judgment is confused. In short, autonomous agents "adopt or acknowledge moral constraints in detachment from the particular ends they desire, and acting autonomously is construed as acting from principles that one would consent to as a free and equal being."[21]

Whereas we share our rational nature, we are divided—marked as different from one another—by our desires and inclinations. Kant treats these as "slavish and burdensome,"[22] expressions of our empirical personality, our temporality, and our idiosyncrasies. Moral action is possible only if the moral law can motivate us independently of all inclination. Kant believes such purely moral motivation is possible. That is, he believes that "Of itself and independently of everything empirical [pure reason] can determine the will. This it does through a fact wherein pure reason shows itself actually to be practical. This fact is *autonomy in the principle of morality* by which reason determines the will to action."[23] It is this sort of "disinterested obedience to Law as such, [and the] independence of Reason in influencing choice without the intervention of sensible impulses"[24] that marks agents as autonomous.

Kant's analysis of autonomy yields counterintuitive implications. Consider, first, that for Kant, personal autonomy is possessed only by moral agents insofar as they act from the faculty of reason; the rational being is autonomous only if his desires cohere with the authority of the moral law and only if his will is determined by the moral law. The agent who rejects the moral law or seeks anything not morally permitted, or who allows his actions to be determined in a "heteronomous" fashion by factors such as pleasure or desire "repudiates himself as a rational being" and suffers a loss of autonomy.

Kant is not making the modest claim that autonomy is a matter of choosing and acting upon desires, attachments, and values that are reasonable in the sense that they have survived critical appraisal, or that the autonomous agent is rational in the sense that her motivational psychology consists of beliefs, desires, attachments, and values

---

19 The definitive volumes of Kant are the 1785 *Groundwork of the Metaphysic of Morals*, tr. H.J. Paton (New York, 1964), and the 1775–80 *Lectures On Ethics*, tr. Louis Infield (Indianapolis, 1963).

20 Kant, p. 114, *Groundwork*.

21 Thomas Hill, "The Autonomy of Moral Agents," *Encyclopedia of Ethics*, Lawrence C. Becker and Charlotte B. Becker (eds) (New York, 1992).

22 Kant, *The Critique of Practical Reason*, tr. Lewis White Beck (New York, 1956), p. 122.

23 Kant, *The Critique of Practical Reason*, p. 43.

24 Henry Sidgwick, "The Kantian Conception of Free Will," *Mind*, 1888, vol. XIII, no. 51. Reprinted in *The Method of Ethics* (New York, 1966), p. 513.

that are coherent with one another. Critical appraisal could be desire-based, after all, and idiosyncratic psychological states could be coherent. Rather, Kant assumes that if a person is to be autonomous, reason must determine the person's choices and actions. Sentiment, the Kantian might charge, is and ought to be the slave of reason. But if the intuitions for autonomy sketched in section one are sound, autonomy does not require an agent to act solely from a reason-based moral code. A person can be self-governing even if her actions are prompted by desires, attachments, and values that are unique to her.

Kant's account is counterintuitive in a second, related way. Kant's view is that an autonomous person directs his or her life according to formal, universal, and impersonal principles of reason. Let us call this the *impartiality thesis*. While factors such as desire, sentiment, and personal attachments may in fact influence the choices and actions of human beings, autonomy requires that a person's will express her rational nature—the nature she has in common with other moral beings—rather than whatever particular desires or attachments she happens to have.

But the impartiality thesis is troublesome. The Kantian may be correct in asserting that impartiality is morally required in many circumstances. But we would be mistaken to say that a person must act impartially if she is to be autonomous. A theory of personal autonomy that discounts the role partiality plays in our moral development and autonomous moral choices is implausible. It is implausible because to accord impartiality this weight is to deny certain obvious and desirable features of human beings.

It is obvious, for example, that people act autonomously, or exhibit self-directedness, while following the dictates of their feelings. Consider Huckleberry Finn, whose affection and concern led him to protect his friend Jim, a slave.[25] The decision not to reveal Jim's whereabouts to slave hunters—indeed, to lie about Jim's whereabouts—was clearly Huck's own, voluntarily and independently formed even though Huck thought he was acting wrongly. In fact, Huck's sentiment-charged decision to act out of friendship could have been born of reason.

Autonomous agency is therefore compatible with influences such as desire and emotional attachment. In the real world, sentiments and desires play a central navigational role in our lives. It is unnatural to think that the autonomous individual must judge possible courses of action in a thoroughly impartial manner. Each of us is a distinctive person with distinctive personal attachments wrought by friendship, compassion, and partiality.

Thomas Hill, Jr. argues that impartiality provides a crucial aspect of the ideal perspective from which moral problems can be adjudicated, stating that "When the moral grounds and limits of personal responsibility are called into question, the discussion moves to a more abstract level in which impartiality plays an important

---

25 Jonathan Bennett, "The Conscience of Huckleberry Finn," *Philosophy* 49 (1974): 123–34.

role."[26] More specifically, Hill believes that Kant's views about the role impartiality plays in autonomous action have been exaggerated by critics of Kant. Hill states that,

> The impartiality thesis ... does not assert, with Kant, that basic moral principles are grounded in pure reason, independent of all contingent features of human nature, that they admit no exceptions, or that they command only our wills and not our feelings. Our thesis does not imply that self-sufficiency is better than dependence, or that the emotional detachment of a judge is better than the compassion of a lover. No one is urged to live with his or her eyes fixed on abstract moral principles, still less with concentration on their justification from an impartial perspective ... Impartiality has its important place, but its place is not that of a model for moral sainthood.[27]

This version of Kantianism is better suited to our idea of autonomy naturalized even if, so revised, less of Kant may remain than Hill allows. In any case, the lesson is that allowing factors other than the rational and detached elements of one's personality to be involved in determining the course of one's life (including one's moral choices) need not diminish one's autonomy. In fact, a robust depiction of the self-determined person demands that reference be made to the emotional attachments, traditions, rituals, and social roles that permeate life.

A third way in which Kant's analysis is counterintuitive is that it seems to rule out the idea of an autonomous moral offender.[28] Kant fails to explain how persons freely choose evil over good. Hill's Kantian account permits us to describe as autonomous the person who acts from friendship and loyalty rather than the dictates of the moral law. But if "man's free power to defiantly reject the law is an ineradicable fact of human experience," it is also a fact that a plausibly naturalized theory of autonomy must recognize.[29]

From the perspective of the intuitions laid out above there is a fourth concern, one that stems from the metaphysical peculiarities of Kant's view. Consider that we can only be aware of ourselves on the basis of how we appear to ourselves; our knowledge of ourselves as autonomous agents must be empirical. But on Kant's account, as members of the "phenomenal" or empirical realm we function heteronomously and so we could not be autonomous. The will is autonomous only insofar as it belongs to the "noumenal" realm, but because this realm transcends human cognizance, we cannot have empirical knowledge of our autonomy.

---

26 Hill, Jr., "The Importance of Autonomy," pp. 46–7, in E.F. Kittay and D.T. Meyers (eds), *Women and Moral Theory* (Totowa, N.J., 1987). Reprinted in Hill, *Autonomy and Self-Respect* (Cambridge, 1991). All references are to the latter text.

27 Hill, Jr., "The Importance of Autonomy," p. 47.

28 Suggestions that Kant wishes to address the problem of responsibility for evil are apparent in his later work. See Kant, *Religion Within the Limits of Reason Alone*, tr. T.M. Greene and H.H. Hudson (New York, 1960).

29 John R. Silber, Introduction to Kant's *Religion Within The Limits of Reason Alone*, p. cxxix.

There is a fifth, final sense in which Kant's account of autonomy is counterintuitive. Kant's description of moral autonomy presents a rather gloomy picture of the level of well-being or satisfaction associated with autonomous agency. Quoting Kant from the *Groundwork*, Jeremy Waldron points out that "morality is 'the direct opposite of … the principle of one's own happiness [being] made the determining ground of the will.'"[30] In fact, Kant appears to claim that the greater obstacles a person faces in doing something, the more autonomous he is in the act:

> The more I have to *force* myself to do an action, the more obstacles I have to overcome in doing it, and the more *wilfully* I do it, the more it is to be accounted to me … the greater the fight a man puts up against his natural inclinations the more it is to be imputed to him for merit.[31]

We are more autonomous "the more [we] give way to moral grounds of impulsion"[32] even though we may face these moral demands with reluctance or distaste. But what of the person whose inclinations fortuitously coincide with the moral law? According to Kant, this individual lacks the chastened spirit and the sort of strife in her motivational psychology that marks her as virtuous. The virtuous person faces a "burden of discontent," and so can hardly be said to be happy.[33] On the off chance that the union of inclination and morality is a harmonious one and results in happiness, happiness will diminish the burdensome element required for virtue. Because the ideally autonomous human is one who prevails against the all too natural temptation to pursue one's desires, needs, and inclinations to perform the moral act, autonomy is likely to come at the cost of personal happiness. The happy person, certainly, will not be ideally autonomous.

Political Autonomy

The idea of political autonomy or liberty can be specified in more than one way, but however it is interpreted, the idea depends on the status of the individual in relation to the state and to institutions of public and civic authority. It is open to question whether politically autonomous citizens must be self-governing or globally autonomous in the sense that concerns me in this book. However, many of the reasons for valuing political autonomy are related to the value of personal autonomy.

As members of societies, particularly liberal democracies, persons ideally possess certain legal and political rights in relation to the state. Among these are the rights to own property, the right to move about freely and to speak freely, to be granted due process under law, to practice religion without fear, to educate one's children,

---

30 Waldron, "Moral Autonomy and Personal Autonomy," in *Autonomy and the Challenges of Liberalism: New Essays*, p. 309.

31 Kant, *Lectures On Ethics*, p. 63.

32 Kant, *Lectures On Ethics*, p. 29.

33 Kant, *Critique of Practical Reason*, p. 122.

and to not be subject to unlawful detainment, search, and seizure of property. Arguably, the idea that we should have these legal and political rights rests on an idea about personal autonomy—on the idea, that is, that persons enjoy an inherent dignity in virtue of which they are entitled to a certain status before the state. As persons we have a standing that constrains both how we are to be treated and what we are permitted to do and expected to do *vis à vis* one another. As Robert Nozick reminds us, "What persons may and may not do to each other limits what they may do through the apparatus of the state, or to establish such an apparatus. The moral prohibitions it is permissible to enforce are the source of whatever legitimacy the state's fundamental coercive power has."[34]

My goal in this section of the chapter is to sketch a variety of theories about political autonomy (or, liberty—the terms tend to be interchangeable in these theories) in order to highlight the points at which the conceptions of political autonomy in these theories differ from our conception of global personal autonomy.

Anarchy and Libertarianism

Both political anarchists and libertarians or right-liberals embrace a conception of liberty as non-interference and both express concern about the invasive quality of social and political institutions upon the freedom of individual citizens. Both treat the ideal of non-interference as a constraint that any institution must respect. But the two differ in what they claim is implied by—indeed, mandated by—the ideal of political autonomy. The concerns of the anarchist are voiced with chagrin by Robert Paul Wolff, who notes that:

> In politics, as in life generally, men frequently forfeit their autonomy. There are a number of causes for this fact, and also a number of arguments which have been offered to justify it. Most men, as we have already noted, feel so strongly the force of tradition or bureaucracy that they accept unthinkingly the claims to authority which are made by their nominal rulers. It is the rare individual in the history of the race who rises even to the level of questioning the right of his masters to command and the duty of himself and his fellows to obey.[35]

Wolff believes that men forfeit their autonomy under the state when they recognize and comply with the commands of a political authority for the sole reason that compliance is the will of the political authority. On Wolff's view, the agent retains his autonomy in the face of moral and legal authority to the extent that he recognizes no moral code, and no legal or political or social body of authority, other than what he himself has determined is justified. Indeed, "For the autonomous man, there is no such thing, strictly speaking, as a command."[36] Any capitulation to a body of authority independent of the agent effectively undermines his autonomy.

---

34 Robert Nozick, *Anarchy, State, and Utopia* (New York, 1974), p. 6.

35 Wolff, *In Defense of Anarchism* (New York, 1970), p. 16.

36 Wolff, *In Defense of Anarchism*, p. 14.

The libertarian conception of political autonomy is a by-product of the libertarian tenet of an individual's right of self-ownership. Nozick sums up the libertarian position when he says "Individuals have rights, and there are things which no person or group may do to them (without violating their rights). So strong and far-reaching are these rights that they raise the question of what, if anything, the state and its officials may do."[37] Interferences with a person's decisions and behavior must be minimalized. Like the anarchist, the libertarian takes the ideal of political freedom to consist in non-interference. Unlike the anarchist, the libertarian allows that an individual's right of self-ownership permits him to relinquish his personal autonomy by voluntarily consenting to do so.

The anarchist and the libertarian views seem discordant with some of our beliefs about personal autonomy. Wolff, for example, fails to account for the fact that people who obey the law because it is the law often take this behavior as compatible with their status as self-determining beings. The patriot views her respect for her country as properly influential upon her way of life. Anarchical self-governance of the sort Wolff recommends does not seem necessary for personal autonomy. Certainly anarchical self-governance is not sufficient for personal autonomy. The individual who accepts no command may have a capacity for autonomy without being globally autonomous for she may not be self-aware and self-managed with respect to matters of fundamental consequence to human agency, and she may be constrained by social roles and arrangements.

Similarly, a person who counts as politically autonomous by the libertarian's criteria might not be globally autonomous. It would be consistent with the libertarian conception of freedom that persons live in ways that abridge their capacity for self-governance. The person who willingly opts for a life of drug addiction is a case in point. On both the anarchist and the libertarian accounts, a person who has political liberty might be left adrift, lacking the wherewithal for self-governed living.

Left-Liberalism

The tradition of western political liberalism can be described as "left-liberal" to distinguish it from its libertarian-liberal cousin. I will focus attention on its contemporary articulation. One central idea of left-liberalism is that personal autonomy is something of value. Recent proponents of liberalism such as John Rawls draw on Kant's belief that persons have an inherent dignity in virtue of which they are entitled to certain rights and liberties which protect their autonomy. Yet political liberty as granted by liberal theory does not suffice for personal autonomy. In general, liberals hold that it is not the business of the state to advance a particular conception of the good as the common good, nor to support a particular conception of personal autonomy.[38] Rather, the goal of the liberal state in promoting political liberty is to safeguard the ability of its citizens to judge for themselves the merits

---

37 Nozick, *Anarchy, State, and Utopia*, p. ix.
38 Liberalism's fidelity to anti-perfectionism will be addressed in Chapter 5.

of different conceptions of the good life, provided these fall within parameters that respect the intrinsic moral worth of all individuals.

However, to safeguard this ability does not ensure personal autonomy. Ensuring personal autonomy may require that the state favor particular conceptions of the good and foster policies that grant certain ways of life a political edge. In addition to the ability and the right to judge for themselves the merits of various ideas of the good life, perhaps people must be encouraged to assume an active role in influencing and fashioning the institutions—economic, educational, legislative, social welfare, media, and so forth—that shape their lives. To further global autonomy, the state might need to promote establishment of the kind of society that accords people the status they need to be autonomous, by promoting, say, economic equity, health insurance, and mandatory education. Perhaps, unlike libertarian-liberalism, left-liberalism would not merely champion freedom from interference but would act to forge policies and institutions that facilitate global autonomy.

Feminist Criticisms of Liberal Political Theory

Feminist political theory charges that the ideal of liberty and the principle of self-ownership at the foundation of liberal, libertarian, and anarchist political philosophy were developed with the interests of men in mind—they reflect a male perspective. In pursuing the aim of eradicating unjustified differential treatment, feminists charge that liberals have overlooked two facts.

One fact is that most socioeconomic inequalities between men and women exist because of the social positions women occupy. The liberal response to inequality is to attempt to create equality of opportunity by "erecting a wall (of rights) between the individual and those around him,"[39] but this will do little to advance the self-determination of persons, such as women, whose social roles historically have not empowered them to realize these rights in practice.

The second fact noted by feminists is that conceptualizing autonomy as something to be attained in separation from the family and local community—the intimate ties that bind—is contrary to the historical experience of women. Liberals focus attention on the civic or public sphere, regarding the "private spheres" of family and community to be off-limits to the intrusive business of politics. But in their concern to leave the private realm free from politics, liberals have overlooked the fact that it is within precisely this realm that the work of women traditionally has been done. This tendency to ignore the familial and the communal spheres central to women's experience is as true of liberalism in its recent incarnation (for example, in the work of Rawls) as it was of the classical liberalism of Locke and Rousseau. Not only have the activities of women tended to be relegated to the private sphere, but their activities in that realm have been devalued in comparison with those that take place in the public realm—devalued in the sense that liberal politics has ignored them.

---

39 Jennifer Nedelsky, "Reconceiving Autonomy," *Yale Journal of Law and Feminism*, 1/1, Spring 1989: 7–36.

The result is that liberal theory leaves women with truncated opportunities for self-determination in both the civic and the private arenas.

Liberal political theory must accept the fact that, insofar as much of the political experience of women is grounded in activities that transpire in the private sphere, protecting this sphere from state interference will have the unfortunate result of marginalizing the lives of many women. Jane Mansbridge and Susan Moller Okin argue that

> [R]ethinking autonomy from [the feminist perspective] means discarding the concept of a "true" or "authentic" self that is revealed when interference (in the liberal tradition) ... is removed ... [A]utonomy cannot be gained simply by shedding adverse socialization. Autonomy must not be a state, but a practice, embedded in existing power relations.[40]

The inherent dignity and self-ownership of all persons is an idea at the foundation of liberal political theory. Yet autonomy for women may require the eradication of unjustified differential treatment in the family and the community, as well as the civic body. Autonomy is not just a value in the public sphere; it has value in the private spheres of home and intimate community as well.

Communitarian Political Theory

Liberal, libertarian, and anarchist theories operate on the ahistorical assumption that there exist human interests of universal importance independent of cultural circumstance. Communitarianism focuses, however, on the way humans are "inevitably embedded in particular historical practices and relationships" and on the fact that "the identity of individuals and their capacity for moral agency is bound up with the communities they belong to, and the particular social and political positions they occupy."[41] Communitarians argue that the existing practices of the community anchor the good for the community and provide a yardstick against which the projects of individuals should be appraised and ranked; hence, resources should be distributed in ways that encourage the development of projects most amenable to the culture. In a nutshell, communitarians charge that the liberal politics of rights, including rights to freedom and to autonomy, should be secondary to—if not jettisoned in favor of—a politic of the common good.[42]

The communitarian position on autonomy—political as well as personal—is very different from that of the political liberal, the libertarian, and the anarchist. Michael Sandel claims that, insofar as liberalism operates with a vision of the self as "unencumbered," liberalism adopts a false view of self-determination,[43] the view that autonomy is the expression of a self that chooses who and what and how to be.

---

40 Jane Mansbridge and Susan Moller Okin, "Feminism," in Goodin and Pettit (eds), *A Companion to Contemporary Political Philosophy*, p. 279.

41 Will Kymlicka, *Contemporary Political Philosophy* (Oxford, 2002).

42 Kymlicka, *Contemporary Political Philosophy*, p. 212.

43 Michael Sandel, *Liberalism and the Limits of Justice* (Cambridge, 1982).

Indeed, Charles Taylor charges that in order for people to define themselves they must first be provided concepts and ideals about which lives are worth living, and they must be granted the resources needed to discuss these ideals with others. (The target of Sandel's criticism and of Taylor's is political liberalism, but presumably, libertarianism and anarchism would be vulnerable to similar charges.) Like the feminist, the communitarian points out that self-determination is exercised within social roles and arrangements; in deciding how to live, we cannot help but bring to bear our culturally given understandings. Autonomy can happen only after a person's identity has been formed by such culturally given understandings.

Autonomy and Political Liberalism

The concerns levied by feminists, communitarians, and others against the liberal, libertarian, and anarchist conceptions of politically autonomous agents deserve more attention than I can provide in these pages. However, I think the charge that liberalism views the self as "unencumbered" is unwarranted and I will return to address this charge in Chapters 5 and 7. I will argue that we should not condemn the liberal view of political autonomy in its entirety, nor the view of personal autonomy upon which it relies. Not every species of political liberalism neglects to account for the social dimensions of personal autonomy. In civic republicanism, for example, we find a version of liberalism that embraces the idea of robust personal autonomy while taking quite seriously the interdependence of individuals and society.

Though there are clearly cultural influences on what we value, and while we are not creatures divorced from social roles *tout court*, an important element of personal autonomy is the power it grants us to examine the communal values we absorb and the roles in which we discover ourselves. It is important that we understand the social roles we inherit. Our embeddedness in a shared social context is not so complete that we cannot judge the worth of these roles for ourselves. It is essential for personal autonomy that we assume an active part in assessing and, if necessary, replacing what is deemed of value by the local community. On this point Jennifer Nedelsky correctly notes that,

> The value of autonomy will at some level be inseparable from the relations that make it possible; thus there will be a social component built into the meaning of autonomy ... [But] the presence of a social component does not mean that the value [of autonomy] cannot be threatened by collective choices; hence the continuing need to identify autonomy as a separate value, to take account of its vulnerability to democratic decision making, and to find some way of making those decisions "accountable" to the value of autonomy.[44]

That we are rooted in community does not mean we cannot grow and branch out; that our self-governance is situated does not mean it is bounded. We can recognize our social identities without relinquishing the task of reasoning about how we should live our lives. There is merit to the liberal idea that we exercise self-determination by

---

44 Jennifer Nedelsky, "Reconceiving Autonomy," pp. 35–6.

standing back from particular socially and politically given roles and relationships, questioning these and subsequently affirming those that are congruent to our interests, making our distinctive identities in the process.

Summary

We are seeking an account of autonomy as a global property of persons who have *de facto* power and authority over choices and actions central to the direction of their lives. Such an account must be naturalized; the properties which constitute autonomy must be natural properties, verifiable through the senses or by introspection, and autonomy must be regarded, in part, as constituted by social relations that are extrinsic to facts about the psychological states of the individual. The condition of being autonomous must be distinguished from a capacity for autonomy.

I have explored aspects of the relation between personal autonomy and moral autonomy and aspects of the relation between personal autonomy and political autonomy or liberty. Moral autonomy is a matter of making one's own decisions about what is morally correct. Political autonomy or liberty is a matter of having a status that accords one certain rights *vis à vis* the state. Both the idea of moral autonomy and the idea of political autonomy or liberty draw on suppositions about personal autonomy, but both are thinner than the idea of personal autonomy.

The next two chapters will be devoted to examining various attempts to characterize the concept of personal autonomy. The goal is to develop a theory of autonomy that is both conceptually plausible and of use in illuminating the moral, social, and political concerns of humans. A plausible account must explain how autonomy is compatible with the acceptance of certain objective standards of correct behavior, an adherence to principles of morality, a commitment to religious practices, to rituals, to tradition, and to other persons. I will evaluate proposed accounts of autonomy in light of the degree to which they capture the intuitions laid out in the beginning of this chapter, as well as the ideas I have just introduced. With this in mind, let us turn to one very popular way of thinking about personal autonomy.

Chapter 2

The Inner Citadel:
Autonomy as Psychological Authenticity

Introduction

In recent years, attention has focused on two types of psychological authenticity accounts of autonomy. The first, earlier models offer "internalist" interpretations of self-determination. Internalist views are Cartesian in that they make the autonomy of persons derivative of specific psychological conditions. What goes on in the mind of the individual (or the soul, if you like) rather than what goes on in the world around her decides her standing as self-governing or not.[1]

Later models supplement or modify this basic idea by introducing (or highlighting) an historical criterion. This is done by introducing certain constraints on the procedures a person employs in decision making and in acting. We will refer to these as "procedural authenticity" or "proceduralist" accounts of autonomy as psychological authenticity. The general theme of all psychological authenticity accounts is that a person behaves autonomously when "she chooses or acts in accord with wants and desires that she has self-reflectively endorsed, and her endorsement is somehow a part cause of her behavior."[2] A person is autonomous to the extent that she rules herself; self-rule allegedly occurs when the person executes the skills needed to direct her behavior in light of values, principles, beliefs and desires that she has authenticated and so made her own.

Structuralist Accounts

The primary as well as the earliest internalist models understand personal autonomy to depend only on the structural character of an agent's psychological states and

---

1 The term "internalist" is similarly employed in the philosophy of mind, where "internalism" and "externalism" characterize different views about the propositional content of belief states. Though the analogy is not exact, philosophers such as Tyler Burge maintain an externalist's stance by contending that having a belief is a function of the causal relationship between the content of the agent's mental states and the world. In contrast, philosophers such as Jerry Fodor offer a more internalist analysis, and declare that what qualifies as a belief can be decided simply on the basis of what can be said of the agent's mental states themselves. See Burge, "Individualism and the Mental," *Midwest Studies in Philosophy*, vol. IV (1979).

2 Marilyn Friedman, *Autonomy, Gender, Politics* (New York, 2002), p. 5.

dispositions, and on an agent's judgments about these states. The distinctively "hierarchical" conceptions of autonomy independently advanced by Gerald Dworkin and Harry Frankfurt are quintessential structuralist accounts. According to these accounts what is central to the status of persons as autonomous agents and as freely-willing agents can only be explained by appealing to a second-level (or multi-leveled) psychology of "preferences about desires to do X." Dworkin and Frankfurt contend that, suitably explained, the possession of a hierarchical psychological structure is necessary and sufficient for personal autonomy and for autonomous action.[3] Agents are said to be autonomous when, first, the lower-order desires that move them to act cohere with and are confirmed by desires of a higher order and, second, an attitude of "identification" with or satisfaction with or concern for these desires ensues.[4]

Although Frankfurt does not always characterize the theory he develops as one of personal autonomy, his explication of the psychology of responsible persons who act freely can be read as an effort to do so. Indeed, Frankfurt's effort to discover the kind of freedom relevant for responsibility leads him to a conception of free will that he himself likens to self-control or autonomy.[5] Additionally, Dworkin's employment of the hierarchical apparatus to explain a conception of autonomy suggests that similar use of this tool could have been made by Frankfurt.

Frankfurt's project consists in an exploration of what must be true of persons in order for them to be appropriate subjects for moral responsibility and, in particular, to be the sort of entities accessible to the attitudes and actions which we take towards uniquely responsible agents.[6] What makes a person the sort of creature suited to actions of punishment and reward, for example?

Frankfurt states that the minimal necessary condition for responsibility is that the entity be a person, an individual endowed with a certain psychological capacity.

---

3   The concepts of personal autonomy and of autonomous choice or action are conflated in most authenticity accounts. This conflation is a mistake and generates problems for these accounts, as we shall see.

4   Though there are passages which suggest that Dworkin and Frankfurt may well disagree over the details of which persons are to count as having met these criteria and over the circumstances in which the criteria are met, their views are sufficiently similar to characterize both as hierarchical. Frankfurt's work spans several decades and can be found in his collected essays, *The Importance of What We Care About* (Cambridge, 1988) and *Necessity, Volition, and Love* (Cambridge, 1999), and in his book *The Reasons of Love* (Cambridge, 2004). For Dworkin's position, see *The Theory and Practice of Autonomy* (New York, 1988).

5   Most recently Frankfurt writes that "What really counts, so far as the issue of freedom goes … is autonomy. Autonomy is essentially a matter of whether we are active rather than passive in our motives and choices—whether, however we acquire them, they are the motives and choices that we really want and are therefore in no way alien to us." *The Reasons of Love*, p. 20, note 5. Also see Frankfurt, "Coercion and Moral Responsibility;" "Three Concepts of Free Action;" and "Identification and Wholeheartedness." These essays are reprinted in Frankfurt, *The Importance of What We Care About*. All references are to that text.

6   In this sense his work is sympathetic to the general project begun by P.F. Strawson in "Freedom and Resentment," *Proceedings of the British Academy*, 48 (1962): 1–25.

Specifically, a person is a being capable of forming volitions of a "second-order" or a "higher-order." Higher-order volitions are preferences that one of the person's lower-order desires to do some action be effective and so be her "will." The will is understood as that first-order aspect of the individual's preference-based psychology that directs a person's choices and motivates her to act. Through the formation of a second-order volition, a person identifies herself with a particular first-order desire, and makes that desire more truly her own.

Having second-order volitions signals that a person is able to reflect upon and evaluate her lower-order desires. Because Frankfurt believes moral responsibility is compatible with causal determinism, he makes reflection a necessary condition for moral responsibility but does not claim that the capacity for revising lower-order desires is needed for a person to be responsible. In virtue of this reflective activity, a person is marked as one who cares about the desires upon which she acts; she is not neutral with regard to their importance. Contrasted with a person is the "wanton" creature who, lacking second-order volitions (though perhaps having second-order preferences), is indifferent about which of her desires or impulses lead her to act.

In virtue of having second-order volitions, two varieties of freedom—freedom of the will, and the ability to act freely—are available. According to Frankfurt, a person's will is free only if, given any one of his first-order desires, the person can either choose that desire as his will or can opt for some other first-order desire as his will. Having freedom of the will means that the person "is free to have the will he wants" ... "The will of person whose will is free could have been otherwise; he could have done otherwise than to constitute his will as he did."[7]

Frankfurt's view is that freedom of the will is not required for either responsible action or autonomous action. What autonomous action calls for, contends Frankfurt, is *acting freely*. A person is said to act freely or of her own free will when she secures conformity between her second-order volition and her will, such that the lower-order desire to do some action is one with which she identifies or is "wholehearted" about. However fortuitously conformity is obtained, the result is that the person is moved by the will she wants and so no longer bothers to raise the question whether to be so moved. Frankfurt's approach is admittedly ahistorical; the focus is on features of the "current time-slice"[8] within which the agent acts, as this rather lengthy quotation makes plain:

> What is at stake ... is not a matter of the causal origins of the states of affairs in question, but [a person's] activity or passivity with respect to those states of affairs. A person is active with respect to his own desires when he identifies himself with them, and he is active with respect to what he does when what he does is the outcome of his identification of himself with the desire that moves him in doing it. Without such identification the person is a passive bystander to his desires and to what he does, regardless of whether the

7 Frankfurt, "Freedom of the Will and the Concept of a Person," in *The Importance of What We Care About*, pp. 11–25. Here at p. 24.

8 The phrase "current time-slice" to describe such models of responsible agency was coined by John Martin Fischer and Mark Ravizza.

causes of his desires and of what he does are the work of another agent or of impersonal external forces or of processes internal to his own body ... To the extent that a person identifies himself with the springs of his actions, he takes responsibility for those actions and acquires moral responsibility for them; moreover, the questions of *how* the actions and his identification with their springs are caused is [sic] irrelevant to the questions of whether he performs the actions freely or is morally responsible for performing them.[9]

In an effort to distinguish between the responsible (because allegedly autonomous) and the non-responsible (because allegedly non-autonomous) agent, Frankfurt invites us to consider the cases of the unwilling and the willing drug addicts. Neither the willing nor the unwilling addict has free will, because neither is free to choose which of their first-order desires shall translate into action. In both cases, "the desire to take the drug will be effective regardless of whether the addict wants this desire to constitute his will or not, i.e., regardless of his second-order volition. Both lack the power to avoid being moved into action by a certain lower-order desire."[10] What each does is largely determined by the addiction each has.

But where the unwilling addict wishes he were not pushed around by his addiction, and finds that his addiction undermines his ability to pursue his preferred plan of life, the willing addict has no quarrel with his manner of living and, moreover, would live exactly as he does even if it were the case that his actions were not in the slightest manner necessitated by his addiction. In the willing addict's case, his addiction causes him to lead a life identical to the one he would pursue if drug free. His addiction might be thought of as a feature that simply enhances his motivational system, and lessens the trouble to which he must go to execute a certain action. Frankfurt's view is that the willing addict acts freely, and is thus autonomous, because he secures conformity of his will to his second-order volitions. Even supposing that the addict could have had a different will and could have acted differently, the critical fact for deciding autonomy is that the addict would not have wanted his will to be any different. What matters for autonomy is that the person's action springs from those essential features of his character without which the person cannot be who he is— and these are characteristics of a person's will with respect to which the person has no ambivalence.

By contrast, the unwilling addict suffers an assault to his self-determination and, more fundamentally, to his personhood. For not only does the unwilling addict lack free will in that he is not free to have the will he wants, the unwilling addict does not act freely. The unwilling addict struggles against his first-order preference to take the drug and succumbs to it as to an alien impulse. In this case, the inner circumstances of the addict's action are autonomy-defeating.[11] It is because the unwilling addict

---

9   Frankfurt, "Three Concepts of Free Action," in *The Importance of What We Care About*, pp. 120–21.

10   Fischer, "Introduction: Responsibility and Freedom," in Fischer, ed., *Moral Responsibility* (Ithaca, 1986), p. 45.

11   Having "placed himself wholeheartedly behind one of his conflicting impulses, and not at all behind the other ... the tendency that the person has come to oppose—by having

does identify with a particular lower-order desire that he feels violated by his behavior. This addict is motivated because of an irresistible first-order desire which has defeated and is discordant with his second-order volition and by which, given the possibility of alternatives, he does not want to be moved. He therefore wishes to dissociate himself from what he actually does.

Acting freely or autonomously does not mean that a person acts willingly. A person might confront a state of affairs discordant with her desires and resent this, since it presents a set of alternatives from which the person does not want to choose. Nonetheless, the person might prefer without reservation one of the available choices over another. If so, Frankfurt's view is that the person would act freely, albeit grudgingly. That is, she would act autonomously within the limits of an unsatisfactory set of alternatives and would bear responsibility for the choice. The person who acts unwillingly, as is possible of the person who acts prudently under coercive conditions, is autonomous if the person does not act solely because of the undesired states she confronts and if the person prefers the alternative she selects to any other option, though she desires none of them.

In a nutshell, Frankfurt's position is that to act freely is to act wholeheartedly, and wholeheartedness is sufficient for personal autonomy. It is here that certain problems stemming from the conflation of autonomous choice and action with the autonomy of persons first become noticeable. If Frankfurt's concern is only to address local autonomy over particular actions and choices or autonomy with respect to certain roles, then acting freely might well suffice for autonomy. Because the bulk of Frankfurt's discussion is on moral responsibility for instances of choice and action we might think his interest is restricted to local autonomy. Frankfurt's famous counterexamples to the Principle of Alternate Possibilities and the numerous Frankfurt-style counterexamples generated in light of his work are intended to show that, intuitively, an agent who has no options for choice or for action can be responsible for her actions. Because global autonomy, unlike local or episodic autonomy over choice, calls for the ability to have the "regulative control" necessary to alter aspects of one's circumstances, it is not a straightforwardly compatibilist concept, as acting freely is intended to be.[12]

But matters are not so straightforward, for the following reason. Frankfurt is not concerned merely to delineate the state of affairs that exists when an attribution of responsibility arises, for presumably there will be occasions when it makes sense to say of a wanton, or an unwilling addict, or a very young child that each is answerable

---

made a decision, or in some other way—is in a sense extruded and rendered external to him … If the alienated tendency proves nonetheless to be too powerful, what it overcomes is not, then, just an opposing inclination. It overcomes the person himself." Frankfurt, *The Reasons of Love*, pp. 91–2.

12 I borrow the term "regulative control" from John Martin Fischer, who develops the idea in "Responsiveness and Moral Responsibility," *Responsibility, Character, and the Emotions: New Essays in Moral Psychology*, Ferdinand Schoeman (ed.) (New York, 1987), pp. 81–106. Also see Fischer and Ravizza, *Responsibility and Control* (Cambridge, 1998) for development of this concept.

for his conduct; each will exhibit local autonomy or will appear to act freely with respect to episodes of behavior. It is, rather, the general conditions for free agency— an effort to distinguish between the autonomous and the non-autonomous agent and, more ambitiously, to articulate the concept of personhood functioning at the core—that commands Frankfurt's attention. This suggests that Frankfurt regards self-determined choice and action as evidence of the global or dispositional variety of self-determination, evidence that is fully forthcoming in the attitude an individual takes to herself and to her motives for action.

Admittedly, characterizing Frankfurt's interest as directed at global or dispositional autonomy as opposed to the local variant is controversial. But there is evidence that the phenomenon of global autonomy is his concern. Frankfurt's point and the point of Frankfurt-style counterexamples appear to be that autonomy is constituted by nothing more than a person's attitude to what may or may not be a causally determined situation.

The Limits of the Hierarchy

Any account that makes autonomy incumbent upon hierarchical congruity alone faces what has become known as the authority problem. In a nutshell, the problem is that such accounts fail to explain how a person's highest-order values, in virtue of which the authenticity of the agent's choice is determined, can themselves be autonomous. Wholehearted identification is not enough to meet our intuitive judgments about autonomy, for the acts of identification by which lower-order desires are considered to be one's own might be motivated by "choices which manifest mindless conformity to convention [and tradition]."[13] The authority problem is thought to be especially pronounced in desire-based hierarchical models because akratic or incontinent desires can be the catalyst for a coherent hierarchical structure. If autonomy follows from identification and identification follows from the structural coherence of psychological states and nothing more, then identification can be induced by techniques such as psychological manipulation. But the authority problem also exists for hierarchical models of autonomy that are not desire based. Indeed, given the prevalence of socialization, the authority problem might be ubiquitous. The problem arises because it seems a person cannot be autonomous with regard to the will that moves her to act if, due to a process of social enculturation, the higher-order principles that inform and govern her will have been socially implanted. Clearly, the higher-order mental states that motivate a person may be as much a product of socialization as are the person's lower-level motivations.

---

13   Friedman, "Autonomy and the Split-Level Self," *Southern Journal of Philosophy* 24/1 (1986): 20. Jon Elster raises a similar worry in his claim that a person's preferences can take on a coherent, integrated character simply through a process of automatic adaptation to circumstance. See Elster, *Ulysses and the Sirens* (Cambridge, 1979) and "Sour Grapes—Utilitarianism and the Genesis of Wants," in A. Sen and B. Williams (eds), *Utilitarianism and Beyond* (Cambridge, 1982).

To what extent, then, is the notion of wholehearted identification helpful in singling out those agents who are autonomous from those who are not? What guarantee is there that one who wholeheartedly identifies with her motives is in actual and rightful control of her decisions? What guarantee is there that one who wholeheartedly identifies with her motives leads a life that is free of consistent and pervasive coercion or manipulation and is in possession of the power to determine how she shall live? Wholehearted identification stipulates that one's volitions are reflective and unequivocal, but little is said about the etiology of the second-order volition itself, and of the status of the individual to whom this volition belongs.

Perhaps the authority problem can be avoided by denying that hierarchical congruity of the volitional elements of a person's psychology in accordance with higher-level standards of assessment is a necessary condition for the attainment of autonomy. Perhaps it makes more sense to ensure autonomy against the threat of untoward influences by requiring that various elements of a person's psyche— cognitive as well as conative—are holistically integrated rather than hierarchical positioned. That is, rather than treat the hierarchical supremacy of some desires over others as the locus of free agency or autonomy, we should locate autonomy in the successful integration of a variety of elements of a person's psychology. Rather than take higher-order principles and pro-attitudes as providing the test against which a person decides which of her motives for action best authenticate her will, we might look to a person's longings and anxieties and the incentive to change one's life that derives from them as providing the most accurate representation of what is important to the individual.

However, it is not clear that one can avoid the problems that beset hierarchical views simply by assuming a more holistic and inclusive approach to the psychological economy of the autonomous person. A person's wholehearted identification with or satisfaction with a certain holistic configuration of desires, beliefs, emotional commitments and the like might be produced by inauthentic means, thus leaving the authority problem intact. There is no reason why a person's inclination to embrace this rather than that configuration of desires, beliefs, and emotional commitments offers a stronger case for representing the authentic motivations of the individual than do principles of reason at the apex of the hierarchy. The problem of authority might persist if it remains open to question whether a holistic configuration of motives for action has assumed a particular shape because of forces beyond the ken and the control of the individual.

Perhaps the solution to the authority problem lies elsewhere. Gary Watson argues that the problem of authority arises because hierarchical theories oversimplify the motivational psychology of persons by analyzing autonomy exclusively in terms of a person's desires.[14] In response, Watson offers what has been called a *Platonic* view, according to which a person's motivational psychology involves a valuational component and an appetitive component. The valuational system consists in the set

---

14 See Watson, "Free Agency," *Journal of Philosophy*, vol. LXXII, no. 8 (1975). I will use the terms free agency and autonomy interchangeably in discussing Watson's account.

of ends and principles around which normative judgments about alternative states of affairs are generated. Watson concedes that value judgments which motivate action are connected with second-order volitions; to value an action is to desire that it be effective and that conflicting desires be ineffective. To this extent Watson's view maintains a connection to the hierarchical machinery. At the same time, Watson points out that a person who is free in the sense that he is able to follow certain desires is not necessarily free in the sense that he is able to do what he most *values*. And it is this latter variety of freedom—the freedom to be motivated by what one values— that is necessary for free agency. A person acts freely when the faculty of reason determines value among various states of affairs and motivates action in light of this determination. When a person's valuational and motivational systems fail to coincide, the person is "motivated to do things that he does not deem worth doing. This possibility is the basis for the principle problem of free action: a person may be obstructed by his own will."[15]

While Watson has not repudiated this account of free agency,[16] he has recently offered an elaborated "self-disclosure" analysis of responsible agency that "goes naturally with a view of free action and free will as autonomy."[17] Watson has argued that the "notion of responsibility central to ethical life and ethical appraisal"[18] is concerned with and is anchored to conduct that makes known a person's evaluative allegiances and so a person's distinctive character as an agent. Watson calls this the aretaic (or attributability) face of responsibility—the perspective which discloses the agent's virtues and imperfections. To be attributed with responsibility for conduct or character from the aretaic perspective is to be recognized as an agent—that is, as an individual with a moral capacity to "adopt certain ends among others" as one's own and thus "to declare what one stands for."[19] In so acting, a person reveals her quality of character and opens herself to a legitimate variety of moral evaluation.

If autonomy is connected with free, responsible agency is this in virtue of the aretaic face of responsibility alone? Watson allows that even if an actor "owns" her behavior and traits of character as the aretaic analysis mandates, it will not be fair to hold her accountable unless she can control her behavior. One to whom character and behavior is rightly attributed might be normatively incompetent, incapable of

---

15 Watson, "Free Agency," p. 213. Watson's view finds support from Thomas Hill, Jr., who points out that, on a conception of autonomy that emphasizes the capacity humans have for valuing, what an individual wants as an expression of her selfish interest may not be what the individual chooses as an autonomous being. What will color one's self-determined selections will be what the person most values. See Hill, "Autonomy and Benevolent Lies," *The Journal of Value Inquiry* 18 (1984): 251–67.

16 Watson continues to offer this account as representative of his views. See *Free Will*, 2nd edition, Gary Watson (ed.) (Oxford, 2003), p. 18, where he describes his as an account of freedom as the capacity for rational self-governance.

17 Gary Watson, "Two Faces of Responsibility," *Philosophical Topics*, 24/2 (Fall 1996): 227–248; at p. 227.

18 Watson, "Two Faces of Responsibility," p. 229.

19 Watson, "Two Faces of Responsibility," p. 233.

controlling his ends (or his character) by attending to what are morally appropriate constraints upon behavior. The other face of responsibility, which Watson labels the accountability perspective, is intended to guarantee control of this sort, the sort that makes deserved retribution and compensatory justice plausible. According to Watson, both perspectives are needed for ascriptions of responsibility—perhaps in conjunction they suffice for autonomy.

Let us defer for the moment the question of whether Watson's account of free will and free action captures the essence of autonomy and focus on the question of whether Watson's analysis represents a real departure from the hierarchical view of autonomy Frankfurt defends. With respect to the first face of responsibility, the aretaic face concerned with a person's moral character, Watson sounds quite sympathetic to Frankfurt. Here, with Frankfurt, Watson contends that a person acts freely when she acts on preferences that are her own because she cares about them. (The second face of responsibility may call for the availability of alternatives for choice and action, if these are needed to ensure the agent control over her behavior. If alternatives are necessary, then Watson's account, unlike Frankfurt's, is not plainly compatibilist. However, Watson's picture of human motivation may make the hierarchy superfluous for acting freely, thereby circumventing some of the problems that beset it. According to Watson, a person acts freely when her actions express what the person most values—what she identifies with—but this can reveal itself at the first order, thus rendering higher-order volitions, and indeed the entire hierarchical apparatus, dispensable. A similar point was noted by the late Irving Thalberg who complained that hierarchical theories of free agency were encumbered by an explanatory structure that was recursive and superfluous.[20] It is unnecessary to explain cases of compulsion or hypnotically induced desires by saying the victim

____

20 Thalberg, "Hierarchical Analyses of Unfree Action," *Canadian Journal of Philosophy*, vol. VIII, no 2 (June 1978). Reprinted in Christman (ed.), *The Inner Citadel: Essays on Individual Autonomy* (New York, 1989), pp. 123–36. All further references are to that volume. Strictly speaking, Thalberg does not offer an alternative to hierarchical theories but rather criticizes a hierarchical account of unfree action. Thalberg argues that if nothing ensures that a higher level of identification is decisive, why bother to pursue the hierarchical method at all? Why not stop at the ground floor and seek the real or authentic agent there? Thalberg makes the point by examining instances of action under coercive circumstances. In such cases, it is unnecessary to equate a person's unwillingness to comply with a first-order desire by which, as a prudential concern, he is moved into compliance with a second-order aversion to that desire. Unfree action can be explained simply by showing that a person finds his reasons for acting painful even while the person acts only because of these reasons. The principle object of the constrained person's aversion is not a first-order desire to act, but the coercive situation itself. Since it is not the desire that the individual objects to, but the action or coercive situation itself, it is that phenomenon which contains the freedom-undermining element. In fact, the desire to comply may be one the individual has no wish to abandon; it may indeed be a motive that he wants to approve and ought to approve for the very reason that it is prudent. Thus, "Dworkin and Frankfurt are mistaken when they suppose that what the constrained person doesn't want is for some desire or other to move him." Thalberg, "Hierarchical Analyses of Unfree Action," p. 128.

is pushed around by a first-order desire where there is a higher-order preference that opposes it. A one-level analysis of unfree action can be given. These are simply cases in which none of the person's desires can be attributed to him as his own—they are, rather, the wishes of his manipulators. Nothing like a complicated hierarchical story is needed to explain why this agent is unfree.

Theories of free agency such as Watson's enable us to understand Frankfurt's conditions of wholeheartedness, decisive identification, and authenticity as expressions of a person's evaluational systems. But Watson's view confronts its own set of difficulties. One difficulty is that Watson's self-disclosure account does not settle the question of authority that bedevils hierarchical accounts. Watson tells us that the locus of free agency is that part of a person's psychological economy that expresses the person's evaluative allegiances. By claiming ownership of certain values a person gives expression to her free, autonomous agency. But it remains possible that an individual can be motivated by what she most values even where her values result from situations where violations to global autonomy are rampant. This is counterintuitive. Surely the agent must not be said merely to act from her values, but from values that are not produced in autonomy-undermining ways. And, just as surely, the agent must be able to execute those values—to give expression to them—in an environment where her autonomy is not constrained.

A second problem affects Watson's account of free agency as much as it might affect a hierarchical view. This problem is that while people frequently experience a psychological struggle—a struggle of the will—between what they most want and what they value, it is false that every unresolved conflict indicates a lack of freedom agency on the part of the agent. That fact that I am often conflicted about pursuing what I desire (say, a slice of chocolate mousse cake) and what I value or most desire (a healthy cholesterol level) does not make me any less autonomous, or any less of a free agent, in my choice of cake or in my life overall. I might even be weak-willed about avoiding chocolate mousse, yet weakness of will does not make me non-autonomous with regard to that fondness. Important values compete for supremacy within the catalog of things a person cares about quite often, and this competition may remain unresolved.

Sartre reminds us of this with his classic tale of the man who values fidelity to his aging widowed mother at the same time that he values committing his time to securing the independence of his country, a value that can only be secured by sacrificing the value of maternal fidelity. Both constitute practical reasons and the agency of the person is, in part, intimately bound by each. The tension one experiences between these values is one's own, yet one is "wholehearted" with respect to neither. But if a person sees the merit of each and is pulled in opposite directions by both, why is the person less autonomous for this fact? And why is the person's choice to realize one value over the other less autonomous because of the conflict? My belief is that conflicted values, desires, and kindred psychological states curtail autonomy only where, first, they are individually emblematic of a person's identity and, second, they are of key importance to the execution of activities fundamental to human agency or, third, they engender conflict of a sufficiently comprehensive kind to render any semblance of an agent impossible. Ambivalence by itself need not be the antithesis of free agency. In numerous ways and to various degrees a person can be autonomous at the same time she can find herself acting in ways that appear to alienate her from some of the things she cares about.

Autonomy and History

A different set of concerns for Frankfurt's account of free agency results from of the ahistorical character of this account. Frankfurt makes a person's autonomous choice and action conditional on the individual's attitude towards her motivations, quite independently of the circumstances under which that attitude arises. The criteria for responsibility and autonomy are largely indifferent to questions about the developmental history of the person's desires and the attitude of identification toward these desires. Presumably, we are to take Frankfurt at his word when he tells us that,

> A person may be capricious and irresponsible in forming his second-order volitions and give no serious consideration to what is at stake. Second-order volitions express evaluations only in the sense that they are preferences. There is no essential restriction on the kind of basis, if any, upon which they are formed.[21]

In "Three Concepts of Free Action" Frankfurt suggests a thin historical constraint for autonomy.[22] Specifically, he alleges an individual's attitude of higher-order approval with respect to an addiction will not suffice for autonomy when the higher-order desire follows from the constant intervention of an alien entity. (In this case, that entity is a fanciful Devil/neurologist.) Constant intervention would make the activity of critical reflection upon one's preferences, and the settled satisfaction with these, impossible. It is as important that an individual's desire to Φ stems from a stable situation as it is that the individual assumes an attitude of approval toward that desire.

It is not entirely obvious why Frankfurt believes this constraint on continual intervention is necessary. Barring cases of severe psychosis sufficient to render the very activities of evaluation and satisfaction or identification impossible, a person can identify just as easily with an episodic history, with a history that is heteronomously induced, or with the products of such a history as she can with a more uninterrupted coherent pattern of motivations. Whether intervention is frequent, constant, or a one-shot event may affect the likelihood of satisfaction or identification but should not decide its possibility.

---

21 Frankfurt, "Freedom of the Will and the Concept of a Person" p. 19, footnote #6. Most recently, Frankfurt repudiates a historicity condition in his "Reply to Fischer," in Buss and Overton (eds), *Contours of Agency: Essays on the Themes of Harry Frankfurt* (Cambridge, 2001).

22 I call this a suggestion on Frankfurt's part since he seems unwilling to commit himself to this view, pursuing an ahistorical account of autonomy for the most part.

Frankfurt's nod to stability aside, history does seem relevant for autonomy. It is implausible that a person is autonomous provided her will conforms to a higher-order evaluation even though the first-order desire which is her will stems from an addiction or from a coercive situation where there are no welcome alternatives for action. Presumably the historical genesis of a person's operative motivational psychology is relevant for assessing genuine control of choice and genuine authenticity of values. Gerald Dworkin appreciates this. Like Frankfurt, Dworkin's hierarchical account of self-determination is a theory about "internal, psychological freedom."[23] Unlike Frankfurt, Dworkin conceives of self-determination as the second-order capacity of an individual to evaluate and, if necessary, revise her reasons for identifying with a particular first-order motivation. He states that "It is not the identification or lack of identification that is crucial to being autonomous, but the capacity to raise the question whether I will identify with or reject the reasons for which I now act."[24] When this reflective and revisionary capacity is exercised, "persons define their nature, and take responsibility for the kind of person they are."[25] This marks the "authenticity" requirement of autonomy. In addition, Dworkin requires that a person identify with her desires under conditions of "procedural independence." Together, authenticity and procedural independence provide "the full formula for autonomy."[26]

Dworkin offers several reasons in support of his charge that identification alone is too weak to capture the essence of self-determination. First, he believes a capacity condition better captures the global view of autonomy than does a locally oriented or episodic experience of identification.[27] Second, if it were the case that coherence alone between levels of a person's psychology determined autonomy, a person whose psychology fails to be congruent in the manner required of identification could merely alter or reject her desires of a higher order so as to achieve coherence. But it is counterintuitive that "one becomes more autonomous by changing one's higher-order preferences."[28] Third, identification can occur even in situations where interferences to autonomy are evident. As Frankfurt's examples show, a person can evaluate and approve of her motives for action in a manner consistent with identification even while subject to coercion or manipulation. A corollary of this is that the act of identifying, and the state of identification, can be induced in ways that offend self-determination. What is violated or interfered with in these circumstances

---

23 Dworkin, "Acting Freely," *Nous* 9 (1970): 367–83.

24 Dworkin, *Theory and Practice of Autonomy*, p. 15.

25 Dworkin, *Theory and Practice of Autonomy*, p. 20 and p. 108.

26 Dworkin, "The Concept of Autonomy," in *Science and Ethics*, ed. R. Haller (Rodopi Press, 1981). Reprinted in Christman (ed.), *The Inner Citadel* (1989), p. 61. All references to this text.

27 Dworkin explicitly interprets self-determination as a characteristic of an individual's entire life rather than a feature of the person at a particular point in time, stating that "autonomy seems intuitively to be a global rather than local concept." *Theory and Practice of Autonomy*, pp. 15– 16.

28 Dworkin, *Theory and Practice of Autonomy*, p. 16. Also see Elster's "Sour Grapes" for a discussion of this phenomenon.

is not the act or the condition of identifying, but rather the capacity to make authentic identifications.

By itself, of course, the capacity condition is insufficient for autonomy. A general capacity-to-Φ can be induced in ways that compromise autonomy (by hypnosis, for example), as can the act of identification. What is needed is some assurance that a person's evaluative abilities are her own and can be actualized. Dworkin believes this assurance is forthcoming if we view the capacity condition as entailing the further condition of procedural independence [PI]. According to Dworkin,

> Spelling out the conditions of procedural independence involves distinguishing those ways of influencing people's reflective and critical faculties which subvert them from those which promote and improve them.[29]

A failure of procedural independence occurs when

> [T]he choice of the type of person he wants to be may have itself been influenced by other persons in such a fashion that we do not view [it] as being the person's own ... In this case his motivational structure is his, but [is] not his own.[30]

PI supplies some, although by no means complete, assurance that violations to autonomy will not take the form of attacks upon the ability of the agent to raise critical questions regarding her motives and upon her ability to revise these motives. PI ensures that those higher-order aspects of an individual's psychology which evaluate and authenticate the individual's lower-order reasons for acting have developed in ways that are consonant with action that is under the agent's control. For Dworkin, then, the mark of personal autonomy is not identification *simpliciter*, or the capacity to assess one's reasons for action, but the fact that persons are capable of rendering their higher and lower-order desires coherent via a process of authentication that occurs in a procedurally independent fashion.

It is not clear how we are to know whether the condition of procedural independence has been secured. How do we distinguish subversive influences from their benign counterparts? And how are we to know that a person's critical and reflective capacities have been undermined? We cannot determine either simply by examining the structure and integrity of a person's psychology. Indeed, Dworkin concedes that a person's approval of the hierarchical pattern her desires assume might be prompted by phenomena such as browbeating, self-deception, manipulation, hypnosis, intimidation, addiction, and weakness of will. All are phenomena standardly regarded as threats to the agent's critical abilities and so all are potentially autonomy-undermining.

But Dworkin contends the presence of such phenomena alone does not guarantee that autonomy is undermined. According to Dworkin, that a person has been influenced in ways that might harm her is not in itself a threat to autonomy. Influential

---

29 Dworkin, *Theory and Practice of Autonomy*, p. 18.
30 Dworkin, "The Concept of Autonomy," p. 61.

phenomena threaten a person's capacity for critical reflection only when the person is unaware of their presence and of the effect they have on her. If a person is aware that her choices have been influenced by, say, a deliberate withholding of salient information, and she assents to this influence, recognizing the effect it will have on her motivations and desires, the condition of procedural independence has been satisfied. That is, procedural independence is secured when a person's assessment of her reasons for action and the critical questions she raises regarding her motives for action have not been induced in her by mechanisms she rejects, and in a manner she opposes. A person may correctly acknowledge as her own a desire that has been introduced in her heteronomously. Indeed, she may be autonomous when the entire economy of her desires has been introduced in such a fashion.

If Dworkin is correct, the conditions for an autonomous psychology can be satisfied even in circumstances where factors that typically are taken to jeopardize autonomy are present. Like Dworkin, other philosophers within the internalist tradition claim procedural independence among the necessary conditions of autonomy. But some philosophers contend that procedural independence demands the satisfaction of more fully specified normative and substantive criteria regarding the influences that shape a person's psychological character. Whether a person's desires are formed under conditions that favor authenticity cannot be decided by appeal to the actor's point of view alone. These desires, if authentic, must be the progeny of non-coercive, sober circumstances.

In this vein, several philosophers have found it necessary to emend the hierarchical approach to autonomy. The worry is that the structuralist, ahistorical view of Frankfurt and the minimally historical view of Dworkin fail to make sense of the influence of certain forms of socialization upon an individual's acquisition of preferences and values. Critics agree with Frankfurt and Dworkin that the autonomous agent's actions must be governed by her desires or controlled by her will, and agree that the will of the agent must be governed on the basis of values accepted by the agent following critical appraisal. But they note that this leaves room for situations where we must count as responsible persons who nevertheless suffer from a process of socialization that leaves them insecure or insensitive, plagued by any host of ills that leave them incapable of acting rightly and reasonably, as it were. Dworkin distinguishes cases where an agent's desires are determined by "foreign" forces from those in which desires are determined by the agent's reflective endorsement. But his account does not differentiate between persons (such as ourselves), to whom we have no ambivalence attributing autonomous action and free moral agency, and those persons towards whom such ambivalence is felt because they lack the resources essential to acting rightly and reasonably.

Because a person's operative motives and choice of lifestyle are clearly colored by socialization and conditioning, greater attention must be paid to the history of a person's psychological states and to the person's participation in and attitude towards this history. Taking the idea of procedural independence as their cue, philosophers such as John Christman characterize autonomy of choice and of action as a function of the development of a person's psychological states, of the person's participation in that process, and of the person's occurrent approval of the psychological state and the process leading to its fruition. Christman's theory is one of a kind that claims

> [A] person is autonomous (either *tout court* or relative to a certain characteristic) when she has developed in a way that is "procedurally independent." This means that, irrespective of the 'content' of these processes—of the values, desires, or characteristics embraced by the agent—a person is autonomous when she adopts traits in the proper manner or if she reflectively identifies with the characteristic.[31]

Where autonomy is present, the relationship between a person and the pro-attitudes and affective states that motivate her is marked by the absence of alienation from the state in question; to be alienated is "to experience strong negative affect relative to that characteristic—to disapprove in some manner—and to resist whatever motivational force it may have..."[32]

Christman formulated the historical condition rather differently earlier on. Then he claimed that what counts for autonomy is

> [T]he manner in which the agent *came to have* a set of desires rather than her attitude towards the desires at any one time. The key element of autonomy is ... the agent's acceptance or rejection of the process of desire formation or the factors that give rise to that formation, rather than the agent's identification with the desire itself ... What matters for local autonomy is not whether I am free to do otherwise than have the desire (i.e., not whether I am free to reject or alter the desire) but whether I autonomously have the desire, i.e., whether the process by which the desire developed proceeded against my will.[33]

Christman now claims to have abandoned this view, granting less significance to the developmental character of a person's psychological economy and a person's assessment of the developmental process and emphasizing instead the absence of alienation.[34] However, the condition of nonalienation is not intended, explicitly at any rate, to repudiate the earlier emphasis on resistance to the conditions that precipitated the development of pro-attitudes. Rather, the condition of nonalienation is intended (by Christman's own admission) to avoid the difficulties that beset proceduralist accounts that emphasize identification and actual endorsement of one's motives for action.[35] For this reason, the concerns I want to raise for his account of autonomy remain relevant.

---

31 Christman, "Procedural Autonomy and Liberal Legitimacy," in James Stacey Taylor (ed.), *Personal Autonomy* (Cambridge, 2005), p. 281.

32 Christman, "Procedural Autonomy and Liberal Legitimacy," p. 279.

33 Christman, "Autonomy and Personal History," p. 10; p. 6. Also see Christman, "Defending Historical Autonomy: A Reply to Professor Mele," *Canadian Journal of Philosophy* 23/2 (June 1993): 281–90.

34 In correspondence.

35 Christman, "Procedural Autonomy and Liberal Legitimacy," p. 279. Christman's revision of his account was prompted, at least in part, by certain criticisms pressed by Alfred Mele (Mele, "History and Personal Autonomy," *Canadian Journal of Philosophy* 23/2 (June

Let us note, first, that because Christman's account incorporates criteria that appeal to the developmental environment of the agent we may call his an "externalist" theory of psychological autonomy. Nonetheless, the approach remains firmly within the tradition that analyzes agent autonomy as a psychological phenomenon. Christman, for example, identifies autonomy as "the actual psychological condition of self-government defined as the ability to be self-governing."[36] In addition, he rejects a global conception of "autonomy as an all-or-nothing property of a person's whole life" in favor of a more "localized" interpretation of autonomy as a function of the formation of individual desires.[37] (As an aside, I think this is a misreading of global autonomy. One who is autonomous, or who lives a life in which autonomy is evident, is not autonomous *tout court*, or with respect to every activity. Autonomy is typically a matter of varying scope and varying intensity, as the discussion in subsequent chapters makes plain. In any event, Christman construes global autonomy, a property of a person's life, as just an aggregate of episodes of local autonomy.)

Here is a sketch of the historical approach as Christman presents it. Autonomy transpires when an individual's psychology remains, at least during those junctures where critical scrutiny of a person's desires, values, and motives occurs, free from external factors that illegitimately influence the individual. Christman urges that critical appraisal of the development of a person's cognitive and psychological states must transpire in a climate free of factors that might impede a person's reflective capabilities. Illegitimate influences are those that compromise an individual's ability to evaluate the manner in which the factors that motivate her are formed. Satisfaction of a fourfold test precludes illegitimacy and thereby determines autonomy: (1) the process of critical reflection that takes place when the person identifies certain psychological and cognitive phenomena as her own cannot be caused solely by the influence of factors external to the individual; (2) the process by which a person comes to have certain motives rather than others, and the factors that influence the development of these motives, must be "transparent" to the person—we are autonomous only when the etiology of those factors that serve as our springs of action is epistemically plain; (3) if, at any moment, the person wishes to revise these motives once the manner in which they transpire is evident to her, she must be able

---

1993): 271–80). Like Christman, Mele states his task as one of articulating the sufficient conditions for psychological autonomy and psychological episodes with respect to which the agent is autonomous. This is autonomy over what the agent could intend, choose, or decide to do; "the kind of autonomy open to even a shackled Prometheus" (p. 144, *Autonomous Agents*). But Mele notes that developmental autonomy—emphasizing a person's pro-attitudes towards the etiology of her motivational states—is consistent with a lack of autonomy *vis à vis* the continued possession of a desire (what he refers to as P-autonomy) and with a lack of autonomy over the influence a desire has upon an agent (what Mele labels I-autonomy). See Mele, *Autonomous Agents: From Self-Control to Autonomy*, pp. 185–6.

36 Christman, *The Inner Citadel*, pp. 5–6.

37 Christman, "Autonomy and Personal History," p. 3.

to do so; (4) and the person must be rational, that is, her desires and pro-attitudes must emerge from a consistent set of beliefs.[38]

In commenting on the first of these tests Christman states, "if the critical reflection that takes place as we identify certain desires as truly our own is induced from some outside source, then it would be correct to label the lower-order desire in question non-autonomous."[39] So suppose I desire to do volunteer work (X), and this is a desire with which I identify upon reflection. If I identify with X *only* due to the influence the elders of my church exert upon me (factor Y), and if, having become aware of factor Y, I want to revise or abandon X, then desire X fails the first condition (and perhaps the third condition as well) and is illegitimate.

I am unconvinced that failure of these tests yields failure of global autonomy or even failed episodes of local autonomy. To see why this is so, think of an agent—I'll call her the reluctant careerist—who develops a desire to leave her children in the care of another person so as to pursue full time employment. Let us imagine that she has no objections to the desire itself. She might even be satisfied with the desire. The reluctant careerist is attentive to the formation of this preference, and notes that her acceptance of it derives from her envious observations of other people engaged in lives of conspicuous, luxurious consumption. Although she does not come to reject or revise the desire, she does oppose its genesis. Her opposition might stem from her belief that desires of this sort—ones that will, after all, affect her life quite significantly—should never be prompted by such selfish yearnings. Christman must say the agent fails to be autonomous because her resistance to the manner in which her desire is formed signals the presence of a reflection-constraining factor. But why say this? We have no reason to think that the development of this woman's desires involves a cognitive failure on her part. There are no factors at work that restrict her critically reflective attitude towards the manner in which the desire develops nor are factors that undermine her occurrent endorsement of the desire present. The woman is neither self-deceived, irrational, or plainly under the influence of factors that inhibit self-reflection.

Even if Christman now repudiates the first and second portions of the test, choosing instead to emphasize the attitude a person experiences subsequent to the development of her motives for action, the result will not be a satisfactory test for autonomy. If autonomy is consistent with resistance to the manner in which one's

---

38 Christman upholds this view in his most recent work. He states "[A] person who, upon reflection, feels no affinity with certain aspects of herself, wants to change or, if that is not feasible, distance herself from them and feels a diluted sense of motivation relative to them is not autonomous. Therefore, a person is not autonomous relative to those aspects of herself that would produce feelings of alienation were she to reflect on them in light of how they came about." See his "Procedural Autonomy and Liberal Legitimacy," p. 280.

39 Christman, "Autonomy: A Defense of the Split-Level Self," *Southern Journal of Philosophy* 25/3: 281–93, p. 289. In this regard, Christman follows the criteria Frankfurt supplies for free action in "Coercion and Moral Responsibility": "We often have to know whether or not specific factors were the *major* causes of a person's action or desire," and this is a matter of empirical discovery. See Christman, "Autonomy: A Defense of the Split-Level Self," p. 290.

preferences have formed then history is less important for autonomy than Christman would originally have us believe. Clearly historical conditions are not sufficient for autonomy; neither, as Christman has described them, are they necessary for autonomy. Far more important for autonomy than approval of preference formation are the reasons that exist for resisting the medium of a desire's development. Far more important for autonomy than absence of alienation concerning the resultant pro-attitudes is the impact alienation has on the person's life. Suppose our reluctant careerist develops a preference to work because she needs to escape an oppressive domestic environment. She might fail to resist the development of this desire; she might even find her incentive to work welcome in that it carries motivational force sufficient to get her out of the home, and into a career. But this in no way indicates that her desire is autonomous and even less that she is autonomous. Neither local nor global autonomy is guaranteed by the failure to resist the development of one's desires nor by a person's pro-attitude or lack of negative affect toward the desire itself.

Approval of the springs of one's actions may be actual or merely hypothetical. The latter is suggested by the conditional construction of the test—"If the person were to resist…;" "If the person wished to revise these motives…"—and is the more credible interpretation. (Recently Christman has stated that "a person is not autonomous relative to those aspects of herself that *would produce* feelings of alienation were she to reflect on them in light of how they came about."[40]) The former would impose too stringent a test. Few people subject the bulk of their motivations to critical scrutiny. But problems with hypothetical tests are legion, as Christman himself concedes.[41] A person's inclination and willingness to survey the genesis of her motives for action is contingent on any number of things, including the person's epistemic state. What are the conditions under which a person would be prompted to appraise her motives for action? Most people are moved to do this only when they have some independent reason to think the motive is of importance for autonomy, or to think the motive is atypical of what the person has come to expect of herself. This suggests autonomy antedates, rather than is created by, episodes of hypothetical critical appraisal.

The modality of the test is uncertain as well. How close to the actual world must the agent's possible acceptance be? Does Christman have in mind hypothetical acceptance of a possible process of appraisal or of an actual process of appraisal? There are, too, issues about how far he intends to press the demand for transparency. To what degree must "the true determinants of an agent's behavior" be known (or knowable) to him?[42] The actual reasons for which the agent performs an action might be very different from the reasons the agent believes are relevant to the explanation of her

---

40 Christman, "Procedural Autonomy and Liberal Legitimacy," footnote 38.

41 Christman, "Defending Historical Autonomy: A Reply to Professor Mele," footnote 5, p. 289.

42 Dworkin raises this as a concern for autonomy in "Autonomy and Behavior Control," *Hastings Center Report* 6 (February 1976): 26.

action.[43] Many of (if not the bulk of) our motives for action are so deeply entrenched in our social history or buried under layers of the psyche as to be inaccessible.

Autonomy as Procedural Competency

Others philosophers who construe autonomy as authenticity focus their attention on the quality of procedural practices exhibited by the agent and are less concerned with whether the procedures at stake bear upon the psychological or the environmental status of the individual. Diana Meyers, for example, charges that autonomy depends on whether a person possesses and successfully uses a "repertory of coordinated skills that make up autonomy competency" coupled with "the collocation of attributes that emerges as a person successfully exercises autonomy competency."[44] Meyers focuses on a triad of tasks—those of self-discovery, self-definition, and self-direction—whose skillful performance enables a person to engage in the enterprise of becoming her own person by defining and redefining her personality into an integrated, dynamic whole. Meyers charges that

> Whether episodic or programmatic, what makes the difference between autonomous and heteronomous decisions is the way in which people arrive at them—the procedures they follow or fail to follow. Autonomous people must be disposed to consult their selves, and they must be equipped to do so. More specifically, they must be able to pose and answer the question "What do I really want, need, care about, value, etcetera?"; they must be able to act on the answer; and they must be able to correct themselves when they get the answer wrong. The skills that enable people to make this inquiry and to carry out their decisions constitute what I shall call *autonomy competency*...[45]

Meyers rightly presses the point that autonomous agency involves the development and realization of skills that depend on the social climate of the agent for their emergence as well as sustenance. Her account better approaches the naturalized ideal of autonomy explicated in the first chapter. Her account avoids the problems of authority that beset hierarchical and platonic models of self-governance and by focusing on practical competencies she moves beyond treating autonomy as a phenomenon predicated solely in terms of a person's cognitive and psychological states. The emphasis remains on autonomy as authenticity of self, but authenticity is described in quite broad terms: Authenticity is in evidence when "action spring[s] from the depths of the individual's being"; when the agent "does what makes sense in terms of his or her own identity"; when the agent is "not so influenced by others that [her] choices seem a committee project"; when she lives in harmony with her convictions and inclinations.[46]

---

43 Stephen Darwall formulates this distinction in *Impartial Reason* (Ithaca, 1983), p. 25.

44 Diana T. Meyers, *Self, Society, and Personal Choice* (New York, 1989), p. 92.

45 Meyers, *Self, Society, and Personal Choice*, pp. 52–3.

46 Meyers, *Self, Society, and Personal Choice*, p. 8.

From the overarching skills of self-discovery, self-definition, and self-direction Meyers distills an impressive but, I think, unwieldy number of competencies falling into three broad categories—communicative, imaginative, and volitional[47]—and alleges these provide for the integrated personality that is the hallmark of the authentic self. Among the competencies, Meyers includes: curiosity about and sensitive to our inner lives; a lively recollection of all of our own experiences and "of human experiences they have learned about through conversation, reading, or the dramatic arts;" the ability to "vividly imagine themselves acting in various ways while anticipating the probable consequences of each; assurance; open-mindedness; resolve; and social acumen.[48] Among the phenomena that undermine autonomy or signal its absence,

> chronic obliviousness to self-referential responses, awkwardness or rigidity in envisaging and appraising options, uncommunicativeness about one's needs, desires, values, and so forth, imperviousness to others' feedback, timidity about acting on the basis of one's own deliberations, and obstinate inflexibility in executing a chosen plan indicate poor development of autonomy competency. These limitations signal the individual's inability to fathom his or her authentic self and consequent habitual indifference to this self, or they signal the individual's inability to project his or her identity in action and consequent repression of this identity. Such people ... do not control their own lives—thus they are not autonomous.[49]

This strikes me as more than needs to be and can be expected for a practical account of autonomy. An analysis of personal autonomy should explain what is assured for an individual whose social and political situation can exert critical weight upon her sovereignty over matters of her body, her intimate relationships, her access to and control over information about oneself, her economic well-being and the myriad phenomena that make up the pattern of her life. This task can be accomplished without mandating that (for example) an autonomous person have a lively recollection of her experiences, or that she be open-minded and deliberative about her decisions and actions. The task of autonomy is not to resolve conflicted feelings or remedy dissonance between values and desires, both of which have been reached autonomously. In addition, not every decision that is capriciously and impetuously formed should be deemed non-autonomous or a threat to self-governance. In and of itself, choosing impulsively and acting in a foolish or even a demented manner have no bearing on the person's autonomy unless choosing in such a manner is symptomatic of a larger inability of the person to direct her own life.

Moreover, the satisfaction of the numerous skills Meyers adduces is not adequate to address counterexamples generated by an earnest acceptance of the conception of self-governance spelled out in the first chapter. The commonplace presentiment is that we ascribe autonomy to a person when we have indication of a life that is self-

---

47 Meyers, *Self, Society, and Personal Choice*, p. 269, note 1.
48 Meyers, *Self, Society, and Personal Choice*, pp. 87–8.
49 Meyers, *Self, Society, and Personal Choice*, pp. 88–9.

directed within social roles and activities of fundamental import to human agency. This entails authority in the form of psychological freedom as well as authority within primary social roles and arrangements. "Living in harmony with one's self" is desirable, but until this idea is fleshed out it will not supply the practical control needed for a self-governed life. If, as Meyers claims, autonomy requires that people display an ability to carry through with their plans while facing opposition or disapproval from others, certain substantive social arrangements and social roles must obtain at the exclusion of others. It will not be enough to claim autonomy is unattainable in the absence of socialization and to note the central place socialization occupies in fostering autonomy competency.

In short, despite her emphasis on competencies Meyers does not succeed in building an account of autonomy sufficiently superior to standard authenticity accounts to capture what we believe is a realistic, intuitively commonsense concept of autonomy as set forth in Chapter 1. Her focus is on competencies of the sort that contribute to the psychological autonomy of the agent, competencies that empower the agent to be assured of (and to assure others of) the authenticity of the springs of action that engage her. Pending information about the agent's interpersonal social circumstances, this yields a commitment to autonomy of an unduly Cartesian variety.

Content-neutrality

All of the accounts of autonomy considered in this chapter defend "content-neutral" or "substance-neutral" explanations of self-determination over rival accounts according to which certain substantive conditions constitute autonomy. Critics charge that substantive conceptions require that an agent is autonomous only if she "choose[s] in accord with the value of autonomy itself, or, at least, choose[s] so as not to undermine that value."[50] Moreover, critics charge, a theory of agent autonomy that imports substantive conditions will be a theory that involves not merely procedural independence but a condition of substantive independence from other persons as well. Such a theory, it is alleged, will restrict autonomous desires, choices, and actions to desires, choices, and actions a person formulates and undertakes independently of other persons. Substantive independence might require, for example, that a person not defer to the directives of others or that a person must not be guided by tradition, ritual, or religious principle if she is autonomous.[51] If substantive independence is demanded, the worry is that very few people will count as autonomous; those who

---

50 Friedman, *Autonomy, Gender, Politics,* p. 19.

51 Substantive independence could be construed far more tepidly, to mean that the agent has not "renounced his independence of thought and action" in the process of developing his motives for choice and action. Though Dworkin employs the phrase in this manner on one occasion ("Autonomy and Behavior Control," pp. 26–8), this is not the sense of substantive independence he makes use of as a rule; he rejects substantive independence construed as independence from others.

do not will be inappropriately subject to paternalistic intervention and autonomy will become an enemy of free choice and of expressions of individuality. It is true that the social-relational account I defend insists upon substantive constraints for an autonomous life. One of these constraints requires that an autonomous agent choose so as not to undermine the value of autonomy. But we will see that this is hardly a disadvantage of the social-relational account. Substantive constraints upon autonomy do not produce the unpalatable consequences critics allege of substantive independence, as the discussion in Chapters 5 and 6 will show.

By contrast with social-relational accounts, proceduralist accounts are neutral with respect to what a person must choose if she is to be autonomous. Proceduralist accounts of autonomy do not require that the agent's interests, choices, and activities be distinct from, or independent of, community-oriented interests, choices, and activities. The social-relational view I advance concurs on this point. But the social-relational view and the proceduralist account part ideological ways where the commitment to neutrality prompts the proceduralist to state that a person "might still be choosing autonomously even if she chooses subservience for its own sake, so long as she has made her choice in the right way or it coheres appropriately with her perspective as a whole."[52] Our ways part where the proceduralist alleges that people can be autonomous "despite having desires for subservient, demeaning, or even evil things."[53] The view of the proceduralist, unlike the social-relational view I advance, is that we can count as autonomous persons who have opted, in a procedurally independent manner, to conform their desires totally to the will of another and to have relinquished themselves to another.

To explain why substantive independence is unnecessary for autonomy and procedural independence is sufficient for autonomy, Christman asks us to consider the case of a person who chooses to join the Marines. The marine expresses a preference to conform to the will of another, and pursues a lifestyle that will compel him to have (or at least give expression to) desires that may not be his own. The marine makes this choice under conditions that meet the criteria for procedural authenticity. If we believe that the marine is autonomous despite his situation our belief cannot depend on the fact that the marine desires substantive independence or that the marine is in fact substantively independent of others. Neither is true of the marine. Indeed, if the situation of the marine is compared with that of a slave, we will find that substantive independence is something they both lack. The marine appears to be autonomous *vis à vis* his choice to become a marine; after all, this choice is prompted by aspects of the social environment which do not impair the autonomous quality of his desires, principles, commitments, or personality. In other words, recalling Dworkin, the marine is procedurally independent. But then what is responsible for the slave's lack of autonomy? Presumably, the slave, too, could have arrived at a preference for slavery under conditions that did not threaten the autonomy of his desires, principles, and so forth. Either neither the marine nor the slave is autonomous or both are. I

---

52 Friedman, *Autonomy, Gender, Politics*, p. 19.
53 Christman, "Autonomy and Personal History," pp. 22–3.

say neither is autonomous; Christman, Dworkin, Marilyn Friedman, and others, it would seem, are committed to defending the autonomy of both, pending evidence to the contrary.

The merit of procedural independence is that it imposes certain requirements upon what is proper and fitting for the development of an autonomous psychology without unduly prejudicing the question of who might qualify as autonomous. By focusing on the relationship a person's pro-attitudes bear to one another or on the relationship a person bears to the genesis of these pro-attitudes instead of focusing on the substance or content of those pro-attitudes, the hope is that a conception of autonomy general enough to circumvent many of the difficulties more substantive conceptions might face will emerge. A conception of autonomy that concentrates on procedural features of a person's psychology will, it is hoped, be theoretically pliable enough to meld comfortably with any number of apparently competing ideologies and cultural practices. Such an account will comport with the multitude of autonomously chosen lives and so offer more viable models for liberal societies to embrace.

But procedural independence will not capture all that autonomy calls for—indeed, it will not capture all that is involved in having an unfettered psychology. It is questionable whether proponents of content-neutral accounts can avoid introducing substantive claims into their theories in spite of their desire not to do so. When we explore the conditions that permit authenticity and independence in the development and appraisal of a person's desires, it is apparent that much depends on two facts that are not content-neutral. These are facts about the social situation of the agent and facts about the character of the agent's desires. When pressed to specify these facts, we cannot help but be selective. Certain substantive conditions are necessary for the genesis of psychological autonomy and for its sustenance; some situations will be amenable to a procedurally independent psychology, while others will not be amenable.

We also need to know which pro-attitudes—desires, values, interests—are consonant with an unimpaired critical psychology. Content-neutral theorists cannot, and have no desire to, comment on this. But it is plausible that a desire for drug addiction (for example), or for enslavement, for systematic deception, for brainwashing, for the restraint of one's civil liberties, or for browbeating and threatening gestures on the part of others is inconsonant with procedural independence and is inconsonant with a person's autonomy. This is true even if these ultimately serve as mechanisms for future enhanced states of autonomy. The individual who favors and pursues a life in which, for example, invasions to her privacy are normal, or in which the potency of addiction overwhelms all else, has, arguably, abdicated her capacity for rational, critical reflection that is necessary for procedural independence. A person who values subservience, addiction, or unquestioned adherence to tradition, or who sanctions threatening measures as most effective in providing the incentives for action she needs will be less likely to be self-directed when making decisions and taking action.

For example, suppose an individual—let us call him Herman—is aware of the fact that he is weak-willed, psychically and socially insecure, and cannot commit himself to any form of employment although he recognizes the need to do so for the sake of his children and his self-esteem. Herman also feels pressed to do so by certain religious tenets he holds. Let us suppose, further, that Herman will succeed in developing the will to secure and maintain employment but only after members of his family browbeat him, inform him that he will go to Hell, and threaten to have his children removed from his care. According to those who defend content-neutral procedural independence as adequate for autonomy, Herman's reflective endorsement of his will to work satisfies the condition for autonomy as long as it is not the product of circumstances that regularly disturb self-reflection. This is decided by means of the following test: "A person reflects adequately if she is able to realistically imagine choosing otherwise were she in a position to value sincerely that alternative position. That is, her reflective abilities must contain sufficient flexibility that she could imagine responding appropriately to alternative reasons (where 'appropriately' and 'reasons' are understood from her point of view.)"[54]

What does this mean? If we are to take seriously the demand that autonomy be construed procedurally, as a content-neutral phenomenon, then whatever a person is influenced by, however the person is influenced, and that the person is subject to these influences are all perfectly compatible with autonomy, provided the person is aware of these influences and assents to (or experiences no negative affect regarding) their presence. In other words, on an account that emphasizes an individual's psychological history, if Herman welcomes browbeating as the catalyst he needs to procure employment, and if he could imagine himself responding "appropriately" to alternative reasons for action, the man is autonomous. But it strikes me as paradoxical to ascribe autonomy to this man. Can a person be self-governing if his motives for action issue from the browbeating behavior of others?

This question can be answered in the negative, although not without argument. A person who submits to measures such as browbeating may be marginally different from the person who elicits the assistance of a demanding coach (athletic conditioning is an apt example) for the purpose of motivational inspiration. Is it a mark of heteronomy to voluntarily subscribe to the "boot-camp" approach when a person knows, rightly, that doing so will help her achieve her goals? I would say "yes," although not necessarily heteronomy of a variety that is objectionable.[55] If a person needs the energy and force of another agent to fill in for her own deficit of motivation, there is want of autonomy but perhaps not of a problematic sort.

On this point, Alfred Mele charges that whether agents who have been subjected to a certain mode of manipulation are deprived of autonomy depends on the effects of the manipulation. In addition to the question whether the manipulation was voluntarily undertaken to promote the person's autonomy it makes a difference

54 Christman, "Procedural Autonomy and Liberal Legitimacy," p. 280.

55 See chapters five and six for discussion of the value of autonomy and legitimate encroachments to autonomy.

for autonomy whether the agent can successfully counteract the influence of manipulation and whether its effects remain in force.[56] Christman is equivocal on the question. Most recently he has asserted that "the hypothetical self-endorsing reflection we imagine here must be such that it is not the product of social and psychological conditions that prevent adequate appraisal of oneself in general."[57] He continues by listing such reflection-constraining factors as "rage, drugs, the programings of a kidnapper, conditions that forbid consideration of anything but a narrow range of options." (In this he sounds oddly like Joseph Raz and myself, although he challenges the requirement of an adequate range of options for autonomy a few pages later.)[58] He concludes that "a fully worked-out notion of 'adequate reflectiveness' could, in principle, be articulated that did not rest on specific contents concerning the values and norms a person is moved by in her reflections, but that rules out cases where reflective self-endorsement *simply replicates the oppressive social conditions autonomous living is meant to stand against*."[59] But this is not to describe autonomous living in this fashion of the proceduralist. In these comments, Christman sounds remarkably sympathetic to the social account of autonomy I have advanced.[60]

What is needed is an account of autonomy that retains the virtue of compatibility with other values while providing flesh to the bones of procedural independence. Such an account of autonomy would not be substantively neutral, for it would rule out certain values and practices. It is doubtful that a definitive test for differentiating acceptable from unacceptable content is possible and, admittedly, it is at this stage that disagreements are bound to surface. Still, there is no reason to require that autonomy be compatible with all possible desires and values, and so no reason to seek a purely formal or procedural conception of autonomy denuded of content. Some desires and values cannot be satisfied if a person is to be self-directed, but it is not apparent that we would want to endorse such desires and values. Other desires and values are such that satisfying them would have no affect on agent autonomy one way or the other. While we may require substantive restrictions of the sort that exclude from the psychological economy of the autonomous agent a desire for heroin addiction, or for slavery, or for browbeating when certain significant matters are in balance, we need not go so far as to require that the autonomous agent never desire personal commitments or that she renounce any form of guidance or the tutelage of others. Certainly, a theory of autonomy consistent with the "communal" virtues

---

56 Mele, *Autonomous Agents*, pp. 148–9.

57 Christman, "Procedural Autonomy and Liberal Legitimacy," p. 280. This is very much in sympathy with Meyers and Friedman.

58 Raz, *The Morality of Freedom* (Oxford, 1986), pp. 373–78.

59 Christman, "Procedural Autonomy and Liberal Legitimacy," p. 280, my emphasis.

60 Marina Oshana, "Personal Autonomy and Society," *Journal of Social Philosophy* 29/1 (1998): 81–102; and Oshana, "Comments on John Christman's 'Relational Autonomy: Some Worries,'" Pacific Division meeting of the American Philosophical Association, March 29, 2003.

of commitment, loyalty, and cooperation more closely approaches the naturalized ideal.

Summary

Internalist and externalist theories of autonomy as psychological authenticity are among the most innovative attempts to understand autonomy. One promising feature of hierarchical theories of autonomy is their tendency toward compatibilism. On the hierarchical view what is important for autonomy is not whether a person can do otherwise, but whether the person really wants to do what she does and whether she identifies with her action, and this is just a function of her assent or dissent to what may well be a causally determined situation. Frankfurt's theory is, arguably, the most interesting attempt to provide a compatibilist understanding of free agency and, derivatively, of autonomy. In itself this is a reason to recommend his theory as a starting point for analysis.

Efforts to arrive at an adequate conception of personal autonomy have led philosophers to modify the hierarchical model in various ways. Some accounts require that the psychological economy of the autonomous person satisfy certain normative constraints or require that they have a certain etiology. All such accounts endorse what I shall call the internalist's premise, even while some deny its sufficiency. That is, they maintain that autonomy is attributed to persons in virtue of the authentic character of the person's psychological states or dispositions. Some of the criticisms generated by alternatives to the initial internalist analyses are provocative, and their recommendations for a conception of autonomy that improves upon the accounts of Dworkin and Frankfurt are often credible.

Nevertheless, none of the alternatives offers a set of conditions for personal autonomy adequate to meet the intuitions of the first chapter. Accounts of personal autonomy framed in terms of the structure of the agent's psychology and the nature and origin of the psychological states of the agent are problematic. The problem is that such accounts are premised on the conditions under which a person's psychological states develop, become authentic, and are realized in the world. Only those factors that impede a person's cognitive and non-cognitive psychological functions are taken to endanger personal autonomy. But people are not psychological states, and their autonomy is a more complicated matter than that of their psychological states. Personal autonomy is not primarily a character trait persons possess in virtue of their psychological history or their psychological competencies or their reflection upon the reasons for which they act any more than autonomy is simply a function of the structure of a person's psychology. Accounts of autonomy framed in terms of a person's possession and exercise of certain skills—in terms of a person's procedural competencies—are problematic as well. Satisfaction of agential skills or competencies of the sort Meyers details are possible in the absence of global autonomy and in the absence of the social, legal, and political conditions that sustain autonomy. In short, even if conditions such as these are necessary for psychological self-definition, richer conditions for *de facto* autonomy must be forthcoming. Chapter three takes up the challenge of developing such an account.

Chapter 3

Social-Relational Autonomy

The Objective

Theories of autonomy as psychological authenticity in effect assimilate autonomy with respect to one's preferences, values, or choices with the autonomy of persons, as if what can be predicated of the former can be predicated of the latter. This assimilation signals the need for an alternate account of self-government. The problem is not merely that such theories lack an adequate analysis of the condition of personal autonomy in terms of something other than the authenticity of psychological states. Rather, they contend that the autonomy of persons is a matter of the condition of a person's psychology—specifically, a person's pro-attitudes (or lack of negative affect) toward her desires, values, commitments and so forth, coupled with dispositional capabilities—and they seek no other account. But while a person's status as self-governing is in part dependent on her psychology, personal autonomy and autonomy *vis à vis* one's psychological states differ in kind; since the subjects vary, the conditions for each may vary as well.

Accounts of autonomy as procedural or psychological authenticity are preeminent, but of late have been challenged by "relational" approaches to autonomy.[1] My aim in this chapter is to defend the claim that personal autonomy, understood as self-government, is a social-relational phenomenon. Autonomy is a condition of persons constituted in large part by the social relations people find themselves in and by the absence of other social relations. Autonomy is not a phenomenon merely enhanced or lessened by the contingencies of a person's social situation; social relations do not just causally facilitate or impair the exercise of autonomy. Rather, appropriate social relations form an inherent part of what it means to be self-directed.

As with accounts that highlight developmental authenticity, the social-relational account contends that factors external to a person's psychological profile are relevant to the formation of autonomy. There are important differences between the accounts, however. On the social-relational analysis I defend, it is possible for two individuals to satisfy all the psychological, historical, and competency conditions we have been discussing but to differ nonetheless with respect to their status as autonomous beings. This difference is explained in terms of some variance in their social circumstances. Thus, in addition to whatever psychological or dispositional

---

1   See Catriona Mackenzie and Natalie Stoljar (eds), *Relational Autonomy: Feminist Perspectives on Autonomy, Agency, and the Social Self* (New York, 2000); and Marina Oshana, "Personal Autonomy and Society," *Journal of Social Philosophy* (1998).

characteristics are required for autonomy, and in addition to whatever can be said of a person's psychological history, there are social criteria according to which we judge someone as autonomous. These external criteria are independent of facts about the individual's internal state. Moreover, they are objective: autonomy is not decided "from within," or on the basis of the evaluational perspective of the individual whose autonomy is at stake. External criteria constitute autonomy and external criteria measure autonomy.

I have called the externalist account I favor "social-relational" by way of contrasting it with a psychological account. By this I do not mean to imply that accounts of autonomy as psychological authenticity ignore relational factors, and that they are flawed for this reason. My complaint about psychological accounts of autonomy is not that they fail to heed the influence of social relations on a person's psychology. Accounts that incorporate an historical element may do this, as will accounts that emphasize the socialization essential to the development of procedural competency or autonomy skills. Rather, my complaints are that such accounts are disproportionately focused on the mental status of the person and that such accounts are largely subjective: The agent's psychological condition alone—specifically, the structural and developmental character of her judgments, preferences, and pro-attitudes in conjunction with the agent's occurrent attitude toward these—is important for her autonomy.

Moreover, the adequacy of a person's psychological state—its success or failure in achieving the desired state—is not a matter for others to decide. Even accounts that claim "the difference between autonomous people and nonautonomous ones depends on the capabilities people have at their disposal and the way in which people go about fashioning their lives"[2] gauge this difference in terms of the point of view of the agent herself: "only individuals can be the measure of their own autonomy."[3] But this is plainly false. Only individuals can be the measure of their sense of autonomy or feeling of autonomy. But sensation and feeling are qualia, and qualia alone do not decide the fact of autonomy any more than a feeling of oneself as nonautonomous

---

2   Meyers, *Self, Society and Personal Choice*, p. 55.

3   Meyers, *Self, Society, and Personal Choice,* p. 82. For example, Christman argues that in order "to capture the idea of self-government that is the motivating concept behind autonomy," the rationality of an autonomous agent must be defined in terms of nothing more than consistency of preferences. No criteria external to the psychology of the agent are allowed for rationality. See Christman (1991), note 18, p. 9 and note 23, p. 14. Moreover, he claims that a person behaves autonomously when she chooses or acts in accord with wants and desires towards which she experiences no alienation, so long as the person has reflected adequately upon this choice, where adequacy is a function of the agent's being able to "imagine responding appropriately to alternative reasons (where "appropriately" and "reasons" are understood from her point of view)." Christman, "Procedural Autonomy and Liberal Legitimacy," p. 280. His account is thus closer to earlier internalist psychological accounts than one might hope given his historicist emphasis; the criteria for rationality are internal to the psychology of the agent, and reflective sufficiency turns on the judgment of the individual.

decides against autonomy (perhaps no more, even, than the feeling that one is or is not a brain in a vat decides that fact). There are guidelines that establish autonomy and its absence, and these guidelines are not oriented around the value perspective of the person whose autonomy is at stake.

The emphasis of authenticity accounts on the subjective point of view reflects the belief that safeguarding the autonomy of persons consists in safeguarding what is symbolically described as the inner citadel. As I noted in the preface, the symbolism asks us to assume for each individual a unique, inviolable heart of agency in virtue of which autonomy is safeguarded. This element is often referred to as the individual's "true" or "real" or "deep" or "authentic" self, and is alleged to safeguard whatever assemblage of interests, values, commitments and skills the individual treats as essential to her identity.[4]

I do not think the imagery of an inner citadel advances our understanding of personal autonomy. My skepticism is due primarily to the fact that the idea suggests a picture of autonomy as relegated to the background of social life—a characteristic that emerges behind an invisible partition that isolates each individual from the rest, overlooking entirely the social and relational dimensions of self-government. There are further reasons to be suspicious of the idea. One reason is that the very idea that human agency centers on a privileged core of the self is empirically suspect. The idea has been contested by philosophers on the grounds that all such depictions falsify the nature of the self and the conditions of its identity and authenticity. Some philosophers charge that the assumption of a coherent self misrepresents persons in presupposing a permanency of identity where in fact the identity of persons is pliant; others chime in that the representation ignores the socially embedded character of human identity.[5] An additional reason for skepticism is that attempts to elucidate the

---

4   Employment of (and, in some instances, defense of) the "deep," "true," and "authentic" self can be found in Thomas E. Hill, Jr., "The Importance of Autonomy," in *Women and Moral Theory*, E.F. Kittay and D.T. Meyers (eds) (Totowa, N.J., 1987), pp. 129–38, reprinted in Hill, *Autonomy and Self-Respect*, pp. 43–51. Hill claims that "self-government" refers to the phenomenon that occurs when the agent is free from internal dissention or conflict. In this state, Hill charges, the agent experiences a sense of psychological unity and well-being, an absence of inner turmoil, and the "true" self of the agent is sovereign. Also see Gary Watson, "Two Faces of Responsibility;" John Christman, "Constructing the Inner Citadel: Recent Work on Autonomy," *Ethics* 99/1 (October, 1988): 109–24; Christman, "Autonomy: A Defense of the Split-Level Self," *Southern Journal of Philosophy* 25/1 (1987): 281–93; Alfred Mele, *Autonomous Agents*; Marilyn Friedman, "Autonomy and the Split-Level Self," *Southern Journal of Philosophy* 24/1 (1986): 19–35; and Friedman, *Autonomy, Gender, and Politics* (New York: 2002). Susan Wolf contends the idea of a true or deep self is underdeveloped and shallow (Wolf, *Freedom Within Reason*).

5   For discussion of these concerns see Linda Barclay, "Autonomy and the Social Self," in Catriona Mackenzie and Natalie Stoljar (eds), *Relational Autonomy: Feminist Perspectives on Autonomy, Agency, and the Social Self* (New York, 2000), pp. 52–71. Diana Meyers questions the plausibility of a cohesive picture of the self, although she accepts the idea of the authentic self. See Meyers, *Self, Society, and Personal Choice*; also Meyers, "Decentralizing

true or the real self have proven notoriously difficult. Even if it made sense to base autonomy upon some core of the individual, it would be difficult to delineate an aspect of the individual (such as rationality) that could lay a legitimate and noncontentious claim to be that core.[6]

Fortunately our discussion does not call upon us to explore the construction of anything as nebulous as a core of identity. The concerns about autonomy I mean to address do not rest on a resolution of the nature and existence of a "self." Even if a core can be identified and an explanation of the true self can be given, having a true self is no guarantee of autonomy—at least, of autonomy as I think we typically understand the concept. The authentic self and the metaphor of the inner citadel enlisted to typify it will not accurately capture the condition of the self-determined agent because autonomy is determined by how a person interacts with others, or so I shall argue.

Case Studies

The social-relational account of autonomy can be illustrated by way of case studies. These serve to document the inadequacies of authenticity accounts and suggest a set of conditions, to be developed in the next chapter, for an adequate account of autonomy. The five studies that follow establish two things in particular. The first is that there is no natural transition from conceptions of autonomy that focus on psychological states or on competencies to an account of the autonomy of persons. The second is that persons who are nonautonomous in certain situations fail to be autonomous because they lack characteristics that only a social theory of self-determination can supply. The first four cases highlight the intuition that autonomy is incompatible with certain forms of constraint—even where constraint is the result of the agent's free, minimally rational choice.[7] They depict persons who satisfy the various criteria for psychological authenticity and autonomy competency but who nevertheless fail to meet the conception of self-government articulated in Chapter 1. To simplify, I consider a hybrid theory of authenticity accounts according to which the criteria are higher-order identification or satisfaction with the operative

---

Autonomy: Five Face of Selfhood" in Christman and Anderson (eds), *Autonomy and the Challenges to Liberalism: New Essays* (New York, 2005), pp. 27–55, especially pp. 32–6.

6   Numerous philosophers have taken special pains to argue that the condition of personal autonomy cannot be described solely in terms of some essential component of the individual such as the "rational self" in virtue of which the individual is self-directing. For example, Mele notes that "On an alternative, holistic view of human beings, the 'self' of self-control is identified with the whole person rather than with reason ... Self-control can be exercised in support of better judgments partially based on a person's appetites or emotional commitments." See Mele, "Autonomy, Self-Control, and Weakness of Will," in Robert Kane (ed.), *The Oxford Handbook of Free Will* (New York, 2002), p. 532.

7   This is consistent with the weak construction of rationality as consistency of belief-desires sets.

desire (or lack of estrangement toward the desire), integration of motivational and valuational systems, planning agency, competencies, and historically proper preference formation. The fifth case establishes that failure to satisfy the criterion of satisfaction with one's operative desire or lack of estrangement toward these need not yield a failure of autonomy.

Voluntary Slavery

Consider the situation of the contented slave.[8] Let us suppose, first, that the decision to become a slave was autonomous in that it met the conditions for psychological autonomy proffered above. This individual has willingly relinquished his rights and has chosen to be a slave under conditions free of whatever factors might impair the autonomy of his decision. Second, assume that a life of slavery is consistent with this person's values and that it satisfies his notion of well-being. The slave is "autonomy competent." The slave is self-directed *vis à vis* his choice of a lifestyle, if we mean by this that he is free from internal dissention or conflict, experiences a sense of psychological unity and well-being, and an absence of inner turmoil. What role do these facts play in determining the autonomy of the slave? Is his autonomy guaranteed by the fact that he possesses an integrated and coherent psychology, and that he has arrived at this preference in a procedurally independent manner? Does the fact that he expresses happiness, satisfaction with, or approval of his situation transform what seems to be a state that violates autonomy into one of nonviolation?

The question of immediate interest is whether the individual who seeks a situation of enslavement, who knowingly, willingly, and freely chooses a life of bondage, is autonomous despite the result. I claim that this person is not. The slave does consent to the state of affairs in which he finds himself, but what he consents to is a loss of freedom.[9] And although the slave may be unhampered in his pursuit of his conception of the good life, what he has in mind for that life, and what he in fact obtains, is a life quite unlike one that captures the conception of autonomy described in chapter one. His interpersonal standing robs him of the *de facto* power to manage phenomena elemental to self-governance.

Whether or not the slave has freely chosen bondage, and whether or not, once he is a slave, he expresses pleasure or displeasure with his status, having become

---

8 The choice of the happy slave, with all slavery connotes, might appear to beg the question of autonomy. I would happily ignore the case were it not for two facts: First, the case baldly exposes the deficiencies of authenticity accounts; unless these accounts are recast they must accept the case of the slave as a plausible test case. Second, the case has been employed by and defended by philosophers such as Gerald Dworkin and Bernard Berofsky who write about the autonomy or persons in exactly this context.

9 As Isaiah Berlin notes, consenting to a loss of liberty does not negate or reverse that loss: "If I consent to be oppressed, or acquiesce in my condition with detachment or irony, am I the less oppressed? If I sell myself into slavery, am I the less a slave? If I commit suicide, am I the less dead because I have taken my own life freely?" Berlin, "Two Concepts of Liberty," in *Four Essays on Liberty* (Oxford, 1969), p. 164.

a slave he has no authority over those aspects of his social situation that influence his will and the direction of his life.[10] Being a slave means that how he shall live is, largely and in key respects, no longer up to him. The slave is denied the possibility of being "an independent participant in the willing, planning, and controlling aspects" of the projects he works on even if he mistakenly sees himself as an independent participant.[11] Instead, the slave is "harnessed to somebody else's ... enterprise as though he were merely a natural force, like a beast of burden or like water-power."[12]

The slave may never actually experience treatment of the sort that provides plain evidence of a failure of self-determination. But why should such evidence be required? The slave might always comply with his master's orders, and as a reward for his obedience he might never suffer punishment (assuming, of course, that his master is reasonable). Nevertheless, servility, degradation, the possibility of punishment, and dependence on the good will of his master are very real, actual properties of his condition, whether or not punitive treatment is ever realized. Being a slave means that he could be punished or mistreated at his master's whim. The fact that he is not autonomous is a fact about the actual situation, the truth of which rests upon the truth of certain counterfactual claims.[13]

That the slave is content does not indicate that he is self-governing. The fact that the slave independently arrives at preferences that mirror those he can realize is a mark of good fortune. But this coincidence will not decide in favor of autonomy. The slave might feel satisfied because the tasks he performs are less menial than are those performed by his counterparts, and for this he is grateful. He may be content because his master allows him the opportunity to learn to read and write, an envied and valuable skill. But the fact that he is better off than are most other slaves, and that his attitude is one of appreciation, does not mean that he governs himself. One might speculate that the slave's *de jure* and *de facto* lack of autonomy are signaled, in part, by the fact that he looks upon literacy as a gift to be thankful for. By contrast, a self-determined man, even if he were grateful to be literate, would likely view literacy as a skill to which he has a right.

One who is sympathetic to accounts of autonomy premised on the authenticity of a person's motivational psychology and or on the attitude a person adopts to the

---

10 Compare Alfred Mele, who notes that one who autonomously chooses a particular state might fail to be autonomous with respect to remaining in that state; an appropriately autonomous history of choice might not be adequate for the continued or occurrent condition of autonomy. Mele's remedy is to seek continued assent; I claim assent makes no difference. See his "History and Personal Autonomy," *Canadian Journal of Philosophy* 23 (June 1993): 271–80.

11 Jeremy Waldron, *The Right to Private Property* (Oxford, 1988), p. 302.

12 Ibid. Though Waldron is speaking of what ought to characterize human involvement in projects of self-assertion upon nature, he takes autonomy to involve self-assertion.

13 As Berofsky notes, though slaves "may possess an enormous amount of positive freedom" and "may have a great deal of freedom of action ... they have powers and skills *they are nonetheless unable to use in ways they might* choose." *Liberation from Self*, pp. 66–7.

states of affairs in which she acts need not claim that the psychological state required for autonomy be one of acceptance. All one needs to do is offer some story about psychological states that is said to explain the autonomy of the person whose states they are. The psychological state in question might be one of resistance. For example, Bernard Berofsky has argued that the contented slave's absence of autonomy is signaled by his acquiescence. (Though he is not a defender of procedural or psychological authenticity accounts of autonomy, Berofsky does construe autonomy in a kindred way, as a matter of a person's psychological freedom upon entering or "engaging" the world.) Berofsky contrasts the complacent slave with the case of "a person forced into slavery who struggles his entire life against this condition, does everything he can to defy his master and thwart his wishes, and tries unsuccessfully to satisfy his own desires, including his desire to escape..." Berofsky alleges that, despite his lack of negative freedom, the rebellious slave "retains a great deal of autonomy. His decisions are entirely his own and, were the world less unyielding, he would be a model of perfect freedom. From an internal perspective, he is a fully self-determining agent."[14]

Well, yes—but this is precisely the problem with internalist accounts of autonomy. When a person's ability and right to exercise control over his life are incumbent upon the independent, effective effort of another person (or persons) who possesses superior and ultimate authority over him, the person's autonomy is lost. The fact is that the world of the slave *is* "unyielding;" the fact is that "he is trapped in an environment which denies him the resources he needs."[15] This being the case, the internal perspective of the slave, whether it is a perspective that speaks of resistance or of compliance, cannot decide the issue of autonomy. The rebellious slave might retain his dignity but he is no more master of his universe than is his easygoing counterpart.

What have proponents of psychological authenticity accounts to say about the autonomy of the contented slave? Christman claims that proceduralist, content-neutral accounts are sturdy enough to filter out the possibility of such cases, but he does not argue the point. Anyone who opts for this life, he suggests, must fail one or more of the criteria for authenticity.[16] It is not clear why a proceduralist would want to say this; if a recruit at a military boot-camp can experience no alienation from his circumstances and can affirm his lack of negative affect to the boot-camp experience

---

14 Berofsky, *Liberation from Self*, p. 22.

15 Berofsky, *Liberation from Self*, p. 22. Berofsky recognizes this, noting that "At some basic level, [slaves] do not choose their own lives. Some things they must do whether or not they want to, and even if they want to please their master and derivatively acquire the desires of their master, they lack independence. In some sense...their goals are not self-determined." *Liberation from Self*, p. 67.

16 John Christman, (1987) and "Relational Autonomy – Some Worries: A Qualified Case for Individualism," presented at a symposium on Relational Autonomy at the Pacific Division Meeting of the American Philosophical Association, March 30, 2003, San Francisco. Revised as "Relational Autonomy, Liberal Individualism, and the Social Constitution of Selves," *Philosophical Studies* 117 (2004): 143–64, at p. 157.

why can't a slave do the same for his own situation? Gerald Dworkin thinks the slave can do this. Dworkin remarks that

> If we conceive of autonomy as the capacity of individuals to critically reflect on and take responsibility for the kind of persons they want to be, then ... there is nothing in the idea of autonomy which precludes a person from saying: "I want to be the kind of person who acts at the commands of others. I define myself as a slave and endorse those attitudes and preferences. My autonomy consists in being a slave." If this is coherent, and I think it is, one cannot argue against such slavery on the grounds of autonomy.[17]

But this is not coherent—not coherent, in any event, if we accept the conception of autonomy laid out in Chapter 1. Dworkin claims that one cannot argue that voluntary slavery offends autonomy, because its voluntary nature renders it consistent with autonomy. But Dworkin's argument is unsatisfactory for the following reasons. First, it relies too heavily on choice as a sufficient condition for autonomy. But choice does not guarantee autonomy, for the person who chooses might be compelled to do so, and to do so from within the confines of a situation that grants her no autonomy; consider Sophie's choice.[18] Even if a person can autonomously select a life that denies him self-determination, the result of that choice will be a situation in which the chooser lacks autonomy. The person who enters "an environment in which external restrictions upon freedom of action are dramatically increased"[19] forfeits negative freedom and suffers a compromised state of autonomy as a result.[20] This loss occurs whether a person freely abdicates autonomy or is forced to so.

The person who chooses slavery is, of course, at least partially responsible for his resulting lack of autonomy. Following the convention adopted in Chapter 1, we may call the slave locally or episodically autonomous with regard to this choice. The slave could be self-governing with respect to those activities or relationships in his life over which he retained control—in his status as spouse, or sibling, or parent, or religious affiliations, for example. But exercising autonomy incrementally, with respect to certain roles, does not make the slave an autonomous person or one who lives an autonomous life. Global autonomy is absent as long as he remains a slave, for he is vulnerable to oppression—indeed, this is a defining characteristic of slavery— and his standing remains one of compliance, submissiveness, and dependency.

This suggests a further point. It is certainly possible that a person could autonomously choose nonautonomy; the example of the Taliban Woman, below, offers a plausible case in point. Some, however, would question whether the person who conceives of servitude as a state that will contribute to his welfare and who pursues that state in light of this belief—who opts for the choice that denies him

---

17 Dworkin, "Paternalism: Some Second Thoughts," p. 111, in Rolf Sartorius (ed.), *Paternalism* (Minneapolis, 1983), pp. 105–11.

18 William Styron, *Sophie's Choice*, (New York, 1979).

19 Berofsky, *Liberation from Self*, p. 21.

20 The link between negative freedom, positive freedom, and autonomy will be addressed in Chapter 7.

autonomy—really is autonomous to begin with. For example, Thomas Hill, Jr. recalls Rousseau's thought that the very idea of consenting to slavery (or, analogously, to torture or imprisonment) is incoherent, since it means that the agent "displays a conditioned slavish mentality that renders [such] consent worthless." Hill argues that "a person's consent releases others from obligation only if it is autonomously given, and consent resulting from underestimation of one's moral status [as a human being entitled to a certain body of rights] is not autonomously given."[21]

Hill's belief merits consideration. For if he is correct, then it is unlikely that truly autonomous desires—desires that meet the hybrid conditions of psychological and procedural authenticity—will be for states of nonautonomy. A person who is autonomous because she meets the authenticity criteria for autonomy will desire situations of autonomy. Equally, a person's desire for nonautonomy will be sufficient to signal her lack of autonomy, or lack of an autonomous psychology, or lack of autonomy-competency. In short, being autonomous (or autonomy-competent or having an autonomous psychology) will turn on having desires of a certain sort. I want to put this concern on hold for the moment, and return to it in considering the next case study. The point to be made at this juncture is that, if Hill's objection holds—if not for the case of the slave then for other, similar cases—it raises difficulties for Dworkin's claim that the slave's desire is consistent with autonomy, and for other proponents of authenticity accounts who make similar assertions.[22] For if Hill's objection holds, the upshot is that substantive content is imported into the condition of psychological authenticity; procedural independence will not suffice to explain autonomy.

Dworkin's analysis of the voluntary slave suggests that the ability to critically reflect in a procedurally independent fashion is sufficient for the condition of being autonomous. This position is shared by others who support a similarly proceduralist approach to agent autonomy. But being able to engage in critical reflection, to take stock of oneself, and to shape oneself on the basis of this evaluation does not guarantee that whatever state of affairs ensues from this activity will be one that permits persons to manage their lives. If being autonomous depends on circumstances beyond those descriptive of a person's psychology, it may still be possible to "argue against slavery on the grounds of autonomy."

The Angel in the House

She was intensely sympathetic. She was immensely charming. She was utterly unselfish. She excelled in the difficult arts of family life. She sacrificed herself daily. If there was chicken, she took the leg; if there was a draught she sat in it—in short she was so constituted that

---

21 Thomas Hill, "Servility and Self-Respect," in *Autonomy and Self-Respect* (Cambridge, 1991), p. 15.

22 For example, see Friedman, *Autonomy, Gender, Politics*.

she never had a mind or a wish of her own, but preferred to sympathize always with the minds and wishes of others.

—Virginia Woolf, "The Angel in the House" [23]

Consider the woman whose role as spouse and as homemaker affords her less recognition and independence than she deserves and than she might otherwise have. Let us imagine that this woman, whom I shall call Harriet, prefers to be subservient. I will assume that Harriet is sober and mature and that we have no reason to suspect any failure on her part to give her preference for this lifestyle whatever measure of deliberation it merits. Nor have we reason to believe that she has failed to evaluate her motivations to whatever extent seems appropriate. Harriet's reasons for her actions are consistent, reflective of her values, and historically sound. She possesses adequate information about, and has taken a critical and reflective stance with regard to, the events that have shaped her character and her desires and she has no wish to alter these events. Let us assume as well that Harriet finds her life gratifying and has no wish to alter it. There is nothing she values more or wants more than to be the angel in the house. She has no evaluative commitments or preferences of a higher order that are somehow ineffective against her will, and she possesses all the autonomy competencies.

Let us return now to Hill's concern about persons who choose nonautonomy. Against Hill, I want to deny that in Harriet's case a lack of autonomy rests on the substance of her preferences and desires—that is, in what she has preferences and desires for—any more than her lack of autonomy would be assured if she had a desire for nonautonomy. (I might sincerely desire to experience the nonautonomous condition of hypnosis, while being autonomous in my wish.) The case of the would-be surrendered woman, below, presses this point. A person's preferences—for religious devotion, for slavery, for subservience, for power—can certainly serve as an indicator of that person's disposition to be self-governing, and some desires more than others are hospitable to autonomy. A person who conceives of herself as does Harriet might exhibit a diminished capacity for autonomy, and if her circumstances nurture this self-conception the capacity will be frustrated. It is likely that a person whose self-conception does not include a commitment to her autonomy, who does not wish to be "an independent participant in the willing, planning, and controlling aspects of her life," will invite others to regard her as a patient rather than as an agent. And this invitation will eventually be accepted, thus eroding the carapace of autonomy as desired.

Harriet's lack of autonomy is not due to the fact that her desire to be the angel in the house emerges from conditions hostile to autonomy. Of course, if Harriet's overarching desire was produced by a socially reinforced belief in her inferior status, then we might be persuaded that her choice was not autonomous. Her lack of autonomy could be traced to an unsupportive history. But we have assumed that such a history

---

23 From "Professions for Women," a speech before the National Society for Women's Service, January 21, 1931, in Virginia Woolf, *The Virginia Woolf Reader*, Mitchell Leaska (ed.) (New York, 1984), p. 278.

is not true of Harriet. In spite of the fact that Harriet's desires may be regrettable, she meets all the qualifications for autonomy as procedural authenticity.[24]

The substantive element of social-relational autonomy is not generally found in the object of a person's desires, and in any event Harriet's lack of autonomy is not due to her lamentable desires. Harriet has the "right" psychology. She satisfies the criteria of psychological authenticity and procedural independence. Nonetheless she fails to be autonomous—not because she *wants* to be subservient, but because she *is* subservient. Her lack of autonomy is due to her personal relations with others and to the social institutions of her society.

Let us assume the social relations Harriet is party to, given her role as homemaker, afford her less financial flexibility, less social mobility, and fewer opportunities for intellectual and creative development than she could have were these relations otherwise. Suppose, too, that in her relationship with her spouse Harriet makes none of the important financial decisions, she does not decide when or where they shall vacation, or where they shall live, and so on. She defers to her husband in matters bearing on their sexual relationship, as with respect to the use of birth control, the type of contraception employed, the frequency of sexual relations, pregnancies, and the like. Absent, too, from Harriet's life are economic and political institutions that might empower homemakers. Although Harriet lives in a manner consonant with her preferences, the choices she makes are guided almost entirely by the judgments and recommendations of others. Taken together, these facts imply that Harriet is not autonomous. But a theory of self-determination as psychological authenticity would characterize her as autonomous, despite her social situation.

We might strengthen this case by assuming that Harriet's regard for others not only exceeds any regard she pays herself, but supercedes or supplants that regard. We could assume Harriet does not think of herself as anything *other* than an other-regarding caregiver, and that she fails to perceive herself as someone whose activities, needs, preferences, and interests have value independently of the value they have for others. Without elaboration these do not seem like evidence of deficiencies of competence and skill, or evidence of an aberrant psychology. So we might go further and describe Harriet as someone who systematically disregards her own counsel. But we need not describe Harriet this way. Harriet's lack of autonomy is not owing to a deficient measure of self-regard, nor to the failure of others to accord her consideration, though it may be fortified by a lack of regard.

---

24 In short I disagree with those who argue that Harriet fails to be autonomous because she has desires that she would not really want were she in full possession of her faculties, and who take the absence of such desires as evidence of an absence of critically reflective activity or of a healthy psychology. (Susan Wolf and Marilyn Friedman offer arguments along these lines. See Wolf, "Sanity and the Metaphysics of Responsibility," in Schoeman, 1987. Friedman's view is found in "Autonomy and the Split-Level Self.") Rationality and the activity of critically evaluating one's motives may lead a person to a variety of preferences—some odious, others admirable—with no promise other than that these preferences are formed in a clear-headed fashion.

The inadequacy of psychological authenticity accounts can be illustrated by contrasting the case of Harriet with that of a homemaker who is self-governing. Both Harriet and her counterpart, whom I shall call Wilma, share the properties touted by psychological authenticity views. Both possess structurally coherent psychologies, both are self-aware, and each offers reasons for her actions that are consistent, value-reflective, and historically sound. Each is a competent planning agent, capable of self-governance. But suppose that the personal relations in which Wilma finds herself, and the social institutions that affect her life, afford her control over her choices. She directs her life from within a range of possibilities that promise economic independence and the opportunity for personal growth. Moreover, although Wilma may view herself as an other-regarding caregiver, she is treated by others as one whose needs and wants deserve to be respected on independent grounds, and this desert is reinforced by her social situation. Dedication to others is consistent with autonomy, but subservience is not. While both women desire to be of service to others, only Harriet finds herself subservient. Wilma can be described as autonomous while Harriet cannot.

The case of Harriet—the angel in the house—may strike many of us as implausible perhaps because it is so exaggerated; we simply cannot envision women in our midst in this day and age living such a life. The case study that follows is true to life and current as well, although distant from the experience of women in the West.

Taliban Woman

Imagine a woman living under a Talibanic regime such as that which controlled Afghanistan until 2001. Suppose that this woman has embraced the role of subservience and the abdication of independence that it demands, out of reverence, a sense of purpose, and an earnest belief in the sanctity of this role as espoused in certain passages of the Qu'ran. Having previously enjoyed a successful career as a physician, this woman has since chosen, under conditions free of whatever factors might disable self-awareness, and with a considered appreciation of the implications of her decision, a life of utter dependence anchored in religious piety. She can no longer practice medicine (indeed, she is no longer permitted access to information about the science of medicine). She is not permitted to support herself financially. She does not have legal custody of her children—that remains in the hands of their father and in his male relatives should he die. She has no voice in the manner and duration of any schooling that her children, particularly her daughters, may receive. She must remain costumed in cumbersome garb—a burqa—when in public. She cannot travel unless accompanied by a male relative (even one younger than she and perhaps dependent on her in other ways, as would be true of a son), and can travel only when granted permission by a male relative or religious elder. She knows that any transgression, any show of independence counts as heretical defiance and invites punishment both swift and harsh. But her life is consistent with her spiritual and social values, provides her with a sense of worth, and satisfies her notion of well-being.

I think it is evident that the Taliban Woman is not autonomous. In a local or occurrent sense of the term, she has chosen her life-plans autonomously. Nevertheless, she fails to be autonomous in a global sense for the obvious reason that the life that she chooses, and towards which she experiences no alienation, is a life in which she is systematically subject to the ultimate will of others. Although the Taliban Woman made her original decision autonomously, and although she willingly renounces her rights and continues to express satisfaction with the life that she has selected for herself, she now has no practical authority over her situation. Any mastery she has over her will is wielded only by the grace of another. What Taliban Woman does coincides with what she decides, but does not depend on what she decides. Taliban Woman does what she wants, but what she wants frustrates autonomy.

It would be a mistake to describe the Taliban Woman as an autonomous woman who supports *Sharia*—the law of Allah that regulates all aspects of religious as well as secular life, including the social, political, economic, and domestic spheres. Taliban Woman is not, for example, a politically empowered member of the Afghan legislature. Conservative women who are members of the Afghan legislature are not themselves operating under the Talibanic model of *Sharia*, for that model would forbid them from occupying this political role.[25]

However, we may want to call the Taliban Woman autonomous because we think of autonomy as a condition relativized to the satisfaction of a person's desires or decided entirely by the stance a person adopts toward her affective states and personal relations. But this, too, is a mistake, one that results from confusing autonomy with one of its potential advantages, namely, that it can lead to personal contentment. I would hardly be the first to point out that there are values other than autonomy and that among the interests of human agents there may well be a desire to sacrifice episodes of autonomy, or occurrent autonomy, in favor of other values. But neither would it be original of me to claim that these interests need not be overarching, that is, they need not be met at the cost of overriding global autonomy. We will return to this point in Chapter 6, where the value of autonomy is examined.

---

25 Not every model of *Sharia* is as fundamentalist as that found in Talibanic Afghanistan or in Saudi Arabia or Nigeria. Even while the early Islamic theocracy in Iran (circa 1979) increased the reach of Sharia law, "the new rulers … emphasized the early Islamic tradition of inclusion of women in civil and political life. The voting right for women was maintained and women were encouraged to participate fully in all forms public life. Consequently a very complex and sophisticated system of inclusion and exclusion were developed." Simin Royanian. Original version 2003–06–27; revised 2005–03–25. http://women4peace.org/women-rights.html Compare the writer Fatemola who, in speaking out against a proposal to introduce Islamic law in Ontario, Canada asked "'How Islamic is Sharia?' [Fatemola] said that Sharia violates the Quran again and again and that it is an institution of political Islam (ref. Maudoodi). 'We don't have to denounce Islam or the Prophet Mohammad, peace be upon him, to denounce Sharia.' He cited several verses of the Quran to illustrate his point." *Synopsis* of the panel discussion on Sharia tribunals in Canada and Women's Rights, hosted by the International Campaign for Defense of Women's Rights in Iran, on March 7, 2004.

As is true of Harriet and of the slave, Taliban Woman has permitted herself to be situated in a flow of events which she lacks the resources to modify, and this lack is due to her relations with others. And, as is true of Harriet and of the willing slave, the Taliban Woman is *subject* to circumstances—she is not the agent of these circumstances. Though the Taliban Woman remains, at least initially, capable of functioning as an agent, the energy that comprises autonomous agency has been arrested by the passivity her interpersonal circumstances impose.[26] Her lack of autonomy is not merely due to the fact that she comes to depend on others. Rather, her lack of autonomy is determined by what this dependency entails for her in her daily life. Whatever may be the character of her will, her life-plan remains in force because of the will of another. The fact that this is consistent with her subjective interest is fortunate—the satisfaction of desires central to her most cherished values is guaranteed. But desire satisfaction is not autonomy.

The fact that Taliban Woman may garner the respect of others neither minimizes her lack of autonomy nor compensates for this lack. It diminishes the concept of autonomy to call a person "autonomous" whose genuine value for subservience leads her to choose to lead a life of dependency and unquestioning adherence to authority. Human beings are distinguished from other creatures precisely because of their heightened deliberative and creative capacities. Moreover, the life-plans of human beings are dynamic and evolving. A life is not one of autonomy is it eliminates the possibility of practical change. For things do change in our lives. Circumstances change. We change. And if we are to be self-directing in these lives we must have the psychological ability to rethink our choices as well as the opportunity to remake our choices and the option to live in a manner that reflects our revised point of view.

The Monk

It is possible for a person to relinquish his autonomy without losing ultimate authority over his condition. A monk, for example, who opts to live under the dictates of a religious order and thereby forego autonomy may nonetheless preserve the power to reinstate his autonomy. Suppose that every year it is up to the monk to decide whether to remain in the order and to continue conducting his life in a manner that denies him a fuller range of freedom. Then, even if the religious order has power over him sufficient to compel him to behave in a certain way, the monk can annul this power annually, in much the same way that individuals have the legal authority to dissolve the terms of certain contracts.[27] The monk has consented to a condition

---

26 I do not claim, and it is not a consequence of my view, that the fully subservient religious devotee is not capable of functioning as an agent. Taliban Woman is not an automaton.

27 Similarly, consider Ulysses' request that his crew physically restrain him when their journey brings them in proximity to the Sirens' songs. While he is bound and restrained, his autonomy is curtailed, for then he lacks control of his fate (and also, of course, command of the ship and crew). But Ulysses' circumstance differs from that of the consenting slave (and more closely approaches that of the monk) in the following fashion. He is not relinquishing his right to determine his course of life; none of his considered options for the future are

that guarantees him ultimate authority over himself on a yearly basis, and he is sovereign—the final arbiter—on this matter.

Unlike the slave and the Taliban Woman, the monk confronts alternative possibilities and does so because the situation he is in, and the relations to which he is a party, permit him the authority to decide whether to remain in the order and to continue living in a manner that denies him comprehensive self-government. Indeed, the monk retains autonomy over a series of ongoing decisions to be subservient, whether or not he considers his commitment to the monastic community to be revocable. A similar claim can be made of the military recruit who accepts conscription for a three year period of service after which she is released from her obligations to the armed forces and is (in theory) free to return to civilian life. Both Taliban Woman and the monk continue to find their behavior governed by their professed values and norms. Like the Taliban Woman, the monk continues to reaffirm his decision to live under the dictates of a religious order. But it is farcical to attribute autonomy to a person who is not at liberty to leave a situation antithetical to self-government, even if the person assents to that situation on a continual basis. Only the monk has the latitude to revisit his life-plan and to effect changes to it. Only the monk retains a right to exit from the order without reprisal. This is key for his potential autonomy and it is due entirely to his social standing.

Of course, the fact that the monk *can* annul his status as non-autonomous does not mean he *is* self-governing. His monastic superiors preserve authority in the interim, for his life is ruled by them on a daily basis. And the nature of the contract, in terms of what is required of the individual, will be important for assessing the autonomy of the monk. Breaking the vow or dissolving the contract may carry a penalty that is sufficiently burdensome to make the quest for autonomy unbearable. (Indeed, the psychological pressure upon young military recruits to reenlist is often great—aggressive and unrelenting. Such pressure highlights the extent to which the experience of a military recruit is antithetical to autonomy at the same time it makes the assurance of future autonomy under a recruitment contract less convincing.) Nonetheless, to the degree the counterfactual "If the monk changes his mind, he will be released from his vows" is true, the monk is within range of autonomy. In light of the social relations he is party to, the monk can become self-governing merely by revoking at the appropriate interval his decision to be subservient.

Would the cultural and social contexts in which persons such as Taliban Woman and the monk (or the military recruit) make their choices modify our assessment of their autonomy?[28] Choosing the role of subservient spouse and religious devotee within the context of a society that typically affords many, if not all, of its citizens rich opportunities for more liberated roles might temper one's judgment that autonomy

---

closed to him since his relations with his crew members remain such that he will resume control at the agreed upon moment.

28 Paul Benson suggested in correspondence that the social context in which a lifestyle is pursued rather than the lifestyle itself informs our judgment that autonomy is preserved or abridged.

was abdicated in a permanent and worrisome way. But that is no guarantee that autonomy was not abdicated, and is no guarantee that autonomy is present after the fact. Certainly the conditions surrounding a person's decision makes a difference to our judgment of the autonomous nature of the person's choice. Evidence that a person chose to abdicate autonomy under conditions of constrained reflection or greatly narrowed options as opposed to careful consideration of a rich array of choice will strengthen our judgment of a lack of autonomy. But it will not be the cause of that judgment. What will cause us to judge that autonomy is absent (or that it remains) will be what life is like for the person following this choice. Similarly, the reasons why a person opts for some arrangements rather than others—noble devotion to a cause as opposed to slothful indifference to his abilities, for example—may count in our assessment of the person's autonomy, not to mention our view of the person's backbone or moral fiber. But whether a person opts for a life of subservience or surrender to another out of high-minded principle or degeneracy is less important for gauging the person's autonomy or lack of autonomy than is what such a life yields for the person on a practical and daily basis.

The Would-Be Surrendered Woman[29]

Consider a person who is autonomous by accident. The would-be surrendered woman shows every appearance of leading a life rich with autonomy. But she has stumbled upon this life without design or effort on her part. She is, she might say, a victim of late twentieth-century child-rearing practices, increasingly imprecise gender-role expectations, and a temperament that has propelled her to a life as a self-supporting, successful professional woman. But absent from this life is what she most wants, namely surrender to the strong direction, or at least the strong arms, of a loving man. Unlike the slave, Harriet the homemaker, the Taliban Woman, the monk, and the rest, the would-be surrendered woman is unable to attain her life plan. Her self-conception is unrealized.

One who contends that psychological authenticity is the hallmark of autonomy would deny autonomy of the would-be surrendered woman. On the face of it, she lacks "a self-chosen identity rooted in [her] most abiding feelings and firmest convictions."[30] Though she creates her character out of her own activity, this character somehow fails to satisfy her personal ideal. But does this misfortune yield an absence of autonomy? If the would-be surrendered woman fails to be self-governing, what is the reason for this failure? Is it because she approaches her life as a sleepwalker might? Is it because her self-conception fails to be satisfied, or because it is unsatisfiable? Is the would-be surrendered woman (figuratively speaking) overwhelmed by her self-governance? Must the option to be nonautonomous exist among the alternatives available to a person in order for us to judge the person autonomous?

---

29 Paul Benson raised the case in discussion.
30 Meyers, *Self, Society, and Personal Choice*, p. 61.

In response to these questions defenders of autonomy as psychological and procedural authenticity might say that we should decline to call the would-be surrendered woman autonomous no matter how independent a life she apparently leads for the simple reason that she is under the sway of forces from which she struggles to be free. I have not characterized the would-be surrendered woman as one who puts up much of a struggle against her position, having envisioned her instead as someone who just finds herself dissatisfied with the status she has. I do not think it would necessarily make a difference for the would-be surrendered woman's autonomy if she did put up a struggle—whether or not she did so might hinge on just how disabled she believed herself to be—although it would certainly make a difference to her happiness and general state of mind. But even if one who is sympathetic to the psychological and procedural authenticity picture conceded that the would-be surrendered woman exhibits autonomy of only a thin, qualified sort they would insist that the alienation she feels toward the facts of her situation signals a general lack of autonomy.

So let us consider this alienation. Does the disaffectedness that marks the would-be surrendered woman's life compromise her autonomy or does it just condition the woman's enjoyment of her autonomy? Diana Meyers insists that "unhappiness with oneself is incompatible with autonomy." Meyers writes:

> People can be unhappy with themselves, or they can be unhappy with their position in the world (or both). Unhappiness with oneself is incompatible with autonomy. For such unhappiness stems either from one's failure to become the sort of person one wants to be (failure with respect to self-definition) or from one's failure to act in accordance with one's authentic self (failure of self-direction). But since autonomous people do not suffer from chronic regret, this type of unhappiness is ruled out.[31]

If Meyers is correct, the would-be surrendered woman is not autonomous. I find this to be curious. It may make sense to claim an absence of autonomy in the case of the would-be surrendered woman if the woman's affective experience of herself is so conflicted as to yield a disintegrated personality, one that makes the sustained exercise of self-government impossible or erratic. But this is not the experience of the would-be surrendered woman. From the fact that a person "fails to act in accordance with her authentic self" and is dissatisfied with her life it does not follow that the person systematically suppresses constituents of her identity, including her desires, attachments, and values, with the result that the person lacks an integrated personality and thus autonomy, as Meyers claims.[32] It does not even follow that the person suffers from chronic regret. Nor is it a consequence of dissatisfaction that constituents of the person's identity are suppressed by others, though if this were a consequence we would have reason to question the person's autonomy, although for reasons that have little to do with her happiness. In short, without further evidence to the contrary we cannot describe the case of the would-be surrendered woman as an

---

31 Meyers, *Self, Society, and Personal Choice*, p. 74.
32 Meyers, *Self, Society, and Personal Choice*, p. 80; p. 73.

obvious example of compromised autonomy prompted by psychological dissonance or conflicted identity.

More generally, it is implausible to deny autonomy of a person simply because the person cannot configure her desires to her situation just as it is implausible to claim autonomy for a person who simply configures her desires to suit an unpalatable situation. Would those who deny autonomy to the would-be surrendered woman claim she would find autonomy if only she succeeded in giving up her unrealized yearnings or if she just fashioned a new self-image for herself? I suspect lives such as the life would-be surrendered woman leads may be self-directed even where these self-directed lives are not expressions of what the individual most wants; they may be self-directed even where the individual suffers tension in her psychological states. Just consider the struggle that confronts the "born again" person who develops a desire to give himself—at least, his conscience—over to God. As may be true of the would-be surrendered woman, the religious neophyte who is accustomed to self-governance may find that surrender does not come easily. But the fact that there is struggle rarely signals a loss of self-government. Indeed, it indicates just the opposite, that the person is disposed to govern himself and that the urge to retain this authority over himself is present.

One who seeks the material for autonomy in the social relations people occupy would likely take unhappiness with one's position in the world to be a better gauge of autonomy than unhappiness with oneself. However, Meyers denies this. The passage above continues:

> [U]nhappiness with one's position in the world is compatible with autonomy. For, rightly or wrongly, the world may be inhospitable to one's true self, and one may lack the power to win it over. Autonomous people may be unable to arrange for a sufficiently receptive environment to guarantee their own happiness, and autonomy may forbid the very compromises with conventionality that would secure contentment.[33]

Certainly, persons need not be happy with the social relations they occupy if they are to be autonomous. Even if some benchmark for how happy a person must be with her situation in the world if she is to be autonomous is essential, we cannot without further information claim autonomy to be absent from the life of a person, such as the would-be surrendered woman, simply because the person is dissatisfied with her situation. However, the fact that a person confronts a world that is "inhospitable to one's true self" where one "lack[s] the power to win it over" *is* relevant for autonomy. To be so positioned surely enervates autonomy for the simple reason that it makes the realization of one's goals more cumbersome. I may be perfectly content with myself, have no regrets about the kind of person I am, but be deeply dissatisfied with my place in the world for no reason other than that it denies me *de facto* power over my life. (Perhaps the would-be surrendered woman, though self-governing according to the social account, lacks the power to win over the world in this sense—she finds that other people, men in particular, are unwilling to or incapable of accommodating

33 Meyers, *Self, Society, and Personal Choice*, p. 74.

her interests, by sweeping her off her feet and transporting her to Cinderella land.) This said, the question to ask in the case before us is not whether the would-be surrendered woman's self-portrait is frustrated, for it is obviously frustrated. The questions to ask are why this is so, and how unrecognizable is the portrait of herself she confronts? And we must ask what effect this has for the would-be surrendered woman's self-government.

Following Paul Benson, it seems correct that autonomy requires that an agent recognizes herself as one who takes ownership of her life—of her choices, motives, actions, relationships—and as one who has the authority to answer for herself. Autonomy requires that the agent has a sense of self-worth—that the agent sees herself as deserving this standing.[34] Does the would-be surrendered woman regard herself in this fashion? She is not, as described, buffeted about by circumstances beyond her power with the result that her self-conception cannot be satisfied by her efforts. If the would-be surrendered woman does not actively suppress her autonomy, then why is it necessary that she assent to her autonomy in order to be autonomous? Aside from the practical efficacy of protecting encroachments upon autonomy—and that is a real concern—is it essential for the satisfaction of autonomy that a person be committed to her own autonomy? It is not obviously necessary that "autonomous people control their lives in ways that obviate [recurrent] regret,"[35] nor is it obvious that the presence of regret signals an absence of harmony between self and action that allegedly is one of the hallmarks of autonomy. The would-be surrendered woman's preferred self-conception fails to mirror her social circumstances, but we continue to call the would-be surrendered woman autonomous because she lives a self-governed life in spite of her desire to do otherwise.

In all of the five case studies we ask what is at stake for the life of a socially situated individual whose interpersonal standing has a significant influence upon self-governance. In the first four cases we find that what the individuals lack is *de facto* power to manage various details of their private and public lives. These details include their intimate relationships, the access others have to information about themselves, their educational and employment options, their mobility, and such. What is salient is that all of these are phenomena that transpire within the context of social, moral, and political frameworks. The social arrangements to which the slave, Harriet, and the Taliban Woman (and, for a period of time, the monk and the military recruit) are subject deny them the ability to govern the management of these phenomena, governance over which is tantamount to governance over their selves,

---

34 See Paul Benson, "Taking Ownership: Authority and Voice in Autonomous Agency," in *Autonomy and the Challenges to Liberalism: New Essays* (New York, 2005), pp. 98–126, and Benson, "Free Agency and Self-Worth," *Journal of Philosophy*, 91(12) (1994): 650–68. Benson contends that this requires the agent to have a sense of herself as deserving or worthy of partnership. John Martin Fischer and Mark Ravizza similarly charge that a person is morally responsible for behavior when it stems from a mechanism that the person has taken responsibility for and, hence, made his own. See their *Responsibility and Control: A Theory of Moral Responsibility* (Cambridge, U.K, 1998), pp. 207–39.

35 Meyers, *Self, Society, and Personal Choice*, p. 34.

or so I shall argue. Each lacks this power of governance in the actual situation in which he finds himself and this lack is due, in part, to the absence of counterfactual power each has to determine his affairs should others attempt to deprive them of their power to do so. Each is vulnerable and their vulnerability is social-relational in origin. By contrast, our would-be surrendered woman is not exposed to such vulnerability by her social relations.

The Consequences of a Social Relational Account

The social-relation account of autonomy has the following consequences. First, the emphasis moves from the autonomy of preferences or values to the autonomy of persons. The case studies illustrate that satisfying the psychological conditions simply will not be sufficient for self-government. We can speak of a person's desires as autonomous, or of a person as autonomous over her desires, even where the person is not autonomous (just as we can speak of a person's desires as satisfied even where the person is not).

Second, personal autonomy cannot be determined solely by reference to a person's history, or to the history of his psychological states, even given a historical account that is sensitive to the person's social-relational background. In general, those who offer a historical account fail to discuss the conditions under which a suitable psychology must develop in terms that are clearly sensitive to the agent's social-relational environment. For example, the "reflection-constraining factors" and "illegitimate influences" which Christman employs to test the autonomy of persons offer no more than veiled references to the social relations that affect the agent's psychological capacities.

It is likely, however, that proponents of psychological authenticity accounts who emphasize history have in mind certain social factors and influences when speaking of appropriate and inappropriate influences. Unlike the structuralist who defends a purely internalist account of autonomy, the historicist might concede that what enables the agent to appraise and, if need be, revise her motivations is not simply the possession of an unimpaired psychology or psychological history but a cooperative, non-invasive network of social relations. He might acknowledge that while personal autonomy supervenes on the psychological condition and the psychological history of an agent, some social contexts will be more conducive to psychological autonomy than others.

But even if he does concede this, it remains the case that the only facts the historicist addresses are facts about a person's psychological history—facts pertaining to the development of the person's capacity to reflect upon, revise, and identify with her psychological states. Historical considerations are germane only to the extent that history produces certain managerial and executive abilities of critical reflection, identification and self-control. The social-relational account claims, however, that to the extent a person's history is important for her autonomy, much more than facts of relevance to her psychological status is at stake. For example, what is historically relevant to the monk's autonomy is that his monastic order permits him to leave after a period of time if he sees fit. What is historically relevant to Harriet's lack of autonomy is a pattern of social practices that have made her subject, rather than sovereign, of her life. The fact that a person's history offers an optimal breeding ground for autonomy, and so is a history happily free of autonomy-constraining factors, is relevant for personal autonomy only if that history yields the kind of social relations and psychological stability that are suitable for self-government.

A third consequence of the social-relational analysis is that authenticity is not necessary for autonomy any more than authenticity or an absence of alienation will suffice for self-governance. To require authenticity is to say that a person is autonomous if she is moved by values, desires, beliefs, and attitudes that have survived unimpaired self-scrutiny and have been embraced in the end. Presumably, the legitimacy of a person's attachments, partnerships, ethnic and cultural identity, and social roles can also be authenticated for autonomy by similar tests. One simply asks how the person regards these phenomena when they are examined in an unblemished, critical light, or how the person would regard them were she to reflect upon their development and their effect upon her. If they are seen as phenomena to which she feels an affinity or as roles she wants to occupy, the criterion of authenticity is met and we can be secure in the thought that the elements that influence the direction of an agent's choices and actions are definitively the agent's own. If, on the other hand, the agent feels disaffected and estranged from phenomena that affect her choices and actions, to the extent that she repudiates them, then (the story goes) autonomy, to some degree, is denied.

I think it is false that a person's autonomy is circumscribed simply because among the values, desires, beliefs and attitudes, attachments, partnerships, ethnic and cultural identity and social roles central to a person's life are those she would disavow or prefer not to embrace. A person even can be autonomous despite the fact that she feels actively alienated from aspects of her character that are essential to who she is and how she conceives of herself. The case of the would-be surrendered woman is instructive in this regard. The woman for whom a life of surrender holds promise can acknowledge the centrality of certain characteristics and relations to her life—in this case, characteristics and relations that mark her as self-governing—and can concede the tremendous social and psychological force of these while valuing neither the characteristics and relations nor their centrality.

The phenomenon of racialized identity exemplifies how a person can be autonomous even while she is inauthentic with respect to a key aspect of her identity, her social circumstances, and her will.[36] Race-consciousness, or awareness of the societal significance of one's race, is inescapable in multicultural societies such as the United States. Persons of color such as myself, in particular, will find our racial identity so ingrained that we cannot "forget ourselves" or fail to appreciate the presence of racial typing. Our autonomy is bound up with our status as persons of color, and as persons

---

36 See Marina A.L. Oshana, "Autonomy and Self-Identity," in John Christman and Joel Anderson (eds), *Autonomy and the Challenges of Liberalism* (New York, 2005), pp. 77–97.

of color we cannot escape the racialized norms that define us and that inform our self-concept, even where we regard these norms as alien. Forgetting one's race involves a lapse of self-awareness. Consciously or not, welcome or not, one's racialized identity contravenes upon numerous aspects of life; it shapes our values, our beliefs and attitudes about ourselves and others, our educational and employment experiences, the attachments and partnerships we forge and the ease we feel in creating these, and so forth. But would forgetting aspects of oneself as integral to one's identity as is race in America rob a person of an authentic psychology, and thus enfeeble autonomy? What effect would a person's disaffectedness about race or her estrangement from her racialized identity have for her autonomy? Must a person be authentic with respect to her racialized identity if the person is to be autonomous?

I suspect an answer to this question will vary depending on what we take authenticity to involve. Certainly authenticity as it is standardly understood is not coextensive with autonomy. If authenticity and autonomy were coextensive then a person could not be autonomous if she felt estranged from the features of her identity, her social situation, and her will that were essential to her life—to how she regarded herself and to what was important to her. We must be very clear on this point. The point is not simply that a person would lack autonomy *vis à vis* some characteristic she happens to have or happens to value. The point is that the person would not be autonomous *simpliciter* because the characteristics from which she was alienated, or which she wished to repudiate but could not, were essential to her status as a self-directed individual.

However, a person's autonomy might be abridged if inauthenticity or estrangement were understood in a stronger sense to mean something like self-deception. For example, if I were to attempt to pass as white because I refused to acknowledge my hybrid African-American/Middle Eastern heritage, my action would signal a kind of self-betrayal, an attempt to defeat my identity. To deny an essential identity-forming aspect of myself would be to falsify myself. Living in denial would require me to conduct myself in an excruciatingly watchful way, at least until the lie ceased to exist for me. Until I had thoroughly forgotten myself, and until all others had forgotten my ethnicity as well—something that is unlikely to happen—a tremendous amount of energy and skill would be absorbed by the task of passing. The effect of this would be a type of practical disability, making self-management a more complicated endeavor.

Thus the attempt to live as something one is not strikes me as adversative to autonomy. Nonetheless it is incorrect that an absence of estrangement from one's social situation, even where this bears on the unforgettable and inescapable aspects of one's identity, is a requirement of autonomy. Rather than demand authenticity or an absence of alienation, autonomy requires that a person be disposed to acknowledge that factors such as these occupy a central role in her psychological economy and practical affairs.

The social-relational analysis yields a fourth result. This is that the social relations in which a person finds himself contribute both causally *and* constitutively to the condition of autonomy. Advocates of a psychologistic approach would, I believe, concede that appropriate social relations contribute causally to autonomy. For assuming that an individual does not suffer from whatever psychological infirmities might make autonomy difficult even in the most hospitable of social situations, a person in appropriate social circumstances is more likely to experience psychological autonomy. The principal psychological characteristics of self-determination—an ability to engage in rational, reflexive self-evaluation, and identification with one's motives—flourish when a person interacts with others in unimpeded ways. Appropriate social conditions thus provide the background against which persons can implement whatever psychological abilities prepare them for autonomy.

But a person need not be in particular social situations in order to meet the requisite psychological and historical conditions and, thereby, be autonomous. For provided that certain psychological and perhaps historical conditions are met, adherents of the psychological and procedural authenticity approach would count as autonomous a person who is physically caged or who is constrained by social prospects. By contrast, an adherent of the social-relational approach will deny autonomy to these persons and will claim that to characterize them as self-governing is counterintuitive.

A fifth consequence pertains to the connection between global and local autonomy. What is at stake in the first four case studies is not autonomy as a characteristic of some choices but not others, or of choices considered individually. What is at stake is autonomy as the general condition of a person's life. What decides a person's autonomy is not simply the interval of time for which a person behaves (or fails to behave) in a self-managed way. Episodes of control do not grant a person a life of self-government any more than the absence of such episodes robs a person of a life of self-government. Just as one who occasionally tells a lie can be an honest person, and one who is occasionally despondent can be a happy person, so, too, can a person be autonomous even though her life might include moments of nonautonomy. The monk (like the slave and the Taliban Woman) fails to be self-governing although on occasion he might be in control of some aspect of his life and although one of the key elements of autonomy is conditionally in his possession. Harriet, the Taliban Woman, the monk, and even the slave may confront choices on a daily basis and may be expected to decide on the basis of these choices. They may be called upon to employ their "autonomy competencies." But they do not choose how or when to put these skills to use. Were they inclined to do otherwise, or were others indisposed toward them, any vestige of control they have would vanish. As a result they lack the authority to determine the employment of these skills—an important range of action remains closed to them as do options for particular goods and states.

The sixth and final consequence of note is this: a social account accommodates the naturalist's demand that an account of the autonomous individual be faithful to empirical fact. By highlighting the "inner citadel" as the locus of agent autonomy, psychological authenticity theories of self-determination tend to diminish the importance of the larger social and phenomenal environment for autonomy. A thoroughly naturalized account incorporates two notions, or "faces," of autonomy. One is an explanatory notion: The concept of autonomy explains choice and the realization of goals. Autonomy is a notion driven by certain facts about the social standing of the agent (such as facts about the range of options available to her) in conjunction with facts about her psychological standing (such as information about her dispositional character). Together, these facts perform the explanatory function. The other notion of autonomy is the alternative possibilities notion. Autonomy mandates the *de jure* right and the *de facto* ability to revisit one's situation and the liberty to exit from it or revise it. The social account of autonomy serves both elements of a naturalized account while content-neutral, proceduralist, psychological authenticity accounts cannot capture either notion in its entirety.

Summary

To sum up the discussion of this chapter: Autonomy calls for a measure of substantive independence from other persons and from social roles and traditions of a variety determined to be inhospitable to autonomy.[37] Hence, autonomy is determined by criteria other than what the agent happens to value. A person cannot be self-directed if her goals have been selected for her, without her input. But setting goals without interference is inadequate for self-government if a person lacks the power to be active with regard to them in the world. She must be able to achieve these goals as well. The proponent of autonomy as psychological and procedural authenticity concedes both points, and believes he can accommodate both. I have suggested that given the commitment to substantive neutrality and the adherence to procedural independence, autonomy as *de facto* self-governance will fail to materialize.

The social account does not claim that the content of a person's choice decides her autonomy, nor that this content must gel with the ideal of autonomy (whatever that ideal is). Rather, substance is introduced as a constitutive element in the social control a person must have if she is to count as genuinely self-determining. The idea is that, whatever the choices of the individual actor, these must be choices that provide her with a modicum of authority over her life. Though the substantively autonomous agent "cares about her own activity of reflecting on deeper, self-defining concerns without impediment and acting accordingly,"[38] the substantivist denies that what marks a person as autonomous is to be equated with what a person happens to care about. The case studies demonstrate just this point.

---

37 The following analogy may help illuminate this point. Consider a legitimate state occupied and controlled by a foreign power. The state has fashioned goals for itself of which it approves, and the foreign occupying force which has usurped it as the governing body upholds these goals. The citizens might never experience hardship or adversity in this situation. All in all, the occupied state does not object to this occupation. Some citizens and their representatives might even welcome the foreign power as providing greater stability or military might against less congenial aggressors. This welcome does not amount to an authorization that the foreign power should assume control, but even if it did the state is nonetheless subject to the dictates of a foreign power and for that reason it still makes sense to deny that the state is self-governing.

38 Friedman, *Autonomy, Gender, Politics*, p. 21.

Nor is it the hallmark of substantive autonomy that "someone choosing subservience would not be autonomous unless she did so for some higher nonsubordinate purpose which continued to be her own purpose even in the condition of servitude" as some claim.[39] This is precisely what proceduralists would aver, and defenders of the substantive social-relational account would deny. A proceduralist would claim that the person continues to be autonomous if she continues to reaffirm her choice, where the substantivist would deny this. Autonomy, for the substantivist, is not a matter of being free to act as one pleases, but a matter of living in a particular way. Autonomy is a notion primarily driven by a conception of the good, by some traits of character rather than others, and by the nondiscretionary presence of substantively specified relations, social roles, and natural circumstances.

One who is procedurally autonomous "is at least minimally self-determining in that the self has defining concerns that determine how she acts"[40] and this is indeed an important element of autonomy. Proponents of a substantively laden account such as myself do not discount such conduct as significant in assessments of autonomy. But we do claim that content-neutrality represents more than just a "lower threshold" of agency.[41] Substantive autonomy is not just an enhanced species of more minimal content-neutral autonomy.

If proceduralist content-neutrality represents a species of autonomy at all, it is a species that fails to motivate the intuitions articulated in Chapter 1. This is a significant failing. These ideas about self-governance are genuinely congruent with commonsense and with the tenets of naturalism. As a result, personal autonomy must be conceptualized as a depiction of what is at issue for individuals who are situated with others in the real-world context of moral, social, and political exchange. The intuitions are not ad hoc and free-floating but rather play the practical role of picking out what is implied for the lives of persons such as Taliban Woman, the military newcomer compelled to experience what may verge on psychic brutality and the incessant muscle of his superiors, and Harriet, our Angel in the House. The question of whether an account of autonomy is adequate depends as well on how successful the concept is in practical as well as theoretical contexts. That is, the adequacy of the account rests on the extent to which the concept makes sense of these cases (and of cases such as that of the would-be surrendered woman).

Admittedly the intuitions might be fail to persuade proceduralists and might not settle the question of autonomy's role in practical affairs. But adjudicating claims to autonomy in the arena of the political, especially where (as in liberalism) autonomy is taken to have its home, relies on suppositions as to autonomy's nature and essence.

---

39 Friedman, *Autonomy, Gender, Politics*, p. 19.

40 Friedman, *Autonomy, Gender, Politics*, p. 20.

41 Friedman characterizes substantive social-relational autonomy as "autonomy with attitude" in which "choices that were made in the right way to reflect what the acting person deeply cares about" are "substantively guided by a commitment to autonomy as a value" such that "autonomy seeking becomes a stable and enduring concern of the agent." Friedman, *Autonomy, Gender, Politics*, p. 20.

I suspect that philosophers who insist upon deciding the merit of an account of autonomy by seeing what the account would imply for political concerns such as the shape of liberal principles and the validation of such principles are not concerned with autonomy but with political theory and what best comports with presuppositions embedded in the theory. Moreover, they fail to notice that reflection on the intuitive character of autonomy is already at work in this task. The undertaking of the following chapter is to strengthen the case for the success of the social-relational account in this regard by developing more precisely the conditions for personal autonomy.

Chapter 4

The Conditions for Personal Autonomy

Naturalizing Autonomy

The discussion of Chapter 3 has left us with the following. An autonomous person not only has the capacity to make independent decisions about matters pertinent to the nature and the direction of her life but exercises this capacity. Such decisions concern, for example, a person's choice of lifestyle, partners, and career. The autonomous person is not inclined to impose impediments to autonomy upon herself; on the contrary, she generally is disposed to live in a self-governed way.[1] She has regulative control over her life, control of the sort that involves the power to do otherwise than one actually does. The possibility of practical change—the ability to revisit values and motives and choices and to live in a manner that manifests this revised outlook—is a crucial component of being an autonomous person.

In Chapter 1, I claimed that if the account of autonomy developed in this book was to be successful in explaining the concept of global autonomy, the account would have to capture certain commonplace ideas about self-governance. These were the ideas that a person is autonomous when she has a kind of authority to govern her choices, actions, and goals, especially those that are fundamentally significant to the direction of her life, and when she has the *de facto* power to act on that authority. In Chapter 3, I argued that the slave, Harriet, the Taliban Woman and, for some length of time, the monk and the military recruit, lack global autonomy. They do so not because (or, not just because) they lack *de facto* power over the actual situation in which they find themselves. Rather, they lack global autonomy, in part, because it is a feature of the actual situation that they *would* lack the power to determine their affairs, governance over which is tantamount to governance over themselves, in the event that others were to attempt to deprive them of the authority to do so. That is, they lack what I have called "counterfactual power" of the sort that regulative control supplies. The slave, Harriet, Taliban Woman, and the like fail to have authoritative control over, or "ownership" of, the management of their choices, actions, and goals. Whatever "authority" each has is unprotected and vulnerable to interference. This vulnerability is due to their social status and relations to others, and it is vulnerability of a sort that makes whatever *de facto* power each of these persons wields insufficient to render them fully autonomous.

---

1 Recall that although the would-be surrendered woman is unsatisfied with her self-governing status she does not take steps to suppress her autonomy. This suggests, if not a disposition to autonomy, then an absence of disposition for its removal.

I claimed that these ideas about autonomy provide a measure against which the plausibility of models of autonomy is appraised. I claimed, moreover, that a plausible account of autonomy must satisfy the requirements of naturalism. It must recognize that the autonomy of persons is partly constituted by the relations they stand in to others, relations that are extrinsic to facts about their psychological history and their occurrent psychological circumstances and competencies. In Chapter 2, various accounts of autonomy were assessed in light of these intuitive ideas about autonomy and the requirements of naturalism and were found wanting. By contrast, the social-relational account introduced in Chapter 3 was found to fare well in both respects.

The task of this chapter is to press this advantage by developing a set of conditions for autonomy premised on the discussion of the previous chapter. These conditions are essential elements of a model of autonomy that is both thoroughly naturalized and that comports with the pretheoretical intuitive ideas sketched earlier. A social-relational account will be a fully naturalized view. The account will explain autonomy in terms of facts about the agent's social status along with facts about her psychological nature. And the account will explain the notion of autonomy as it bears upon alternative possibilities—autonomy as the power and the authority to reconsider one's situation and the liberty to abandon it or rework it.

The Conditions for Personal Autonomy

The case studies indicate the need for the following conditions for autonomy. In conjunction with one another they are sufficient to constitute autonomy. Not everyone must exhibit these conditions to the same degree in order to count as autonomous. As we saw in discussing the capacity for autonomy in Chapter 1, there is a threshold for personal autonomy and autonomy can be had in degrees. An appreciation of the threshold can be had by examining cases in which it is clear autonomy is lacking. But these conditions must be satisfied, each to some significant degree, if a person is to be globally autonomous.

Epistemic Competence

A number of epistemic abilities are required of the person who is autonomous. Most importantly, autonomy requires that a person is epistemically competent in the sense of being self-reflective and self-aware. Self-reflection and self-awareness are multi-faceted. They permit the actor to notice herself as an agent, someone who can deliberate about action and author action. To be self-aware is to be cognizant of who one is—it is to have a sense of self. An absence of self-reflection and self-awareness, and an indifference to one's identity, eclipse autonomous agency. Someone who lacks a desire for self-understanding and who does not, as a rule, acknowledge some cognitive, affective, and behavioral characteristics, and certain attachments as important to her—perhaps as essential to her self-conception—nor concede the absence of others is in a lesser position to assume an active and authoritative voice in the direction of her life. A person of this sort would be disinclined to regard herself as bearing a distinctive identity, as someone whose aspirations, interests, and commitments—whose *raison d'être*, if you will—had not simply been bestowed upon her or borrowed from others. Such a person would be less able to appreciate what she has grounds to do based on the beliefs, values, institutions and relationships she is willing to stand behind and based on reasons for action she is willing to endorse. Epistemic competence provides some assurance—certainly not complete, but essential—that a person's governance over her life is her own and that a person is able to avoid situations that undermine the pursuit of her life-plans.

Self-awareness is, of course, a matter of degree, and no person is completely self-aware. Self-awareness does not mandate utter transparency, as elements of our psychology are obscure, inaccessible, or elusive. Moreover, I am not claiming that an autonomous individual needs to be self-aware at every juncture. Indeed, persons who are constantly attentive to themselves are not thought to possess a healthy consciousness of themselves but rather are self-conscious or in a state that tends to hamper confidence in oneself.

The prototypical ideal of autonomy requires that a person conceive of herself as someone who can affect the world in light of a perspective and plan for life that is of her making. Without self-reflection and self-awareness, a person cannot embark upon a life of autonomy in the global sense, and autonomous choice and action cannot commence nor be sustained. A person gains self-awareness when she critically appraises her motivations and actions and the environment in which these develop. Critical reflection permits an individual to be knowledgeable of her circumstances and of the effective forces that are operative in these circumstances. Part of what critical competence amounts to is sensitivity "to environmental circumstances so as to allow oneself as much elbow room as possible."[2] On the basis of this appraisal, the individual is better positioned to determine whether and when her particular actions, and the actions of other beings, will comport with, advance, or frustrate her more global interests. As a result she might accept her motivations as her own and treat them as reason-giving. Or she may decide they require correction or revision.[3]

We may say that the reasons for which the autonomous agent acts become her own by a compound process of maturation and critical reflection. But the fact that autonomous persons may affirm as important to them the proattitudes and beliefs that engage them in action does not mean that autonomous persons must embrace these proattitudes and beliefs as ones they most want to have or as ones with which they unequivocally identify or are unambivalent with respect to or even regard as

---

2   Daniel Dennett, *Elbow Room: The Varieties of Free-Will Worth Wanting* (Cambridge, MA, 1984).

3   Along these lines, Waldron remarks that autonomy involves "the ability to stand back from one's occurrent desires, to determine in some way—on the basis of a thought-out conception of the good—which desires and preferences one wants to be motivated by ... With this done, choice, decision, and action are a matter of responding to values and to desires that have been given this reflective precedence..." Jeremy Waldron, *The Right to Private Property* (Oxford, 1988), p. 305.

desirable. Motivational states such as proattitudes and beliefs are important to a person because the person treats them as central to her will and to her life. But a person can be autonomous *vis à vis* these states even where she harbors ambivalence toward them or repudiates their ancestry. We will return to this point in discussing procedural independence, below, and again in Chapter 7 when exploring the topic of self-creation.

Rationality

Rationality is a species of epistemic competence but of a sufficiently distinctive and important sort that it merits special mention. Autonomous agents are rational in at least three ways. First, they are rational in the sense that they are attuned to their internal and external environment—the spheres of the psychological and of the social. Second, autonomous agents are rational in the sense that they can formulate, and are disposed to follow through with, plans for action that are conducive to the realization of ends important to them. Autonomous agents are not disposed to frustrate successful means-end reasoning in pursuit of their interests. Satisfaction of rationality as competence in prudential reasoning may be as simple a matter as having a coherent belief-desire set. Third, persons who are self-governing must be rational in the sense that they are able to distinguish from among the multitude of possible choices, activities, and relationships in their lives those that are favorable to self-governance from those that disadvantage self-governance. Robert Young captures the importance of rationality so understood when he states that:

> [B]eing rational can be seen as significant [to autonomy] in the following two positive ways. First, it brings coherence into the relationship between a person's general purposes and his or her particular actions. Some degree of understanding of this relationship will be needed to ensure that actions performed on particular occasions do not seriously thwart or impede more dispositional concerns. Second, and more importantly, perhaps, rationality equips a person to assess critically the advice tendered by others, an increasingly important safeguard given the extent to which we are reliant on the testimony of others about matters of great moment like health, welfare, education, economic and political affairs and so on.[4]

Procedural Independence

That an individual happens to reach, via critical reflection, certain conclusions about the influences which affect her decisions, choices, and reasons for action is not sufficient to determine whether she is autonomous. For a person can decide, mistakenly, that she has not been affected in ways that jeopardize the autonomy of her decisions, choices, and reasons for action even where she has in fact been so

---

4   Robert Young, *Autonomy: Beyond Negative and Positive Liberty* (New York, 1986), p. 13.

affected. Phenomena that impair a person's critical judgment may be psychological, consisting of obstacles such as neurotic compulsion, excessively low self-esteem, systemic weakness of will, or addiction. Of course, qualitative distinctions need to be drawn: some types of obsessive behavior will make little difference to a person's successful management of her life, whereas neurotic behavior of other sorts or on a greater scale will impede successful management. Compulsively checking the water faucets for drips every time a person prepares to leave home will in all likelihood have little affect on the autonomy of one's critical choice-making abilities; obsessing about which route to take to work each day, on the other hand, may impair the same abilities to a degree that greatly undermines a person's prospects for self-government.

Hence the need for a condition of procedural independence, suitably revised from its original formulation. Recall that procedural independence is satisfied when a person's critical faculties (a) have not been introduced in the agent by mechanisms she rejects (or would not reject, were she aware of their presence) and (b) have not been influenced in ways that undermine the legitimacy of the motivations that are appraised by those faculties. This description is underdescribed as it stands. In the first place, a person might welcome the introduction of certain critical powers where these are owing to phenomena that arguably subvert autonomy. A case in point would be the browbeaten provider described in Chapter 2. So the second component of the condition must be restated as follows: (b*) a person's critical faculties have not been introduced or influenced in ways that undermine the legitimacy of the motivations that are appraised by those faculties, even if the person approves of the process and regardless of the person's lack of resistance toward the process. Recall that both Dworkin and Christman concede that a person's approval of her motivational and valuational psychology might be generated by phenomena such as browbeating. Dworkin goes further and includes self-deception, manipulation, hypnosis, intimidation, addiction, and weakness of will among the permitted generators. Christman contends it is enough for autonomy that we grant that a person is attentive to these motivational phenomena, that the person occurrently condones (or would condone) the influence they exert upon her, and that she counterfactually could envision herself taking action were suitable alternatives presented. But browbeating and the rest are phenomena customarily viewed as detrimental to our critical capacities, even if they ultimately engender a state of enhanced autonomy in the person subject to them.

The original characterization of procedural independence is underdescribed in a second sense. As it is originally characterized, the condition of procedural independence is not clearly distinguished from the condition of authenticity. But the distinction needs to be made. It needs to be made clear that procedural independence is a condition that describes the cognitive and evaluative *activities* of the individuals whose autonomy is at issue. It is a condition that pertains to the process or manner in which evaluation and adoption of autonomy-salient beliefs, values, and dispositional states transpire. By contrast, authenticity is meant to be a characteristic of the products or the results of this activity—a characteristic of the beliefs, values, and dispositional states themselves—and, more narrowly, of the attitude taken to these by the person whose beliefs, values, and dispositional states they are.

Procedural independence is no guarantee of authenticity so understood. Procedural independence does not guarantee that a person approves of or embraces the beliefs, values, and dispositional states that emerge from the evaluative process. The point of procedural independence is not to secure for the individual satisfaction with her beliefs, values, and dispositional states. The point of procedural independence is simply to assure us that the psychological economy of the individual is "her own"—"authentic" in a sense different from one that of having a positive attitude of endorsement (or absence of a negative attitude)—only because the contents of her psychology have a particular etiology.

I press this point simply because it is false that a person must have a positive attitude toward her beliefs, values, desires, and the like—call it identification, or satisfaction, or lack of estrangement—in order to be self-governing. Whether it is necessary that a person actually approve of the formation of her goals, values, desires, and so forth if she is to be autonomous remains an open question. I claimed in the preceding chapter that the experience of disaffectedness from or inauthenticity *vis à vis* certain aspects of one's motivational and valuational psychology does not yield diminished autonomy. The key for autonomy is not whether a person feels alienated from those characteristics of her psychology that affect her choices and actions but whether the person refuses to acknowledge the centrality of these characteristics in her psychological economy. That would indicate self-deception, and the effect would be an impediment to self-governance.

The description of procedural independence calls for clarification on a third, minor point, a point where I take issue with Dworkin. I would not accompany Dworkin in demanding that any factors that influence a person's reflective and critical faculties "must promote and improve these faculties rather than subvert them" if procedural independence is to be satisfied. I suspect people live quite robustly autonomous lives despite having been influenced in ways that blunt, though not to the point of subverting, their reflective and critical powers. Given the fact that we have little say over how our faculties are molded, this component of autonomy can be—indeed, typically is—heteronomously shaped.

A fourth, final clarification is in order. Procedural independence allegedly guarantees the integrity of a person's critical faculties while preserving neutrality with respect to the variety and content of social and psychological circumstances that are conducive to such integrity. Those who embrace diversity as a value are eager to allow for variety in the choices an autonomous person might make, and they hesitate to delimit a set of social roles as ones that are intuitively consonant with self-governance. Hence, defenders of neutrality tout neutrality as a virtue. I do not see neutrality in quite so glowing and benign a light, nor do I think an account of procedural independence can be neutral. In general, the requirement of procedural independence incorporates certain rather open-ended standards of historical and social-relational legitimacy into the criteria for personal autonomy. These standards characterize substantively the manner in which the autonomous individual relates to others in the world. If procedural independence is to be a meaningful criterion of autonomy, we have to modify procedural/psychological authenticity accounts so as to incorporate certain content-laden stipulations about the nature, origin, and plausibility of a person's motivational and valuational states. These concerns are especially pressing when questions about the practical role of autonomy and the value of autonomy are raised.

Self-Respect

Respect is a form of valuing. It finds expression in the attitudes one takes to oneself and others, in the treatment one accords oneself and others, and in the expectation of a certain level of regard which one believes oneself and others to be entitled. To respect a person is to look upon that person as possessed of intrinsic value; it relies on recognition of a particular kind and of a particular caliber from others—a recognition of something remarkable about humans, namely the fact of their inherent dignity or worth. To recognize this worth is to refrain from treating oneself and others (or permitting oneself or others to be treated) as of derivative value or as of subjective value only, entitled to consideration merely to the extent someone views us as worthy of note, or of use.

So understood, to respect a person is (at least) to refrain from treating a person in a manner that makes light of her autonomy. It is to refrain from damaging the person's autonomy and the extended conditions that sustain self-governance. One who fails to respect herself or who lacks the respect of others regards herself or is regarded by others as less worthy of being accorded the sort of treatment to which persons are entitled. The concepts of respect and self-respect share a distinctive and indissoluble connection with the concept of personal autonomy in the moral theory of Kant, who famously insists that persons are to be respected (and are to show themselves respect) solely in virtue of their status as autonomous, rational beings.[5]

Certainly, how a person regards herself colors the choices she makes, the activities she pursues, and the desires she has.[6] One mark of deficient self-regard is seeing greater value in others who are no different from oneself as far as their

---

5   In pressing the importance of self-respect for autonomy we do not have to follow Kant who regards servility as a violation of the requirement of moral law, any more than we need to follow the utilitarian who might regard servility as a state of character that detracts from the social good. We must, however, accept as primitive an undefended assumption that persons are entitled to a basic level of equality and dignity. Some may take this to be a controversial supposition.

6   For an examination of the relationship between autonomy and self-worth, see Paul Benson, "Free Agency and Self-Worth," *Journal of Philosophy*, vol. XCI, no. 12, (December 1994): 650–68. Robin Dillon notes that this raises the question whether there are "objective conditions—for example, moral standards or correct judgments—that a person must meet in order to have self-respect, or is self-respect a subjective phenomenon" such that a person has self-respect provided that she believes she is not being treated in ways or behaving in ways that denigrate her and is not tolerating such treatment, the accuracy of her judgments about

humanity is concerned, or seeing oneself as different (as less human, less deserving of concern) where this judgment is mistaken. When a person's feelings of inadequacy cause her chronically to make "choices which call for submission to humiliation or maltreatment,"[7] autonomy is impossible. Similarly, self-respect is needed to inspire others to reciprocate with a similar attitude of respect toward oneself. The person who, for example, constantly reneges on, or is inconsistent about, the personal values he establishes for himself exhibits no respect *qua* commitment to these and so cannot expect that others will take his expression of these values seriously. Although a disinclination to uphold a set of professed values is not inconsistent with autonomy, a commitment to these is a mark of someone who has forged for himself a distinct identity and who takes this identity seriously enough to expect that others will acknowledge it. The individual who is indifferent to his values might be regarded by others as less than committed to self-government (or to the idea of himself as a self-governing party) for this reason.

This does not imply that anyone who regards someone or something else (a deity, perhaps) as of superior value to himself in some way and as deserving service due to this superiority fails to respect himself and suffers diminished autonomy as a result. Nor does every abdication of autonomy signal a diminished level of self-respect or a decrease in respect from others. The self-respecting evangelical Christian, for example, gives her faith up to Jesus Christ and puts herself in his hands and finds in this transference enhanced self-worth. In doing so she surrenders to a foreign (in the sense of external and supernatural) element over which she lacks control. The element is foreign to her even if she does not regard it as such; after all, Jesus is not literally identical with who she is. Her attitude towards Jesus Christ informs her beliefs about the place she and others ought to occupy in the community. But the surrender of the evangelical Christian need not cause her to view herself as less entitled to moral standing than that which is owed to others—in fact, it may have just the opposite effect. Nor need it prompt her to abdicate autonomy in a far-reaching, general way. And certainly the phenomenon to which the evangelical Christian devotes herself need not insist upon servility. As Hill reminds us, servility is distinct from a willingness to sublimate one's personal desires for the sake of another. Servility involves a failure to regard one's own interests and needs as important and deserving of being met.

In many cases, however, even if giving oneself up to another person or to a creed is not marked by a profession of lesser worth or experienced as a denigration of one's intrinsic worth, nonetheless it is to behave in a way that may belie self-respect. For to give oneself up to another or to surrender oneself to a foreign element over which one lacks control is to make oneself less visible at some level. Even if persons such as Taliban Woman and Harriet lead satisfying lives, they behave in ways that suggest a failure to appreciate themselves as warranting a certain caliber

---

herself aside. Robin S. Dillon, "Respect," *The Stanford Encyclopedia of Philosophy (Fall 2003 Edition)*, Edward N. Zalta (ed.), 2003.

7   Thomas Hill, Jr., *Autonomy and Self-Respect* (Cambridge, 1991), p. 6.

of recognition and as having a native standing in virtue of which certain treatment is beneath their dignity. Perhaps they have no desire to be regarded differently or perhaps they simply do not believe that the treatment to which they are subject renders them less visible, or that it is degrading, disrespectful, and inappropriate. The result in any case is they have no inclination to protect incursions to their lives and no disposition to resist their relative invisibility. Persons such as Harriet and the Taliban Woman may legitimately request that we accord them a certain level of respect. This request might be founded upon entitlement to a status more primitive than autonomy. Children have this status, for instance; non-human animals (or some class of these, such as primates or domesticated species) may enjoy this status as well. But as a "claim" this request has no teeth. It is up to the rest of us to decide how to treat such beings.

Control

Some philosophers suggest that a weak form of control suffices for autonomy—or, more properly, for moral responsibility—charging that a person can remain in "guidance control" of his choices, actions, and will even when subject to conditions that could undermine self-governance.[8] For example, the person who, for reasons of psychosis, duress, subordinate rank, and so on could not do otherwise than perform a particular act (attempt to fly without any apparatus from roof tops, surrender his vehicle to an armed carjacker, execute a military order) might nevertheless be deemed in control of his actions and responsible for them if he would have performed the act of his own free will anyway, independently of the external operative condition. The idea is that guidance control is possible even in the face of factors that are sufficient to determine one's actions.

While guidance control might suffice for responsibility or for local autonomy, personal autonomy requires control of a more vigorous variety. To claim global autonomy is to claim that a person has the power to determine how she shall live. This power can be compromised where coercive impediments to self-government are merely likely, or where it is possible although unlikely they will be put into effect. For this reason, autonomy necessitates a fairly robust variety of control of a sort that must be effective within a person's social situation against the presence of counterfactual impediments. We cannot sensibly claim a person is autonomous if she is party to social relations or institutions that would enfeeble her ability to determine how she will live if it were the will of others that they do so. We cannot claim that a person is self-governing if her efforts to determine how she will live would have

---

8   "Guidance control" is a term of art coined by John Martin Fischer, and I am being liberal in my appropriation of it. Strictly speaking, guidance control refers to the properties of mechanisms for action, such as normal practical deliberation, and is determined by a counterfactual sensitivity of the mechanism from which a person's actions originate to reasons for action. For an extensive discussion of guidance control, see John Martin Fischer and Mark Ravizza, *Responsibility and Control: A Theory of Moral Responsibility*.

been thwarted had she tried to act differently with respect to activities relevant to the direction of her life.

But this is precisely what is true of the case of the slave, the subservient housewife, the Taliban Woman, and it is what accounts for the diminished autonomy of the monk, and the military recruit. Each might enjoy a modicum of free reign, but because each fails to have counterfactual power over the management of their choices, actions, and goals, someone else is in the saddle. And in each instance, this lack of power or control—the terms are interchangeable in this context—is owing to the social situation. This suggests that a person who is autonomous must enjoy a social status that safeguards her right to manage key aspects of her life against other persons or institutions that might attempt to wield coercive control over her. The autonomous person must be empowered to challenge others who might attempt to direct her against her wishes, or who might aim to dominate her, even if she never has cause to do this. Moreover, autonomy fluctuates according to the number and the nature of uncontrollable intrusions in the life of the agent—intrusions whose operation the agent cannot control even counterfactually. The metaphysical demands that accompany the requirement of control will be explored in Chapter 7. To anticipate the discussion of Chapter 7, let us note that the condition of control highlights the aspect of autonomy that is concerned with alternatives possibilities.

Access to a Range of Relevant Options

Procedural authenticity theorists believe that restrictions upon a person's options compromise autonomy when the person regards them as having done so. Their view is that narrowed options circumscribe autonomy only to the degree they are felt to do so by the individual; having the option to modify one's situation is relevant for autonomy only when a person is alienated from the situation.[9] Perhaps all that is necessary for autonomy, then, is that a person is happy with the range of options in his life.

As a proponent of a social-relational account of autonomy, I maintain that the self-governing individual must have access to an adequate assortment of options, yet I deny that the adequacy of options can only be decided by the individual whose options they are.[10] I also deny that the availability of options only is important for autonomy to the degree the individual regards options as important. Of course, people will regard very differently the range of choices they confront, and given their

---

9   Christman explicitly holds this view. See his "Liberty, Autonomy, and Self-Transformation," *Social Theory and Practice* 27/2 (April, 2001): 185–206, and his "Procedural Autonomy and Liberal Legitimacy," p. 284.

10   Joseph Raz formulates the condition of access to a range of options but in stronger terms than I think are necessary. He states that, in order to be autonomous and live autonomously, a person must face a range of options that "enable him to sustain throughout his life activities which, taken together, exercise all the capacities human beings have an innate drive to exercise, as well as [have the option] to decline to develop any of them." Raz, *The Morality of Freedom* (Oxford, 1986), pp. 373–78.

very different values and commitments will experience these choices as autonomy constraining, or as meaningful and liberating, or neutrally. This is hardly surprising. In light of the variety of lives we lead, the choices presented to us can make all the difference or none to our autonomy. For example, if I am a farmer, dependent on the land for my sustenance, it will matter for my self-governance whether or not the option to produce a certain crop and to distribute it at the local market is available to me. If I am a college professor, this option is meaningless for my autonomy. If I am a Taliban Woman it will make less difference to me—it will be of less value to me—whether my environment is one of rich opportunity of choice.

The argument of the social-relational theorist is that autonomy will depend on an improvement or decline in the assortment, quantity, and arrangement of options we confront. Deliberate acceptance of a particular state of affairs as one that offers an adequate range of choice does not prove autonomy any more than repudiation or disavowal of the same state of affairs establishes a lack of autonomy. It is not enough for autonomy that a person acknowledges the social state of affairs in which she finds herself as one she would consent to even if she were lacking any other options, for the fact that a person finds her social situation acceptable does not mean that hers is an acceptable situation.

Some options essential for self-governance are clearly adapted to the needs and interests of a select group. Other options are more generally imperative for the ability of anyone, farmer or professor or religious devotee, to live a self-directed life. Because self-governance is governance over matters of central importance to human life, the options available must be relevant to the development of a person's life and they must be ones a person can genuinely hope to achieve. At a minimum, a person must have among her options the opportunity to develop her capabilities (to hone her autonomy skills, if you like) and she must be involved in doing so. This is not characteristic of the contented slave, Harriet, the Taliban Woman, or (in some instances) of a military recruit or of a monk.

There is some fact about the extent to which a person can suffer restricted options and still maintain her autonomy. An assortment of options is not adequate if a person can only choose nonautonomy: The option to choose nonsubservience must be available. Nor is an assortment adequate if the agent's choices are all dictated by duress (be it physical, emotional, economic) or by bodily needs. A person is not autonomous if driven by luck to the only option that happens to be open, even if it is an option the person likes. Because humans are not brute creatures, but are individuals whose autonomy depends on the ability to engage the body and the mind variously and creatively, keeping options open in general better comports with autonomy than does a willingness to commit oneself to a life of circumscribed options. Restricted options can change the explanation of the agent's choice from one that highlights autonomy to one that marks its absence, as Hurka notes:

> Imagine that one person chooses life *a* from among ten life options, while another person has only life *a* available. It may be true of each that she has made *a* the case and is in that sense responsible for it. But there is an important difference between them. The first

or autonomous person has also made nine alternatives to *a* not the case: If her options included *b*, *c*, and *d*, she is responsible for not-*b*, not-*c*, and not-*d*. The second person did not have this further effect. Her realization of *b*, *c*, and *d* is due, not to her, but to nature or whatever person limited her options. This difference is important because [it] involves expressing intentions in the world and determining what it does and does not contain. The autonomous agent, by virtue of her autonomy, more fully realizes this ideal. When she makes choices, she has two effects: realizing some options and blocking others. She has a more extensive causal efficacy than someone who lacks options, and a higher score on the practical dimension of number. By letting her determine what she does not do as well as what she does, her autonomy makes her more widely active and more practically efficacious ... Individually discriminated options increase agency.[11]

Social-Relational Properties (Substantive Independence)

Unless these options are had by one who is socially autonomous, they will be moot. In order to be autonomous, a person who is in a society must find herself within a set of relations with others such that all of the following are true:

a. The social background, where this includes social institutions, is such that the person can determine how she shall live in a context of at least minimal social and psychological security. The minimum level of security necessary for autonomy is whatever it takes for an individual to shield herself against (or be shielded against) and to challenge the arbitrary attempts of others to deprive her of the *de facto* and *de jure* power and authority characteristic of global autonomy, where and when such attempts arise, without undue cost. These will vary given the circumstances. The minimum of security might be quite great depending on the probability of interference a person faces. A person who resides in a high-crime area or someone who has lived a very sheltered life may need greater than average assistance in achieving the social and psychological security to pursue her goals.[12]

At a minimum, borrowing from the account of "republican freedom" or "social freedom as non-domination" developed by Philip Pettit, we might characterize autonomy as a social standing people possess "when they live in the presence of other people and when, by virtue of social design, none of those other dominates them."[13] As is true of the social freedom Pettit extols, autonomy calls for security

---

11 Thomas Hurka, *Perfectionism* (New York, 1993), p. 150.

12 Mandating the absence of probable interference for autonomy draws on a republican or neo-Roman tradition that makes a person's freedom depend on security against interference. It is not clear, as Pettit reminds us, why the requirement of protection against possible interference should count against a theory of freedom (or, I would add, of autonomy). See Philip Pettit, "Freedom and Probability," presented at the 4th Conference on Moral Theory and Practice, Granada, Spain, June 2005, p. 16.

13 Pettit, *Republicanism: A Theory of Freedom and Government* (Oxford, 1997), p. 67; also see p. 122. The account of social-relational autonomy defended in this book was developed independently of the theory of "full social freedom as non-domination" Pettit defends in political philosophy. It is nonetheless gratifying to discover that many of his ideas support my own views about personal autonomy. But as a cautionary note, the fact that I

from interference of a sort that is forthcoming only when others with whom a person dwells and works and interacts are dispossessed of arbitrary power over the person.

b. The individual can have, and can pursue, values, interests, and goals different from those who have influence and authority over her, without risk of reprisal sufficient to deter her in this pursuit.

c. The individual is not required to take responsibility for another's needs, expectations, and failings unless doing so is reasonably expected of the individual in light of a particular function. It is reasonable, for example, to expect that a parent is responsible for fulfilling the basic needs of his children; it is reasonable to expect an attorney to serve the needs of her client. An expectation is not reasonable if it issues from the whims of other persons or if it requires a person to live "in uncertainty under the shadow of another's presence."[14] An expectation is reasonable, in addition, if it is one the person has a fair opportunity of meeting, and if it does not deprive the person of the ability to care for herself.

d. The individual enjoys a level of financial self-sufficiency adequate to provide the material capital to be independent of others. Diana Meyers correctly notes that "People seek economic self-sufficiency to rule out the possibility that others might gain control over them through their needs. If one can take care of oneself, one is beholden to no one—neither to the state nor to any other individual."[15] Economic autonomy is a requirement of personal autonomy.

e. The individual is not subject to misinformation about what she is able to do. Deceit or deprivation of information truncates a person's opportunity to control her life. We will return to concerns about autonomy and informational management in Chapters 5 and 6.

Together, a–e describe the social-relational features of the seventh condition for autonomy, that of *substantive independence*. To repeat, the seven conditions for autonomy are *epistemic competence, rationality, procedural independence, self-respect, control, access to a range of relevant options*, and *substantive independence*. These conditions will inevitably appear somewhat underdescribed. But I do not see how this can be otherwise. Underdescription is the risk every attempt at conceptual analysis confronts, and the risk is amplified where the concept at issue is one that draws from such a range of social and cultural relationships. Such is the case with the concept of autonomy.

What the conditions do yield is a naturalized model of autonomy that exemplifies the pretheoretic intuitive ideal. Autonomous persons have *de facto* power and

---

employ aspects of Pettit's analysis of social freedom in explaining social-relational autonomy does not mean Pettit would do so or that he would approve of this appropriation. In fact, he offers an account of "autonomy as orthonomy" that is very different from the analysis I propose here.

14 Pettit, *Republicanism: A Theory of Freedom and Government*, p. 5.

15 Meyers, *Self, Society, and Personal Choice*, p. 12. Meyers characterizes economic autonomy as a phenomenon distinct from personal autonomy, charging that while the focus of the former is the conditions that constrain the liberty of people, the concern of the latter is positive, amounting to a statement of how people should live if they are autonomous.

authority over the management of their lives within a framework of standards they establish for themselves and their autonomy is partly constituted by exogenous phenomena—that is, by relations extrinsic to their psychology. And, because it is essential that persons who are autonomous are party to ongoing social relations that enable them to direct their lives with a minimum of interference, autonomy means having counterfactual power or influence across a range of neighboring possible worlds wherein others are able to intervene capriciously in a person's affairs.

Interferences threaten autonomy when they relegate persons to a position whereby, in order to live in a self-managed, self-directed fashion, persons must resist the interference, or at least resist the temptation to regard the interference as normal and legitimate, even as they adapt to its presence. As evidence let us look to one well documented, much studied phenomenon. Consider the series of adaptations and constant vigilance to one's public behavior in the face of potential interferences required of black Americans during the years of Jim Crow. A more recent example of similar adaptation and vigilance is found in response to the phenomenon of racial profiling known as "Driving While Black."[16] Statistically, African-American men (and darker complexioned men, more generally) are subject to arbitrary stop-and-searches by law enforcement officials to a disproportionate extent, frequently while commuting to and from work.[17] The men might be informed that officials have been directed to keep an eye out for suspicious looking persons (persons who look as if they do not "belong" in the area), or they might be told they fit the description of suspects wanted in a series of felonious assaults. The drivers might be advised to keep clear of the area for the time being. Some might argue that isolated incidents of this sort will not affect global autonomy; perhaps even repeated and expected incidents need not undermine a person's autonomy. After all, persons might come to accept such interrogations as a fact of life, or they might come to regard stop-and-searches as no more than minor irritants. They might devise ways of minimizing the likelihood of stop-and-search incidents, such as seeking alternate routes to and from work so as to make themselves less visible. They might be driven to use guile or, worse, ingratiation to achieve their ends. In short, they might employ strategies of prudential rationality to accommodate this phenomenon.

But the impact of arbitrary stop-and-searches upon autonomy is plain if we compare the African-American driver with his white male counterpart. Assume both men choose the same routes to and from work based on considerations of expedience and safety. Both drive the same model and make of vehicle. Both are similarly attired. But the social standing of each man is quite different. Few law enforcement officials are disposed to interfere with the white man's choice of route, perhaps because he

---

16 Other up-to-the-minute examples might be "Flying While Muslim" or "Serving in the Armed Forces While Gay."

17 *New York Times Magazine*, Sunday, July 16, 2000: 83. Also see the online archives of the American Civil Liberties Union at http://archive.aclu.org/congress/dwbstories.html and *Counter Punch*, Alexander Cockburn and Jeffrey St. Clair (eds), "Driving While Black," http://www.counterpunch.org/drivingblack.html.

is seen as having a right to be driving in the area. But law enforcement officials are more disposed to interfere with the choice of the black man. Here is what Pettit says about the comparative social freedom of each. Let X represent the white man, Y the black man, and A the choice of the commuter's route:

> Now imagine that X and Y each succeed in enacting that choice: X succeeds unsurprisingly, of course, while Y succeeds because of managing to avoid detection or interference, whether through duplicity or cunning or sheer good luck; Y may succeed, not just in doing A, but in enjoying a high accidental probability of non-interference. Should we say in such a case that X and Y were equally free to do A: that they enjoyed and exercised the same social freedom in respect of that choice? Surely not ... There is nothing paradoxical about saying that although successful in doing A, and although having a high accidental probability of succeeding in doing A, Y did not have the social freedom to do A. As a standing feature of an agent, the social freedom to do A is akin to a disposition or capacity. And just as you may occasionally manage to do something that you are not generally disposed to do, or for which you do not have a standing capacity, so you may manage to perform a given action without exercising or displaying the social freedom to act that way.[18]

People adapt, often in ingenious way, in the face of incidents that question their global autonomy. But the fact that the victim of racial profiling is shrewd and knows how to make the best of a bad situation will not resolve his autonomy in the situation. The "sour grapes" phenomenon—adjusting one's attitudes or preferences so as to eliminate psychological dissonance and increase psychological freedom—cannot alter a person's social environment or social status, transforming a situation of constraint into one of independence.[19] While such interferences do not approach the magnitude of deprivation of which he speaks, Amartya Sen makes a point that illustrates the inadequacy of trying to salvage autonomy by this means:

> A thoroughly deprived person, leading a very reduced life, might not appear to be badly off ... if the hardship is accepted with non-grumbling resignation. In situations of long-standing deprivation, the victims do not go on grieving and lamenting all the time,

18 Philip Pettit, "Freedom and Probability," p. 9.
19 On the sour grapes phenomenon see Jon Elster, "Sour Grapes—Utilitarianism and the Genesis of Wants" in A. Sen and B. Williams (eds), *Utilitarianism and Beyond* (Cambridge, 1982). Pettit notes the irony of making it possible to become socially free simply by adopting postures and attitudes grossly antithetical to autonomy: "You could make yourself free just by adjusting you attitude and address towards the powerful. You can self-censor any displays or choices that might put them offside and you can ingratiate yourself with them by resort to charm and cunning, fawning and flattery, even perhaps toadying and kowtowing ... [But] adjusting so as to keep the powerful sweet involves an embrace of servility and self-humiliation that is directly at odds with the idea that social freedom gives you a degree of immunity against the interference of others. Having the ability to be suitably servile and to avoid interference even in the event of others turning sour is not equivalent to being socially positioned so that even if they turn sour they are unlikely to be able to interfere." Pettit, "Freedom and Probability," p. 15.

and very often take great pleasure in small mercies and cut down personal desires to modest—realistic—proportions. Indeed, in situations of adversity which the victims cannot individually change, *prudential reasoning* would suggest that the victims should concentrate their desire on those limited things that they *can* possibly achieve, rather than fruitlessly pining for what is unattainable. The extent of a person's deprivation, then, may not at all show up in the metric of desire fulfillment.[20]

What is at issue in the case of racial profiling and similar states of affair is not simply the frequency or the predictability of interferences, nor that a person's self-determination is abridged in what some regard as relatively minor ways, nor that only certain persons suffer such abridgements to a disproportionate extent. Rather, the issue is that these persons are socially positioned such that they *must* adapt to being a person subject to profiling, by resistance, or by cunning, or ingratiation. How the African-American driver gets to work—what he does with respect to an activity central to his livelihood—is decided by facts about others who have preemptive and unwarranted power over him. He cannot govern himself. No matter how successful a person might be at liberating himself from the psychological and practical encumbrances of practices like racial profiling, and despite the fact that being black is not in itself antithetical to autonomy, racial profiling narrows the range of one's autonomy: "To be a black driver in America is to invite police scrutiny."[21] Indeed, as Kwame Anthony Appiah charges, in the context of a racist society "it will not even be enough to require being treated with equal dignity despite being Black for that will require a concession that being Black counts naturally or to some degree against one's dignity. And so one will end up asking to be respected *as a Black*."[22]

In cases such as this, where one person or one class of persons "looks with a degree of apprehension on a master who holds power … over them,"[23] persons can only minimize interference in their lives by surrendering to inegalitarian circumstances. By accepting the denial of their right of global or comprehensive autonomy and their capacity for comprehensive autonomy, these persons deny autonomy of themselves. The social climate, in sum, not only affects the ease or the difficulty one confronts in exercising one's right of autonomy, but is the source of reduced autonomy as well.

Natural Impediments to Autonomy

That personal autonomy is built upon social protections of a fairly robust sort is unsurprising. Neither is it surprising that many of the conditions for autonomy are interpersonal. But it might come as a surprise that the conditions for autonomy include the absence of impediments other than those of an interpersonal variety. In

---

20 Amartya Sen, *Inequality Reexamined* (Oxford, 1992), p. 55.

21 Cockburn and St. Clair, "Driving While Black."

22 Appiah, "Identity, Authenticity, Survival: Multicultural Societies and Social Reproduction," in Amy Gutmann (ed.), *Multiculturalism* (Princeton, 1994), p. 16.

23 Pettit, *Republicanism: A Theory of Freedom and Government*, p. 132.

part, autonomy is measured by the extent of independence granted a person by her natural circumstances (her physical abilities and limitations, for example) and by the natural world.

If autonomy is a social-relational phenomenon, why should natural phenomena obstruct it? Pettit argues that natural phenomena cannot obstruct social freedom although natural phenomena may be among obstacles to "outright" or "overall" freedom of choice. A person is free outright or in an unconditioned way, he claims, only in the indistinctive sense in which all persons are free—that is, in the sense in which persons are protected from obstacles of any variety that might hamper the way in which their choices are made, the range of choice that is available, and their successful execution of the choice. Pettit notes that if we are interested in a person's freedom of choice, it makes sense to focus on the plethora of obstacles a person confronts in availing herself of options—obstacles of a natural as well as social sort—rather than restrict our interest to the freedom a person confronts within a particular sphere of activity *vis à vis* the agency of others.

But, Pettit continues,

> If our interest is in social freedom, then ... forms of interpersonal interference will be the primary object of attention. Other hindrances will be seen as factors that do not reduce social freedom in itself but only the range over which, or the ease with which, it can be enjoyed: they will be taken to affect the worth of social freedom, not its presence or absence; they condition freedom as distinct from compromising it ... [T]here is every reason for focusing on social obstacles, if our interest is in how far a person has a standing amongst others that gives them a presumptive immunity, partial or total, to such obstacles.[24]

In the context of this discussion, Pettit notes, rightly I think, that there is a distinction to be drawn between freedom of choice and freedom of choosers. The distinction marks a salient difference between the social-relational approach to autonomy and rival procedural authenticity accounts. Procedural authenticity accounts make freedom of choice tantamount to autonomy, and this choice-based approach has come to dominate debate about autonomy.[25] But as Pettit notes, adopting a choice-based view would yield a counterintuitive result for social freedom:

> On a choice-based view, the social freedom of a person would depend only on how far their choices happened—perhaps as a matter of sheer luck—to be socially unobstructed; choices would be free so long as they escaped interference and choosers would be free as far as their choices were free.[26]

---

24 Pettit, "Freedom and Probability," pp. 2–3.

25 Pettit contends that while the history of political theory (notably the republican tradition he embraces) has emphasized social freedom, "the choice-based way of thinking about social freedom has come to predominate [liberal] political philosophy." Pettit, "Freedom and Probability," p. 4. Perhaps this is one reason why a choice-based way of thinking about autonomy has come to dominate the debate.

26 Pettit, "Freedom and Probability," p. 3.

I would claim a similar counterintuitive result is generated by a choice-based account of autonomy. It is counterintuitive to think the power, authority, and control emblematic of self-determination are forthcoming when phenomena that preempt choice are serendipitously forestalled, or forestalled at the behest of someone other than the agent whose self-governance is at stake. So I would agree that the concern of autonomy is the chooser as opposed to the choice. If the concern of autonomy is primarily a concern for how far choices are unobstructed—for how procedurally authentic they are—it would appear we will have little cause to concentrate our attention on social obstacles, as these are just one among a number of factors that might impede choice. But since the concern of autonomy is *not* primarily a concern for how far choices are unobstructed, we appear to have considerable cause to concentrate our attention on social obstacles. After all, the concept of global autonomy is concerned with a key status a person has amongst other persons. The autonomous person has a status that protects her against obstruction of a kind that is uniquely directed at choosers, namely, obstruction that emanates from interpersonal contact.

However, social-relational autonomy differs from social freedom as Pettit characterizes the latter in at least one notable respect. Pettit contends that freedom in the agent contrasts "with freedom in the environment of the agent" when what is at stake is not the curtailment of activity by the presence of other agents but "how many and how significant are the options made available by the impersonal parameters within which the agent exercises his or her freedom: say, the parameter dictated by a harsh natural order or a constraining social system."[27] But where the autonomy of persons is at issue, a similar distinction cannot be so neatly drawn. The number and significance of options made available in the environment of the person are salient concerns for autonomy, and if a person is to be autonomous and not just socially free, myriad impediments within the environment of the agent must be contained. These include impersonal natural impediments and circumstantial impediments as well as interpersonal impediments.

Certain natural phenomena—physical ability, for example—do not simply condition the exercise of global autonomy; by increasing or by diminishing "the range over which, or the ease with which, it can be enjoyed," these phenomena yield global or dispositional autonomy of a more resilient or more enfeebled form. As with interpersonal relations, these natural phenomena are constitutive of autonomy at the same time they serve to elevate or diminish the quality of autonomy a person enjoys. Because autonomy is a matter of degree, these conditions constitute a threshold for autonomy, and their absence means the demise of that threshold. The extent and variety of impersonal environmental freedom needed for global autonomy will vary depending on what a person will need in order to be able to control her life by means of her own authority. I will say more on this last point when we return to address the interface of autonomy and freedom in Chapter 7.

---

27 Philip Pettit, *A Theory of Freedom: from the Psychology to the Politics of Agency* (New York, 2001), p. 4.

In sum, freedom of choice is relevant for autonomy and freedom from impediments to choice are important for autonomy, but an account of personal autonomy must be an account of autonomous choosers rather than an account of autonomous choice. While the conditions for global autonomy emphasize social freedom and the interpersonal aspect of life, impersonal natural and environmental forces must be counted among the possible hindrances to self-government. Pettit's account of social freedom brings us close to the concerns of personal autonomy, especially in the political realm that is his focus of interest. But social freedom does not deliver autonomy in its entirety. The idea of social freedom captures some, but not all, of the ingredients of autonomy.[28]

Apples and Oranges

The task of the next chapter will be to turn a critical eye to some of the challenges the social-relational account confronts. Before turning to these matters, we should consider the possibility that further evaluation of the merits of social-relational accounts against psychological authenticity account of autonomy is uncalled for. For one might raise the "*Apples and Oranges*" objection. One might object that two separate notions of autonomy are at issue, and accuse me of having equivocated between them. While some define autonomy in terms of psychological conditions, one might say I am developing a different notion of autonomy. Perhaps one could concede that a social-relational analysis plays a useful role in certain contexts, but contend that the conception of autonomy as psychological authenticity is legitimate in its own right. It is not incoherent or improper to analyze autonomy in a Cartesian fashion.

In support of his complaint, the authenticity theorist may deny he shares my belief that the pretheoretic idea of autonomy really is commonplace or that it really does capture ordinary intuitions about self-government. Believing that personal autonomy consists in the integrity of the inner citadel, he will find his own criteria for autonomy quite adequate: autonomy is a condition that supervenes on psychological states, and the presence or absence of social-relational conditions, if relevant at all, is useful only as a way of explaining what is required for the exercise of autonomy understood as the realization of these psychological states.

I doubt different notions of self-government operate here. It is true that the idea of autonomy declared in Chapter 1 does not concern the autonomy of one's preferences and the conditions that make that possible but rather the autonomy of persons who have certain preferences, and who pursue certain options. But this is not autonomy of a different sort than the autonomy that psychological authenticity accounts

---

28 Pettit would agree. Treating self-mastery as a species of personal autonomy, he notes that "freedom as personal autonomy … is a richer ideal than that of freedom as non-domination; there can certainly be non-domination without personal self-mastery, but there can hardly be any meaningful form of self-mastery without non-domination." *Republicanism*, pp. 81–2.

analyze. The advocate of autonomy as psychological authenticity is not attempting to explain something other than the autonomy of persons, such as psychological freedom *simpliciter*. In all instances the object of concern is the status of persons. What is distinctive about the advocate of autonomy as psychological authenticity is his attempt to explain the autonomy of persons in terms of autonomy with respect to psychological states such as freedom of choice. (Even Harry Frankfurt describes the freedom responsibility calls for as "autonomy," and analyzes the conditions for moral responsibility as conditions of the autonomy of persons. So I am confident he would accept the claims about what personal autonomy is and about the work autonomy is intended to do.) The problem is that defenders of autonomy as psychological authenticity maintain that the autonomy of persons is a function of the state of a person's psychology, and they ask for no further explanation.

Summary

Let me summarize some of the ideas developed in this chapter. To be autonomous is to stand in a certain position of authority over one's life with respect to others. Persons cannot be autonomous unless the satisfaction of certain social conditions is guaranteed, and this guarantee demands that the conditions are protected for a variety of counterfactual scenarios. Thus, if a person is to be autonomous, the circumstances to which he freely and authentically assents must grant him the latitude to choose and to live in a fashion that does not hinge on the consent of others. A self-governing person must be able to evaluate his reasons for action in a psychologically and socially unfettered way. Moreover, the choices he makes and the goals he sets as relevant to the direction of his life must emanate from a variety of acceptable alternatives, and the individual must be able to pursue these choices without undue social or psychological cost.

The discussion may suggest that a lexical priority to the enumerated conditions is warranted. Is it more important for autonomy that the person "take ownership" of his choices as epistemic competence provides, or that he be positioned to do practically so? I am not inclined to defend any ranking since in my estimation the conditions stand together and fall together.

Although only the seventh condition of personal autonomy is explicitly labeled "social-relational," all seven conditions contribute to a conception of self-government that is distinct from an account of self-government premised on psychological and procedural phenomena. The fourth, fifth, and sixth conditions (of self-respect, control, and access to options, respectively) represent departures from the depiction of self-government as psychological authenticity. And while the criteria distinctive of psychological authenticity accounts, critical reflection and procedural independence, are retained their content as well as their successful function is measured in socially richer terms of epistemic competence and substantive rationality.

Satisfaction of the conditions for personal autonomy does not guarantee that a person will be autonomous with respect to every element of his life. I might meet these conditions and so be an autonomous agent, but at the moment be too distraught by some crisis to function in a self-directed way. The role of these conditions is not to account for the means to securing control over one's immediate situation but to illustrate what is absent in the lives of individuals like the slave, the subservient housewife, the Taliban Woman, and to a lesser degree the monk and the military recruit, and what is present in the life of the would-be surrendered woman.

Now let us turn to some of the criticisms levied against the social-relational account of autonomy.

Chapter 5

Objections from Liberalism

Introduction

This chapter will address two objections to the social-relational account of autonomy. The first objection is that the social account is unduly perfectionist. By imposing certain substantive and value-laden constraints upon autonomy, the social account will fail to accommodate the multiplicity of lifestyles central to a liberal society. A second objection follows on the heels of the first. This is that the social-relational account of autonomy incorporates an ideal of what a self-determined life looks like. The result is a diminished account of autonomy, weakened in particular with respect to its traditional role of defining the limits within which a person is protected from paternalistic incursions. These objections are, of course, related and I will address them as such.

The Social Account is Perfectionist

The social account makes autonomy possible only within a rather limited range of circumstances. For example, persons whose freely formed desires lead them to embark upon lives of servitude cannot be autonomous. Is the social account too restrictive to be of great use as a result? Does its exclusivity speak to a need to redesign the view with a more generous boundary? What is wanted, after all, is not simply a theoretical analysis of an ideal of personhood to which individuals might aspire and against which the cultural institutions that shape them are judged. What is wanted is an analysis of a concept of practical value and currency. What is wanted is an account of autonomy that is latitudinarian, an account that can address the various lifestyles and self-conceptions embraced by competent, independent adults. Meyers claims this commits us to the view that

> [O]nly individuals can be the measure of their own autonomy. Apart from the formal good of an integrated personality, and the procedural good of autonomy competency, autonomous lives are remarkable more for their differences than for their similarities. To affirm a list of universal personal goods or an account of an objectively good personal life and to maintain that every autonomous life must realize such goods is to deny the uniqueness of individuals. It is to create a mold that autonomous lives must inevitably break.[1]

---

1   Meyers, *Self, Society, and Personal Choice*, p. 82.

As we saw in Chapter 3, this view is common among defenders of procedural authenticity accounts of autonomy. But there are flaws with this view. Even granting autonomy competency and an integrated personality, an individual's assessment of what make for permissible or impermissible limitations to self-governance will not decide the matter of her autonomy. In what follows I want to pursue the claim that while a viable analysis of autonomy must certainly affirm the distinctive lives agents can lead, it must do so within the confines of objective requirements of the sort Meyers and other proponents of content-neutral authenticity accounts claim are inconsonant with autonomy.

But let us begin with a set of specific questions which appear as possible worries for the social account I advance. Autonomy as I have characterized it concerns authority over a person's affective and cognitive states as well as authority over the social roles and relationships that define the agent and that sustain her in her various endeavors. But in order for autonomy to guarantee that will and action exist under the *de facto* authority and *de jure* entitlement of the agent, specifications pertaining to the interpersonal or social environment of the agent as well as to her natural environment must be included among the conditions of autonomy as conceptually necessary or constitutive elements rather than as mere causal or contributing factors. What does this imply for the autonomy of Berofsky's rebellious slave or that of the Jehovah's Witnesses who maintained a remarkable integrity of spirit despite internment in the concentration camps during World War II? Does the social account produce "the odd result that dispossessed social reformers and rebels such as Gandhi and Martin Luther King, Jr. are less than fully autonomous?"[2] Christman believes this is exactly the result. His concerns are summarized in the following statement:

> It is one thing to claim that social conditions that enable us to develop and maintain the powers of authentic choice and which protect the ongoing interpersonal social relationships that define ourselves are all part of the background requirements for the development of autonomy ... It is another thing, however—and a more dangerous and ultimately problematic move, I have argued—to claim that being autonomous *means* standing in proper social relations to surrounding others and within social practices and institutions. Taking this position, I have argued, turns the concept of autonomy into an unacceptably perfectionist idea that carries with it the danger of exclusion and overarching paternalism that attention to autonomy should well protect against.[3]

Christman claims that defining autonomy, as I do, in terms of social dynamics of particular sorts has (at least) two troubling implications. First, the perfectionist strain of the social account excludes from the democratic political process the voices of those who, by their own agency and in an unconstrained, reflective fashion,

---

2   James Stacey Taylor posed this question in personal correspondence.

3   Christman, "Relational Autonomy," Pacific Division Meeting of the American Philosophical Association, March 30, 2003, San Francisco. Revised as "Relational Autonomy, Liberal Individualism, and the Social Constitution of Selves," *Philosophical Studies* 117 (2004): 143–64, at p. 159.

embrace a way of life grounded on strict obedience or subservience to others, just as it excludes the voices of the marginalized and the systematically discriminated against and, presumably, just as it might deny autonomy to politically dispossessed persons such as Gandhi and King. Second, the social account of autonomy imports an ideal of self-government. As such it undermines the traditional function of the concept of autonomy to demarcate the confines within which paternalistic intrusion is impermissible.

Christman's worries reflect the suspicion that the social version of autonomy I advocate is antithetical to liberalism (in some of its guises) as a legal and political ideal. The assumption is that liberalism relies on autonomy as a basis for political participation. Liberalism is grounded on the beliefs that human beings have a moral right to be in command of their own destiny, that "individuals are self-creating, that no single good defines successful self-creation, and that taking responsibility for one's life and making of it what one can is itself part of the good life."[4] But this is just to say that liberalism is grounded in beliefs about the value of some variety of autonomy. Political liberalism, or a distinctively liberal political theory, is the view that "the content of [the] goals [of liberal society] can only be set by attending to the opinions of all the people under [the authority of the government] ... To exclude anyone's view is to devalue them; it is also to deny what liberalism relies on for its effect as a moral argument, the claim that we are born free and equal."[5]

So one objective of liberalism is that all should have a voice in the political process. Does it follow that the liberal must not describe autonomy in a way that imports value-laden or content-laden constraints, including checks on social-relational circumstances, into that condition? Proceduralists such as Christman, Friedman, and Meyers believe this does follow: The liberal cannot say, as I do, that in order to be autonomous one must be in certain sorts of relations, which I define broadly as relations that do not subordinate one party to the will of the other and that do not constrain future choice. To respect autonomy is to permit persons to fashion and pursue their own conceptions of the good, but an account such as I advance requires that a number of ways of living—those in which a person's status and circumstances are marked by constraint—will be irreconcilable with autonomy, regardless of the manner in which a person came to the circumstances and regardless of whether the person opted for the status. If the concept of autonomy is not comprehensive in the variety of lifestyles it permits, there is the risk that the voices on the fringe—especially the fringe of social and political power—shall be silenced. By contrast, a comprehensive approach to autonomy invites these voices to be heard. And, these critics continue, a comprehensive approach to autonomy must be an account limited to procedural authenticity.[6]

---

4   Alan Ryan, "Liberalism," in Robert Goodin and Philip Pettit (eds), *A Companion to Contemporary Political Philosophy* (Oxford, 1993), p. 292.

5   Ryan, "Liberalism," p. 299.

6   For instance, Friedman states that "[I]f content-neutral and substantive accounts are roughly equally convincing on conceptual and intuitive grounds, then a content-neutral

Let me answer this charge by employing one of the case studies of Chapter 3. Recall the Taliban Woman, an amalgam of subservient spouse and religious devotee. Taliban Woman has chosen a family situation in which her religious leaders, her husband, and her male relatives, in that order, make all significant decisions for her. She has embarked upon a life in which devotion to a system of belief means that she will do what the system, through the voice of other persons, bids her to do without quarrel. Despite her authentic, competent, and sober acceptance of such situations, I contend that her lack of relational autonomy means that she is not self-governing.

Now, if classical liberalism as a theory of limited government is also the liberalism that says the government may not champion a perfectionist view of the liberal individual—to wit: it is not the role of the state to set up institutions that enable the pursuit and realization of some ways of life at the expense of others— then, Christman charges, the defender of a social view of autonomy confronts an ironic result. Christman states:

> [U]se of a substantive conception of autonomy in order to exclude those participants living under (arguably) oppressive value systems B such as women under some versions of religious fundamentalism for example B implies that the *victims* of oppression have lower moral status, are less morally responsible for their choices, and (depending on one's view) less eligible for participation in democratic deliberation (if autonomy is necessary for all these) *than their oppressors*. For the latter will presumably enjoy the freedom from restrictions, abilities to resist authority, and the like which merit the label autonomy in a substantive, relational sense (depending on the details of those views).[7]

Let us focus on the question of the autonomy of oppressed persons, deferring the question of their diminished moral responsibility to Chapter 8 where the nexus of autonomy and responsibility is examined. With respect to the autonomy of oppressed persons, Christman is absolutely correct. However, the ironic result he notes is not brought about by the social theory of autonomy, nor should it be remedied by redefining autonomy, extending its boundary to include persons who obviously are *not* self-governing. The most straightforward way of characterizing the result of a version of liberalism that insists upon value-neutrality is that it says "everyone should have a voice, even those who are not autonomous!"

It is true that Taliban Woman does not enjoy autonomy (not even *de jure* autonomy), and it is true that she finds her voice barred from "deliberations about the meaning of equality and legitimate authority" despite being "competent and authentic

---

account should be preferred for the fact that it will serve better in one of the normative roles that an ideal of autonomy fills, that of motivating people to treat others with an important form of respect. An account of autonomy that is too demanding will prompt persons to regard a greater number of others as failures at personhood and thereby reduce the number of others they regard as respect worthy. Thus, an account of autonomy with fewer requirements has, independently of other considerations, the advantage of promoting a more inclusive sense of equal worth." Friedman, *Autonomy, Gender, Politics*, p. 23.

7   Christman, "Relational Autonomy, Liberal Individualism, and the Social Constitution of Selves," fn. 38, p. 163.

in ways that procedural accounts of autonomy require."[8] It is true that politically oppressed persons such as the American Negro of the 1950s and early 1960s were dispossessed owing, in large part, to a lack of substantive autonomy. But persons like these, labeled non-autonomous on the social-relational account because of the relations in which they stand, do not lose their voice *because* the social-relational account dubs them non-autonomous. The American Negro, like the Taliban Woman, loses her voice because her social-relational status precludes having a voice. This is not a problem that can be remedied by claiming persons like Taliban Woman are autonomous. We can call Taliban Woman whatever we want, but doing so will make no difference if her social situation and the institutions that support that situation continue to undermine autonomy.

Autonomy demands more of a person and of her environment than does *de jure* autonomy. It appears to be *de jure* autonomy that Christman has in mind when he claims the proceduralist account, suitably historicized, better comports with liberal neutrality. If political liberalism only requires *de jure* self-government, the liberal can count as autonomous some persons who will not satisfy the conditions of autonomy we have been discussing. The procedurally authentic variety of autonomy had by Taliban Woman might substantiate a claim to a right to a voice in the democratic process. I say this with reservation, as it is not clear how autonomy so construed would mandate claim rights of any sort. A moral right to autonomy that even a nonautonomous person claims need not sustain a political right of the sort demanded for involvement in the democratic process. But even if procedural authenticity does substantiate a claim to a right of democratic participation, it does not guarantee people like Taliban Woman a practical voice. One can retain a right to autonomy despite lacking autonomy in fact. While this right deserves respect, it is a right that is unexercised when relational autonomy is absent.

Two points can be made at this juncture. First, unless the proceduralist is willing to make certain other assumptions—such as the assumption that *de jure* autonomy calls for global autonomy—it does not follow that on the social-relational account the Taliban Woman does not enjoy "the status marker of an independent citizen whose perspective and value orientation gets a hearing in the democratic processes that constitute legitimate social policy," as Christman contends.[9] This would follow only if one result of denying global autonomy is that *de jure* autonomy, or the right to be heard, is denied.

Second, it remains an open question whether the right of autonomy will be instantiated despite the treatment forced upon Taliban Woman by her social role. If political liberalism champions value-neutrality, it naturally gravitates towards an account of autonomy that is inclusive. But would its very inclusiveness allow us to count as autonomous individuals who, having satisfied the proceduralist criteria, establish themselves in situations where their abdications of free agency

---

8   Christman, "Relational Autonomy, Liberal Individualism, and the Social Constitution of Selves," p. 157.

9   Ibid.

are irrevocable or where their free agency is practically curtailed—persons like the Taliban woman? The *de jure* autonomy to participate in the political process is of little value when, by virtue of her position, a person lacks not the will but the authority to speak for herself.

I suspect that Christman prefers to represent people such as Taliban Woman as autonomous because he subscribes to a variety of liberalism that conflates personal autonomy with political autonomy. That is to say, it is not personal autonomy that is the subject of the liberal's concern as Christman presents it, but autonomy of some other (political) variety. As we saw in Chapter 1, the central idea of political autonomy concerns a status of the individual against the state or against institutions of public and civic authority. Very generally, political autonomy in its liberal guise is the idea that the justification of political institutions must appeal to considerations recognized as valid by all adult citizens of a society. It is more accurate to claim, following the political philosopher John Tomasi, that liberalism is latitudinarian in its conception of *political* autonomy since it is the function of an account of political autonomy, rather than personal autonomy, to identify the attributes of citizens whose concerns and judgment inform the principles of justice upon which a legitimate state rests.[10]

But, as we have seen, accounts of political autonomy generally are too thin to illuminate a full account of self-determination. Personal autonomy is a marker of one of a wider range of lifestyles political liberalism accommodates, but there may be politically autonomous agents who fail to be personally autonomous in the manner I describe. A politically autonomous person might be ill suited for personal autonomy for reasons having to do with her social situation and physical environment as easily as reasons that bear upon her psychological condition. If autonomy genuinely is a social phenomenon, constituted and not simply facilitated by a distinctive interpersonal status, then certain versions of political liberalism may fail as the philosophical expression of the variety of civic body conducive to autonomous agency.

One option open to the defender of value and content-neutrality seeking an account of autonomy congenial to political liberalism would be to follow the feminist philosopher Uma Narayan, who advocates a very thin construction of autonomy. Focusing on the practices of veiling and *purdah* (seclusion) among women from the Sufi Pirzada Muslim community in Old Delhi, Narayan notes two stereotypical assessments western feminists make of the relatively non-autonomous lives of third world women.[11] One stereotype sees these women are "prisoners of patriarchy," forced against their will to accept oppressive lives. The second stereotype treats the women as "dupes of patriarchy," so dominated by the prevailing culture that

---

10 Tomasi, "Should Good Liberals be Compassionate Conservatives?" *Social Philosophy and Policy*, 21/1 (Winter 2004).

11 Narayan, "Minds of Their Own: Choices, Autonomy, Cultural Practices, and Other Women," in Louise M. Antony and Charlotte E. Witt (eds), *A Mind of One's Own: Feminist Essays on Reason and Objectivity*, 2nd ed. (Boulder, Colorado: Westview Press, 2002), pp. 418–32.

they have lost any capacity for critical, reflective, independent judgment, declaring themselves utterly committed to veiling and *purdah*.

In neither case, Narayan charges, is the experience the Pirzada women have of their own lives and of their relative autonomy accurately comprehended. The Pirzada women register complaints about the practical encumbrance of the veils and the limited social mobility *purdah* imposes at the same time as they exhibit pride in the centrality of these practices to their religious and ethnic identity. Rather than interpret their acceptance of veiling and purdah as evidence of complicity or near enslavement, Narayan charges that westerners would do well to note that these women admit the cultural pressures and constraints to which they are subject at the same time as they recognize their emotional and financial interest in compliance. Perhaps these women are better described as "bargaining with patriarchy"[12] than as dupes conned into turning a blind or taciturn eye to their relative lack of autonomy. This being the case, Narayan asserts that:

> A person's choice should be considered autonomous as long as the person was a "normal adult" with no serious cognitive or emotional impairments, and was not subject to literal or outright coercion from others. On this account, a person's choice could be autonomous even if made under considerable social or cultural pressure, and even if it were the only morally palatable option open to her.[13]

Narayan claims to "be genuinely puzzled" why choices made among morally unacceptable alternatives do not count as procedurally independent or worthy of respect when they are made by women who, recognizing the consequences they face from non-compliance, acquiesce and make the best of a less than optimal situation. She worries that the call to respect the choices of women only when these have been made autonomously relies on an overly demanding conception of autonomy, one that would preclude the choices of women such as the Pirzada, and goes so far as to warn that "If the liberal position is concerned only with protecting individual autonomy and not with protecting liberty more generally ... it would paradoxically have profoundly illiberal effects."[14] But Narayan's response to this worry is explicitly to deny the necessity of three of the most pressing and noncontroversial of conditions for autonomous choice. These are that "the level of coercion, deception, and manipulation [autonomous persons face from media and cultural pressures] must be insignificant," that individual choices must be founded in deep critical reflection rather than unreflective habits, and that "there must be significant and morally acceptable alternatives among which women can choose."[15] In doing so, Narayan's position strikes me as one a proponent of psychological authenticity accounts would not endorse.

---

12 Narayan, "Minds of Their Own," p. 422.

13 Narayan, "Minds of Their Own," p. 429.

14 Narayan, "Minds of Their Own," p. 430.

15 Narayan, "Minds of Their Own," pp. 425–26.

At the same time, Narayan is correct that "Not only is the degree of autonomy evinced by particular agents often difficult to gauge, it is often difficult to generalize about the degree of autonomy different women enjoy with respect to particular cultural practices. The degree to which different agents who engage in the 'cultural practice' regard it as life and self-defining, and the degrees of coercion and constraint that agents experience with respect to the practice, *vary widely*."[16] The case of the Taliban woman illustrates this point. At the same time, the case can be used to contest the idea that chosen social roles of any variety must be permissible if a person is to be self-directed. After all, why should autonomy be a condition compatible with any social role or with every life-plan? The fact that many of us in liberal societies are drawn to the idea that autonomy can, in theory at least, be realized through myriad ways of life, and are wary of the idea that only certain social arrangements befit self-directed agents does not settle the question. It is true that not everyone will include an autonomous life among the goals that he or she regards as integral to well-being, and to suggest that there is an ideal end or way of life is more likely than not to impose our ideal upon others. But it is one thing to say there are a variety of social arrangements that comport with individual ideals of well-being, quite another to claim that each of these arrangements will provide a life of autonomy.

Autonomy is one among a multitude of values. As Robert Kane notes, what has been called "value pluralism," the idea that the legitimate "ends of men are many, and not all of them are compatible with others"[17] need not entail value relativism. Value pluralism "does not imply that any end or way of life is just as good as any other—for all persons, or for a particular person at a particular time."[18] So it is not insensitive to state that the types of lives a properly autonomous person can live are limited. Neither is it incorrect to contend that some ways of life are more preferable than others. At the same time, the types of lives a properly autonomous person can live need not be restricted to an arguably unattractive and unrealistic archetype that reflects the alleged perspective of western society, where autonomy is valorized as a condition of self-created individuals, insulated from the influence and guidance of others.

The culture of the United States accords an extraordinarily high value to the freedom of the individual, or purports to do so. It is a culture premised on the belief that human beings have a right to be in command of their own destiny. Naturally, then, it is a matter of contention whether ours ought to be a culture that espouses the principle that "the best government most promotes the perfection of all its citizens ... the best government is explicitly committed to perfectionist values, or to promoting a perfectionist vision of the good."[19] For the most part, inhabitants of the United States allege to value the ideal of state neutrality, according to which the state remains impartial about what constitutes the good for persons. For the most part, we

---

16 Narayan, "Minds of Their Own," p. 431.

17 Kane, *The Significance of Free Will* (New York, 1998), p. 203.

18 Kane, The Significance of Free Will, p. 200.

19 Thomas Hurka, *Perfectionism* (New York, 1993), p. 147.

believe it is not the task of the state to endorse or endeavor to promote a particular array of personal values over others. Rather, we assume that "[P]olitical decisions must be, so far as possible, independent of any particular conception of the good life, or of what gives value to life."[20]

We can espouse this principle of political liberalism while denying the value-neutrality of autonomy. This principle does not commit us to any particular conception of autonomy. As Waldron notes, "there are reasons for holding the state to a neutrality principle that are not centered on individual freedom or autonomy (the state may be incompetent to make decisions about what makes life worth living), and there may be reasons for opposing neutrality that are not reasons for opposing the [liberal] principle (there may be aspects of the state's other duties that make neutrality impossible)."[21] More important for our purposes is whether individuals and states genuinely value autonomy if it is value-neutral and inclusive of all manner of lifestyles. Indeed, we might ask whether liberalism will best serve as a political expression of autonomy if autonomy is a content-neutral or value-free concept? Or is the conception of autonomy liberals value a perfectionist version such as the model of autonomy developed in the previous chapter?

There is good reason to believe political liberals value a perfectionist notion of autonomy. In the liberal society of the United States, the government does claim that some ways of life are inherently superior to others and frequently aims to promote some ways of life over others. Moreover, the state is regarded as legitimate for the very reason that it does this. Sometimes this is done for reasons other than the intrinsic value of these ways of life, as when the state appeals to the need for social efficiency or solidarity among its citizens. One reason a social-relational "perfectionist" notion of autonomy is valued is that it provides a stronger guarantee of the political participation sought of adult citizens than does a content-neutral notion of autonomy. The former captures our intuitions about the sort of autonomy that animates democratic political citizenship. We will return to this point in Chapter 6, when considering the value of autonomy.

There is nothing inconsistent about holding a perfectionist account of autonomy in conjunction with political liberalism. Steven Wall defends a perfectionist variety of liberalism according to which "political authorities should take an active role in creating and maintaining social conditions that best enable their subjects to lead valuable and worthwhile lives."[22] Even if classical liberalism does not readily accommodate perfectionist autonomy, other models of liberal political theory are perfectionist and will make the accommodation. Egalitarian liberalism of the sort that generated welfare-state liberalism, for example, defends substantive social perfections such as freedom of expression, religious tolerance, and the freedom of association. All of these can be justified by appeal to the intrinsic value of autonomy. And all of these are perfections of the sort that rely on a guarantee that persons will

---

20 Ronald Dworkin, *A Matter of Principle* (Cambridge, MA, 1985), p. 191.

21 Waldron, "Moral Autonomy and Personal Autonomy," p. 314.

22 Wall, *Liberalism, Perfectionism, and Restraint* (Cambridge, U.K., 1998), p. 22.

be party to particular social relations at the exclusion of others. John Rawls allows (admittedly, controversially) that while the justification of principles of justice rests in the neutrality of the original position, the principles that emerge will conform to certain constraints of what is "reasonable." Perhaps, then, it is better to say that what the political liberal opposes is a "thick" variety of perfectionism wherein it is claimed that autonomous agents must have particular values, or preferences, or entertain certain goals and aspirations. But if this is the case, the opposition is not to the social-relational account, for this is not what the social-relational account demands. The social-relational account demands that the autonomous individual is one who is free to choose what sort of social relations to be in. The account also requires that these relations, however else they may differ from each other, are ones that grant the agent substantive power and authority. But it is not contrary to autonomy, standardly construed, to require both.

The idea that persons are autonomous only when they realize certain goals, engage in specific pursuits, or occupy a type of role within particular interpersonal relations might be problematic for different reasons, reasons of a practical nature. If a person's autonomy is restricted by her social relations and these are subject to change then autonomy seems worrisomely ephemeral—episodic, if you will—making global autonomy something that could not be sustained. In this case it might be better to abandon the social model for some version of the authenticity view discussed in Chapter 2. But this is not a serious concern, for two reasons. First, our experience of autonomy within social relationships and roles is not ephemeral but generally quite stable. Second, that autonomy can develop and wither as social roles and relations change is no reason to oppose a social-relational construction of autonomy. To the degree we regard autonomy as a value, it is a reason to oppose particular social relations, and particularly unstable social relations.

Perhaps the resistance to an account of autonomy that embraces perfectionism stems from the fact that perfectionism has been sullied by its legacy of association with politically repressive regimes. Indeed, Thomas Hurka, a proponent of perfectionism, concedes that

> [C]ritics worry that perfectionism is hostile to the modern political values of liberty and equality. Because it thinks some lives are better than others, they argue, regardless of whether people want or would choose them, it favors state coercion to force people into excellence. Also because it thinks some lives are better than others, perfectionism wants the bulk of resources distributed to those who can lead such lives. Instead of equal shares, it wants the material conditions for perfection confined to a small elite, for whose benefit the rest of the population must labor.[23]

Hurka alleges the perfectionist can affirm a version of the liberal principle consistent with classical liberalism. He suggests that perfectionism might avoid the charge of systematically restricting liberty by adopting a broad point of view, one that treats "*autonomy*, or free choice from many life options, as itself an intrinsic

---

23   Hurka, *Perfectionism*, p. 47.

good. If self-determination is itself a perfection, any restrictions on it are *prima facie* objectionable."[24] Moreover, if autonomy is a perfection that involves just a person's inner state of character—if it is a perfection in the Aristotelian sense—then autonomy is not something that can be directly produced in a person by the state, or guaranteed by the forcible or the gentle effort of the state.

Modifying perfectionism in this fashion is unlikely to satisfy either the staunch defender of liberty or the defender of a substantively social-relational account of autonomy. The libertarian liberal will contend, rightly, that broad perfectionism cannot affirm the classic liberal principle of noninterference unconditionally. There will be occasions when it will be advisable to curtail a person's (local) autonomy in the present in order to increase the prospect of future autonomy.[25] A compromised broad perfectionism is unlikely to hold much appeal for the defender of a social-relational account either, since it locates the perfection that is autonomy in the inner character of the individual. Insofar as the charge of perfectionism stands against the social-relational account of autonomy, it is perfectionism of a variety that involves the promotion of certain phenomena external to the individual and the exclusion of other phenomena external to the individual.

Nonetheless, some progress has been made in bringing the social-relational account within liberalism's fold. Political liberals disagree about the kind of autonomy they hope persons will aspire to just as they disagree about the shape a liberal society should assume. But from the fact that political liberalism is comprehensive it does not follow that political liberalism recognizes no symmetry in the experience of autonomy. To be personally autonomous is to be *de jure* permitted and *de facto* positioned to participate in the democratic process, even if politically autonomy only calls for the first. Disparate cultural influences and group membership will vary in their effect on the experience of autonomy and likelihood of autonomy for persons. In addition, people differ in the lives they sincerely wish to experience, and comprehensive political liberalism will defend the right of people to experience these different lives. But liberals can concede that these may well be lives in which the experience of autonomy is absent, as is the case for the contented slave, the Angel in the House, and the Taliban Woman. Liberals can agree that some projects and some ways of life better comport with autonomy and can regard social-relational autonomy as one element of an ideally liberal life.

Moreover, liberals can make value judgments about the variety of autonomous lives. Liberals can uphold the ideas that there is no privileged perspective of the

---

24 Hurka, *Perfectionism*, p. 148. Broad perfectionism is an "inclusive view [of the good for human nature] that values some development of capacities or some achievement of excellence," p. 4.

25 Hurka concedes as much, stating that "A plausible broad perfectionism, then, can treat autonomy only as one good among others, which may sometimes be outweighed. It therefore cannot endorse an absolute liberty principle, but it can endorse a non-absolute principle. If free choice is intrinsically good, any restriction on it threatens some perfectionist cost and is therefore prima facie objectionable. Other things equal, the state should not interfere except to protect the greater liberty of others." *Perfectionism*, p. 149.

good for individuals that state institutions should favor as well as the idea that it is the right of each person to define value for himself and to decide his own conception of the good at the same time liberals judge some of these decisions more estimable than others and at the same time they recognize a particular ideal of self-government. Liberalism might claim good moral reasons or good pragmatic reasons for preferring some expressions of autonomy over others against the good political reasons for allowing the expressions of individualism in the lives of citizens to go unchecked. In short, liberalism need not regard as equally good every expression of autonomy, every way of life, and the multitude of individual interpretations of the good. Even if liberalism treats the idea of personal autonomy rather than the idea of political autonomy as its keystone, it may do so for reasons having to do solely with the political purchasing power of personal autonomy.

The Social Account Invites Unwarranted Paternalism

Because the social account contends that autonomy is not a perfection that involves just a person's inner states, the social account might permit greater paternalistic interference and a wider range of illiberal laws than Hurka's Aristotelian perfectionism allows. This is especially likely if social-relational accounts claim particular ways of life as correct for autonomous agents. Autonomy will then no longer be an ideal associated with self-fashioned individuality and mastery of character but will be a species of self-perfection. People who do not count as socially autonomous might be fair targets for paternalistic intervention as a result.

Let us understand paternalistic action as interference with a person's autonomy that seeks justification "by reasons referring exclusively to the welfare, good, happiness, needs, interests or values of the person..."[26] We offend a person's autonomy by paternalistic means when we endeavor to impose on the person a conception of what is a worthy and proper life. It is irrelevant whether or not we are in fact motivated by concern for the person's own good, and whether or not a person's well-being is actually threatened. We offend a person's autonomy by paternalistic means either by preventing the person from doing whatever she has decided to do or by interfering with the way in which she reaches her decision.

Four things are required in order for an act to be paternalistic:

1. Since paternalism just is that which offends autonomy, those who are subject to paternalistic action must be self-governing or capable of self-government.
2. The act uses compulsion (although not necessarily coercion) to promote the well-being of a subject or to achieve some benefit that may or may not be

---

26 Gerald Dworkin, "Paternalism," *Monist* 56 (1972): 65. I will confine my remarks to what Dworkin calls "pure" paternalism and what Joel Feinberg labels "direct" or "one-party" paternalism, where "the class of persons whose freedom is restricted ... is identical with the class of persons whose benefit is intended to be promoted" by such restrictions. (Dworkin, "Paternalism," p. 68).

recognized as a benefit by the one for whom it is intended.[27]

3. In cases where we wish to protect a person from a harm, incurring the harm requires the active cooperation of the victim.

4. To the extent that the agent is aware of the paternalistic measure, the agent does not want (or would not want) to be treated in this way.

Paternalism usurps autonomy because it substitutes one person's judgment for that of another. Hard paternalism is the view that an acceptable reason for paternalistic behavior is the necessity of protecting competent adults, against their will, from the harmful consequences of even their fully voluntary undertakings.[28] Suppose that a friend in the United States military is torn between his need to be forthright about his homosexuality and his allegiance to the military policy of "don't ask, don't tell" about such matters. If I reveal the homosexuality of my friend to his supervising officer because I believe that doing so will alleviate the anxiety my friend is experiencing and in the long run will best promote his psychological esteem, I invade my friend's privacy and I invade his autonomy. My intervention most certainly invites substantial changes in my friend's life that he might fail to welcome. My motives need not be malicious. But because I have substituted my judgment for that of a competent adult, my action is paternalistic.

One way of determining the circumstances under which a person's right of autonomy may justifiably be violated or rescinded is found in John Stuart Mill's effort to fuse an alliance between the spheres of liberty and authority. The default position is that under normal circumstances, individuality, as a valued manifestation of autonomy, must be protected from the "tyranny" of social custom and the collective authority of society. Since people are members of society (and of narrower, more formal associations), tensions will inevitably arise between the provinces of individual freedom and social authority. Because some threats to individuality are

---

27 To "compel" is to necessitate an action by force of some sort: it may include gentle persuasion or temptation. To "coerce" is to compel behavior by use of pressure, threats, or intimidation where failure to comply leaves the subject worse off. The markers of paternalism are not specified by the manner in which a person is prevented from exercising her autonomy. Paternalism consists in the practice of imposing a putative good on a person when that person does not welcome the imposition, and this can transpire by means as diverse as manipulation, brute force, and rational persuasion.

28 Dworkin distinguishes between "hard" and "soft" paternalism in "Paternalism: Some Second Thoughts," Rolf Sartorius (ed.), *Paternalism* (Minneapolis, 1983). Feinberg also distinguishes between "soft" and "hard" paternalism but, where Dworkin makes soft paternalism a feature of the actor's competence, Feinberg views it as determined by the involuntary nature of the harm suffered by the actor. Feinberg's idea is that we can permissibly protect a person from self-regarding harm only when the harm is substantially nonvoluntary or when intervention is required in order to determine whether it is voluntary or not. Soft paternalism is intended to affect only such "wrongfully" suffered harms, that is, harms the subject does not consent to. (Given that the person fails to consent to the harm, Feinberg rightly questions how action or legislation taken against the harm can truly be called paternalistic.)

unavoidable, the variety of control and the extent of the power that can legitimately be exercised by society over an individual must be ascertained.

To this end, Mill employs the general-interest principle known as the liberty principle. Negatively formulated as the *harm principle*, it states that "the only purpose for which power can be rightfully exercised over any member of a civilized community, against his will, is to prevent harm to others."[29] The harm principle establishes parameters for individual autonomy by showing that autonomy legitimately can be nurtured only within the confines of the rights and concerns of others. When a person behaves in ways that we find injurious to the self-determination of others, either by "doing evil" or by failing to prevent evil, or when a person violates certain accepted codes for social behavior, or abdicates "a distinct and assignable obligation to any other person or persons," even when this action consists of injury the person does to himself, "the case is taken out of the self-regarding class and becomes amenable to moral disapprobation in the proper sense of the term."[30] In these cases, abrogations of autonomy, even where this touches on affairs that are of profound importance and interest to a person, are justified.

Mill's idea appears to be that while the right to autonomy is the stock position, we should not assume that this right ought to be upheld for all persons. There are exceptions to this right. But the exceptions here are not based on considerations of a paternalistic nature. These exceptions to the right of autonomy are premised on the idea that self-determination is a condition to be promoted only for deserving persons.[31] The criterion of desert helps fix the class of persons against whom infringements to autonomy are in general unjustified—person for whom autonomy should be inviolate, all things considered. The default position is abdicated when there is a forfeit of desert. There are probably other negative tests for desert than Mill's harm principle, but let us begin with this as it is well known.

The thought that a right to autonomy is bound up with desert is quite plausible when self-determination is thought of as a characteristic persons develop, exercise, and retain in virtue of their relations to others. But it does not help us understand what might make paternalistic interference warranted. The criterion of desert does not define the limits of legitimate paternalistic interference as persons deserving of autonomy might be plausible subjects of paternalistic intervention. These are the disquieting scenarios—the ones where persons who possess the capacity for autonomy and who have not violated the harm principle are targets of paternalistic intervention. Interferences of this sort are worrying, if only because they threaten to make systematic violations of liberties more acceptable. Thomas Hill, Jr. and Isaiah Berlin join Mill in voicing such worries.

---

29 John Stuart Mill, *On Liberty*, 1859, Currin V. Shields (ed.) (New York, 1956), p. 13.

30 Mill, *On Liberty*, p. 99.

31 Although the focus of our discussion thus far has been autonomy as a global state of persons, the issue of desert arises primarily when autonomy is regarded locally, as a condition predicated of persons *vis à vis* a certain activity or set of rights exercised in a social context.

In speaking of the value of individuality and the nature of self-regarding conduct, for example, Mill tells us that the person most interested in the well-being of an individual is the individual himself. If the individual is a reasonable, mature adult, he should be granted "perfect freedom, legal and social, to do the action and stand the consequences."[32] No other person should tell him "not to do with his life for his own benefit what he chooses to do with it."[33]

Even when persons engage in behavior "which experience has shown not to be useful to any person's individuality," or act in ways that are "injurious to happiness and ... a hindrance to improvement"[34] intervention, says Mill, is permitted only to prevent a graver harm to the larger social body. In order to justify compelling a person to do what another believes is best, Mill adds, "the conduct from which it is desired to deter him must be calculated to produce evil in someone else ... Over his own body and mind, the individual is sovereign."[35]

Hill claims it is irrelevant whether paternalistic intervention is intended to protect a person from discomfort or to augment that person's independence. Consider the act of telling a lie. Lying is emblematic of trespasses upon autonomy. When one knowledgeable, sane person is subject either to deliberate deception or to a voluntary withholding of information by another, "one's opportunity to live in rational control of one's life" is curtailed.[36] This may occur when a lie is told in an effort to shelter a person from pain or worry, and perhaps we are less disturbed by a lie told in such circumstances. But lying also, perhaps less obviously, trespasses autonomy where a lie is told in order to foster autonomy, especially if the desired effect is achieved. That its offensive character may be blunted does not alter the autonomy-robbing function of the lie. The lie is still paternalistic even if its offensive character is commensurate with the intentions of the liar or with the extent to which the activity disrupted by the lie is significant.

Berlin cautions us against paternalistic acts that arise out of a particular interpretation of positive freedom. Specifically, Berlin asserts that the positive idea of freedom, understood as self-mastery, invites unwarranted interference in personal choices when mastery is interpreted as the domination of the agent by his "real" or "ideal" self, as opposed to his baser impulsive and passionate nature. The idea, Berlin states, is that "[T]he self that should not be interfered with is [not] the individual with his actual wishes and needs ... but the 'real' man within, identified with the

---

32 Mill, *On Liberty*, p. 92.

33 Mill, *On Liberty*, p. 93.

34 Mill, *On Liberty*, p. 98.

35 Mill, *On Liberty*, p. 13. Mill's injunctions against paternalism as well as the harm principle emanate from the principle of utility. Berlin points out that other principles, such as the categorical imperative, prescriptions of natural law, or the inviolability of a social contract, might likewise be employed. See Isaiah Berlin, "Two Concepts of Liberty," in Berlin, *Four Essays on Liberty* (Oxford, 1969), p. 127.

36 Thomas E. Hill, Jr., "Autonomy and Benevolent Lies," *Journal of Value Inquiry* 18 (1984): 265.

pursuit of some ideal purpose not dreamed of by his empirical self."[37] The outcome
is that this true self takes on a fetishized character. It somehow becomes identified
with whatever larger social or institutional collective body is given reign over the
expressed wishes of the individual. Berlin remarks that just as

> [t]he reason within me ... must eliminate and suppress my "lower" instincts, my passions
> and desires, which render me a slave; similarly ... the higher elements in society—the
> better educated, the more rational, those who "possess the highest insight of their time
> and people"—may exercise compulsion to rationalize the irrational section of society.
> For ... by obeying the rational man we obey ourselves: not indeed as we are, sunk in our
> ignorance and our passions ... but as we could be if we were rational.[38]

The phenomenon that Berlin describes gives rise to what I will call rational
consent varieties of paternalism. If the rational consent model is correct, then action
on behalf of the individual against his expressed wishes will not be viewed as what
the individual would want were he otherwise, but as what the individual does in fact
really, though not expressly, want. Under such circumstances, argue advocates of
the rational-consent justificatory scheme, no objectionable, no genuine interference
to the freedom of the individual in fact occurs. Since the individual's real, albeit
unrecognized, self by proxy carries out the action against his "less real" self, the
individual is not interfered with by alien factors. Detractors reply that rational consent
models not only severely limit the class of people whom we call autonomous, but
also countenance a state of affairs potentially hostile to liberalism. The idea that
there is a particularly correct way of life and a correct set of creeds that sustain a
rational man's vision of self-government or a vision of self-government held by our
"rational selves" invites intolerance and the suppression of opinions.[39]

The worry of perfectionism, then, has not been discharged entirely: Perfectionism
might permit some restrictions on liberty as when the injury it forestalls is to the
rational personality a person will experience or has the ability to experience at some
future date. If we agree that individuals have a right to autonomy, then perhaps
interferences to this right will be justified only if the state that would obtain in the
absence of the paternalistic gesture is so disastrous as to override the individual's
claim to autonomy as a right. What would count as sufficiently disastrous remains
an open question. Would the self-regarding aim of the individual to destroy his own
autonomy qualify? Is it true that when the aim is to develop our rational nature,
a paternalistic form of illiberality "reduces autonomy only a little, removes just

---

37 Berlin, "Two Concepts of Liberty," p. 134.

38 Berlin, "Two Concepts of Liberty," p. 150.

39 Berlin, for example, worries that the two-self ideal breeds moral and political
despotism. Once the rational consent position is adopted, "I am in a position to ignore the
actual wishes of men or societies, to bully, oppress, torture them in the name, and on behalf,
of their 'real' selves, in the secure knowledge that whatever is the true goal of man ... [it] must
be identical with ... the free choice of his 'true', albeit often submerged and inarticulate, self."
Berlin, "Two Concepts of Liberty," p. 133.

one route to excellence, and leaves considerable scope in the choice among the remaining options?"[40] Can paternalism be justified all things considered if it directs people into more valuable behavior, with the result that, "although perfectionism has a strong general commitment to liberty, it may sometimes favour legal restrictions on especially bad activities," such as those that "are very difficult to abandon once they have been tried?"[41]

It is especially difficult to weigh the value and desirability of autonomy against that of paternalism in situations where a person's self-directed actions threaten the person's autonomy, and where paternalism might avert this threat, when what is at stake are weighty competing values such as a right to privacy and a right to liberty, or individual well-being. Perhaps in such cases we can claim that interference with a person's autonomy is permitted either because of an occurrent or a dispositional defect in the decision-making capacities of the person, and because we believe the person would consent to such intervention were her decision-making capacities revived. This would count as a case of "soft" or "weak" paternalism, a necessary condition of which is that the target of paternalistic overtures is incompetent in some sense.

In cases such as Taliban Woman no obvious credible reason for deeming the agent incompetent and her actions involuntary presents itself. Taliban Woman's failure to be autonomous cannot be traced to a lapse of reason or a mistake of judgment. Thus incursions to her right to realize certain ends central to her life cannot be justified by appeal to soft paternalism. In such cases, we may only be able to defend encroachments upon choices and actions of the sort Taliban Woman makes by a policy of hard paternalism.

Dworkin attempts to avoid the hard paternalistic position by arguing for a "hypothetical consent scheme for justifying paternalism" via the "soft" view. Justifications of paternalism based on hypothetical consent turn on the assumption that, to some degree, competent adult individuals are vulnerable to the same cognitive, emotional, and epistemic failings as are their less competent counterparts. It is also assumed that rational persons wish to protect themselves from cognitive deficiencies and incompetence. Dworkin's idea is that soft paternalism is justified when an agent's action is voluntarily undertaken but poses a significant and genuine risk of which the agent is not aware or does not sufficiently appreciate. Paternalistic protections or limitations on certain conduct are appropriate if they are protections rational individuals antecedently would willingly and collectively establish, and would consent to as "social insurance policies."[42]

---

40 Hurka, *Perfectionism*, p. 155.

41 Hurka, *Perfectionism*, p. 155.

42 Dworkin, "Paternalism," p. 78. The parameters of justifiable interferences will be determined in either of two ways. We might focus on the rationality and competence of the individuals involved or we might examine the decisions the individual makes. On the former approach we ask whether the individual suffers from some degree of cognitive incompetence that causes her to weight abnormally some of her values, or to "discount unreasonably the probability or seriousness of future injury" ("Paternalism: Some Second Thoughts," p. 108.)

Taliban Woman believes that abdicating her right of self-governance to religious
edict has instrumental value—she believes, perhaps, that abdication will maximize
some other, more highly desired good. If we can show that Taliban Woman suffers
from a misapprehension, or a mistaken calculation about how best to obtain the
primary good that she seeks, then we will be justified in imposing certain mandates
regarding her behavior. Doing so "minimizes the risk of harm ... at the cost of a
trivial interference with ... freedom."[43]

Similarly, Berlin believes there are times when it is defensible to compel a person
to do one's will, or the will of a larger group, under the guise of promoting what the
person would, in a more informed, mature and reasonable state prefer. In this case
the difference—which Berlin believes to be a crucial one—is that interference is
made in the name of an action that the individual would want were he otherwise.
Paternalism is warranted in light of presumed future consent, as opposed to the
presence of a "true, rational self." Again, the assumption is that the person will come
to recognize and welcome these interferences as being in his or her best interest.

None of these manage to transform paternalism into something else, something
that does not offend autonomy. When the targets of intervention are adults, the
hypothetical consent model that is invoked to justify soft paternalistic restrictions
lends itself to the worries that Berlin himself voices against true self models. Surely
not every interference with freedom is trivial, especially from the perspective of the
one who is interfered with. Forcing the Taliban Woman to abandon her way of life
counts to her as a substantial harm, the cost of which is her purported flourishing.
It is tempting, even easy, to think that no sane person would choose to live as she
does. Hence it is easy to think that paternalistic measures ought to be taken in her
name to remove her from the grip of Talibanic ideology. As Narayan notes, it is not
uncommon in the West to support the use of compulsory procedures against women
who choose ways of life that fail to comport with a Western ideal of autonomy
"on the grounds that ... cultural constraints render women's decisions to comply
with such practices not really choices in any meaningful sense."[44] Narayan voices
"serious reservations about state-driven agendas to save women from cultural
backwardness,"[45] and echoes Martha Nussbaum's suggestion that women whose
preferences have been "deformed" by patriarchal socialization and who confront
limited opportunities for life should be granted by the state "empowering options

---

On the latter approach we wonder whether the person selects courses of action that are "far
reaching, dangerous, and irreversible" ("Paternalism," p. 80), or are made under conditions of
duress, or involve dangers not sufficiently understood or appreciated. (Ibid., p. 82.)

43 Dworkin, "Paternalism: Some Second Thoughts," p. 110. Dworkin believes that once
the consent of the subject is acquired, "in interfering with such people we are in effect doing
what they would do if they were fully rational. Hence we are not really opposing their will,
hence we are not really interfering with their freedom" ("Paternalism," p. 77). But this avoids
the problem by dissolving it: once consent is granted the action is no longer paternalistic.

44 Narayan, "Minds of Their Own: Choices, Autonomy, Cultural Practices, and Other
Women," p. 426.

45 Narayan, "Minds of Their Own," p. 426.

rather than coercion."[46]   Justifications for weak or soft paternalism based on
assumptions of rational consent or future consent are thus problematic even though,
as Dworkin notes, paternalistic interference is a less bitter pill to swallow where it
allegedly "preserves and enhances for the individual his ability to rationally consider
and carry out his own decisions."[47]

Do there remain cases in which strong or hard paternalistic measures ought to be
employed as a means of discouraging certain self-regarding behavior, of compelling
certain self-regarding behavior, and of enhancing autonomy where the capacity
is present, but unfulfilled? I believe a case can be made that strong paternalistic
intervention is sometimes needed to preserve the autonomy that is threatened by a
competent and deserving person's self-regarding conduct, even where the target of
the paternalistic gesture has not behaved in ways that clearly permit infringements
of autonomy. Robert Young argues for this point:

> Suppose *S* knows that heroin addiction causes severe physical harm and likely death
> before 30 years of age, but still chooses to take the drug because he wants the pleasure of
> the moment more than anything else. Assume, furthermore, that we independently have
> good grounds for believing *S* is emotionally stable and of sound reason. A policy of weak
> [soft] paternalism cannot in such a case justify intervention to prevent *S*'s taking heroin.
> A strong paternalist ... would argue for intervention where the consequences of *S*'s action
> would be to undermine other more dispositional commitments.[48]

Since employing paternalistic measures to compel autonomy seems contradictory,
it is the phenomenon on which I will focus.[49] Recall Mill's argument that because
paternalism affects conduct that is entirely self-regarding, it cannot be justified

---

46 Narayan, "Minds of Their Own," p. 425.

47 Dworkin, "Paternalism," p. 83.

48 Young, *Personal Autonomy*, p. 68. The idea is that while *S* exhibits autonomy of
desire, paternalistic measures might be employed to preserve *S*'s autonomy of future action.

49 Actions taken to compel autonomy, such as prohibitions on consensual slavery, might
be explained by nonpaternalistic reasons, as when the explanation appeals to the interests
of others. We might ask whether the person who happily relinquishes his capacity for self-
determination causes a decline in overall utility within the larger environment in which he acts.
While no definite duty to the public has been abridged, it is plausible that in these instances
(for example, opting for voluntary servitude or life as Taliban women) social offenses have
been committed in collusion with society. If the offense imperils the basis for productive
interchange within the social, political, and economic realms, then the utility principle could
be invoked to support injunctions against the action. Classifying self-imposed slavery as a
social offense of this proportion involves analyzing the implications of self-imposed slavery
for the social structure in which it occurs. The same is true of a society in which 50 percent of
the adult population willingly relegates itself to the status of the Taliban woman. Of course,
a utilitarian calculus could conclude that autonomy is of less value to a society than is the
sovereignty of the individual who chooses nonautonomy; society might greatly benefit from
voluntary slavery and Taliban women. The decision to utilize paternalistic measures will then
depend on the extent to which a society counts autonomy as important for the integrity of
its structure. In a society that bestows less social worth on autonomy, actions that diminish

by citing the need to protect the interests of others. In addition, Mill contends that because the individual is, arguably, the best judge of his own welfare, it is unlikely that paternalism would advance the interests of the individual. Indeed, the opposite is often the case: it is likely that paternalism would produce greater evil than it would prevent. Mill's reasoning is founded on the utilitarian cost-benefit calculus, but the claim he wishes to defend is not supported by the cost-benefit analysis.

First, it is false that adult individuals always know their own interests. As I will argue in Chapter 6, it is in a person's interest to be autonomous. To briefly anticipate, a person who lacks autonomy stands on weaker ground when claiming consideration from others and is less likely to be accorded the presumption of consideration human agents are due. The failure of people to decide accurately about their autonomy might offer one reason in favor of paternalistic interferences, even when a person has decided in what he believes is his best interest. The right to autonomy will be a good that must be preserved, even when it is the aim of the individual to destroy this right in none but himself.

Second, as Mill himself should acknowledge, paternalistic action sometimes constitutes a lesser evil, or a greater good, than would obtain should the action it restrains go unchecked. Allowing a person to autonomously pursue a life in which more dispositional or global interests are circumscribed does not always make the person better off, even if the person is happy with the result. Mill writes:

> [An] ... exception to the doctrine that individuals are the best judges of their own interest, is when an individual attempts to decide irrevocably now what will be best for his interest at some future and distant time. The presumption in favor of individual judgment is only legitimate, where the judgment is grounded on actual, and especially on present personal experience; not where it is formed antecedently to experience, and not suffered to be reversed even after experience has condemned it.[50]

Ironically, then, Mill's version of liberalism imports perfectionist elements. The value that Mill accords autonomy can be used to justify an argument he offers against self-imposed slavery. Mill counts freely chosen slavery among those actions over which the individual is not sovereign, and says:

> The ground for thus limiting [the slave's] power of voluntarily disposing of his own lot in life is apparent, and is very clearly seen in this extreme case. The reason for not interfering, unless for the sake of others, with a person's voluntary acts is consideration for his liberty ... But by selling himself for a slave, he abdicates his liberty; he forgoes any future use of it beyond that single act. He therefore defeats, in his own case, the very purpose which is the justification of allowing him to dispose of himself. He is no longer free; but is thenceforth in a position which has no longer the presumption in its favour that would be afforded by his voluntarily remaining in it. *The principle of freedom cannot*

---

a person's autonomy would then be targets for reproof or regret, but would not be treated as social evils.

50 John Stuart Mill, *Principles of Political Economy*, 2 vols. (1848; reprint, New York, 1900), p. 459.

require that he should be free not to be free. It is not freedom to be allowed to alienate his freedom.[51]

Mill's use of the term "freedom" equivocates between "liberty of action" and "individuality" or "autonomy." His point would be more explicitly made were he to say that people should not be at liberty to relinquish their autonomy. But his point is clear nonetheless. Individuality or autonomy is too important a characteristic for persons to be without. Since it is that element of persons upon which all other forms of freedom are grounded—including the freedom to act—autonomy cannot be something that we are at liberty to dismantle. Respect for persons does not preempt intervention when occurent behavior puts dispositional autonomy at risk. As Robin Dillon notes, "We also respect [people] (positively) by protecting them from threats to their autonomy (which may require intervention when someone's current decisions seem to put their own autonomy at risk)..."[52] Consensual slavery, regardless of the gains it might provide others and aside from any benefit to the enslaved, transforms the human subject into a possession or object of another and accordingly defiles the enslaved person's autonomy. Once autonomy has been cast off, the person is in no position to expect others to treat him with the respect for his individuality that typically disallows paternalism.

Moreover, it is unmistakably Mill's belief that persons care about being autonomous agents, even if, on occasion, they autonomously act in ways that are not expressive of that concern. Mill derides the person "who lets the world choose his plan of life for him" as one who "has no need of any other faculty than the ape-like one of imitation." While such a person might be "guided in some good path, and kept out of harm's way ... what will be his comparative worth as a human being? It really is of importance, not only what men do, but also what manner of men they are that do it."[53]

This being so, it is preferable that people safeguard their capacity for autonomy and do so on willingly, and of their own initiative. "In the best case of all," Hurka remarks, "they choose self-preservation partly for its own sake, as an intrinsically valued exercise of self-management."[54] But when people do not choose self-preservation, as in the case of voluntary slavery, restrictions on autonomously executed acts that eradicate one's dispositional autonomy can be upheld under a policy of judicious strong paternalism that even a staunch champion of individuality such as Mill would allow.

---

51 Mill, *On Liberty*, p. 125, my emphasis.

52 Robin S. Dillon, "Respect," *Stanford Encyclopedia of Philosophy,* Edward N. Zalta (ed.), <http://plato.stanford.edu/archives/fall2003/entries/respect/>.

53 Mill, *On Liberty*, pp. 71–2. In challenging the assumption that autonomy is for Mill to be desired on instrumental grounds alone, James Bogen and Daniel Farrell note that "Autonomy may be desired for its own sake, even if it ceases to produce the mental state for which it was originally desired." See Bogen and Farrell, "Freedom and Happiness in Mill's Defence of Liberty," *Philosophical Quarterly* 28/13 (1978): 334.

54 Hurka, *Perfectionism*, p. 158.

Summary

The arguments that I have considered surrounding paternalism and more general interferences with autonomous behavior lend themselves to the following conclusions. First, it is difficult to assess the extent to which usurpations of autonomy by paternalistic means count as nontrivial losses. Reasonable persons disagree about what will constrain their choices and actions, and they will certainly disagree about when these constraints are and are not acceptable. Some persons resent paternalistic intervention, and will label a class of activity as such, where others will not. Even where it is plain that an interference with autonomy has occurred, disagreement about the permissibility or objectionable character of the intervention is possible. Is it enough that interference owing to the deliberate efforts of others occurs without the authorization of the affected party in order to claim the interference is objectionable? I have suggested that interference is objectionable when it is arbitrary or when it is not on the promise of furthering the affected party's dispositional concerns. As the story of the Taliban Woman suggests, certain attributes that promote or strengthen a person's autonomy might be quite undesirable from the perspective of the person.

Second, there will be occasions where a decision to favor global autonomy must be held in abeyance. Even if dispositional or global autonomy is a good for the person who rejects it, autonomy may not be paramount among a person's set of goods, and it may be better that autonomy is given short shrift in that person's preferred life-plan. Values such as liberty are perhaps as important—maybe more important—than autonomy, and this gives us grounds to consider limits to state interference even if an ideal of global autonomy does not.

An inclination to promote autonomy is tempered by what is gained in its absence. Clearly, there may be attributes of character that exceed autonomy and cognate states such as liberty in importance, at least on some occasions. As Joel Feinberg correctly notes, "autonomy is not the whole of virtue, and may be made to look bad if it keeps bad company. (Imagine an inflexibly conscientious Robbespierre [sic])."[55] A person's way of life might exemplify autonomy without the life being estimable or one we regard as morally right. Even Berlin assumes that there are values higher than autonomy that bear protection, and the protection of which calls for restrictions on individual freedom. He states:

> I do not wish to say that individual freedom is, even in the most liberal societies, the sole, or even the dominant, criterion of social action. We compel children to be educated, and we forbid public executions. These are certainly curbs to freedom. We justify them on the ground that ignorance, or a barbarian upbringing, or cruel pleasures and excitements are worse for us than the amount of restraint needed to repress them.[56]

---

55 Joel Feinberg, *Harm to Self*, vol. 3 of *The Moral Limits of Criminal Law* (New York, 1986), p. 40.

56 Berlin, "Two Concepts of Liberty," p. 169.

Third, there are penumbral cases in which an individual's voluntary abdication of certain liberties may fail to provide us with good or sufficient reason to claim an absence of global autonomy and thereby to attempt a restoration of autonomy on the person's behalf. An example is the life embraced by persons in insular Anabaptist religious communities such as the Old Order Amish, the Hutterites, and the Mennonites. Amish youth are raised according to the congregation's religious beliefs but are not members of the church until they choose to join by way of baptism, usually between the ages of 16 and 21. Until they have made their baptismal vow, all Amish adolescents experience the "running around" Amish rite of passage known as *rum springa*. This vital decision-making phase of their lives begins at age 16 during which time they are in a unique position in the community. Because they are not yet members of the church they are given reign (without reprisal) to explore a life free from the strictures of the community. They have freedom to bend church rules, such as listening to radios or driving cars, without fear of being shunned.[57]

Like Taliban Woman, the Amish join the church as adults and only after reflecting upon their willingness to commit to the community. A majority of 85 percent to 90 percent of the youth enjoy their phase of freedom from the church and then come back to the congregation. Granted, they confront significant social, psychological, and economic pressure to do so. They are surrounded by a culture of close-knit, extended family and if they wish to retain this connection they must marry in the church. Also, the formal education Amish youth have received is inadequate to supply them with the skills they would need to survive in a non-agrarian economy. But there are salient differences between the Anabaptists (or persons in similarly insular societies who have opted for cloistered lives or lives of service to others) and cases like that of Taliban woman with respect to their global autonomy. One difference is that members of Anabaptist colonies preserve a modicum of autonomy despite their centralized form of government and comparatively regimented quality of life, as this description of the Amish path toward marriage indicates:

Although much of everyday life among the plain people is shaped by church rules and traditions, Amish youth in their late teens and early twenties are expected to take more responsibility for their choices. Courtship is one area of Amish life that is left more to the discretion of the parents and the youth themselves.[58] ... Family is the core element in the Amish church, and choosing a mate is the most important decision in an Amishman's life. Boys and girls begin their search for a spouse when they turn sixteen. By the time a young woman turns twenty or a young man is in his early twenties, he or she is probably looking forward to the wedding day. But several definite steps must be taken by a couple

---

57 Joe Wittmer, *National Committee for Amish Religious Freedom*, "Joe Wittmer Responds to Questions Regarding the Amish," http://www.holycrosslivonia.org/amish/.

Wittmer is Distinguished Professor Emeritus of Counseling at the University of Florida, Gainesville and was reared in the Old Order horse-and-buggy Amish faith in Indiana until age sixteen.

58 http://www.amish-heartland.com/?pathToFile=%2F%2Farticles%2F-Amish+Culture %2F&file=Dating.txt&article=1.

before they may marry ... The young man asks his girl to marry him ... The couple keeps their intentions secret until July or August. At this time the young woman tells her family about her plans to marry.[59]

Similarly, alongside the overarching importance of the community and cooperation, evidence of respect for individuality can be found in this description of life in a Hutterite colony:

At the age of 20 or older, we are baptized. This may be [the] most important step in the life of the Hutterite. It is making a great commitment with God. When we [are] baptized we become brothers and sisters to the other members and also to Christ. After baptism is marriage, and our marriages are not arranged ... We try to be open to each other and at the same time we respect each other as individuals.[60]

A second factor that differentiates the Anabaptists from persons such as the Taliban Woman is that the dedication found in the former communities is corrupted into servility in the lives of the latter. While servility cripples the human personality, dedication need not. The lives of the Anabaptists are devoted to and tailored to a set of written and unwritten rules of the community for daily living. But though these rules accord individuality considerably less importance than is desired in liberal society, they do not require that members of the congregation value the submissive personality of the person, or that they value autonomy only in selected persons and on arbitrary grounds. There is less cause to consider pressing a particular configuration of global autonomy on the Anabaptist given that these persons typically find themselves dedicated to social roles and relations that, following Martin Luther King, Jr., "uplift, rather than degrade, the human personality."[61] This is not true of persons such as Taliban Woman, the contented slave, the browbeaten military recruit, and the subservient spouse.

Even when a person's autonomy bears upon only those affairs in her life that are self-regarding and even when a person's autonomy is of fundamental importance to the pursuit and outcome of these affairs, autonomy is not inviolable. I cannot declare with certainty when the value of autonomy should be overridden despite the cost to the individual. If we distinguish global autonomy from local autonomy or personal liberty, it may be that global autonomy is one of those values for which local autonomy or personal liberty can be sacrificed. Interference with affairs that are of profound importance and interest to another person may constitute a violation of a person's right to autonomy and autonomy of choice and must be employed with care. But there are times when we shall be permitted to override a person's right to noninterference, as when there are other, more exacting prerogatives that we want

---

59 *The Amish, the Mennonites, and the Plain People*, "What's an Amish wedding like?" http://www.800padutch.com/amish.shtml.

60 Ruth Walman and Susie Stahl, *Hutterite History: Past and present*, Oct. 5, 1985, Saskatoon Inn, Saskatoon, SK. http://sesd.sk.ca/grassroots/Riverview/page17.html.

61 Martin Luther King, Jr., "Letter from Birmingham Jail," *Liberation* (June 1963): 12.

to protect. There is, as we have noted, tension here that even Mill finds difficult to resolve. The fact that it might be morally and legally incumbent upon us to caution others against their own behavior, to warn them of the punitive consequences that might follow their behavior, and to actually take steps to curtail their local autonomy does not mean that global autonomy is not a valued state. This ideal remains intact, although uninstantiated in certain cases.

Chapter 6

The Value of Autonomy

Introduction

As the discussion of the preceding chapter indicates, assertions about the value of autonomy are often problematic. They are problematic because they concern the kind of value autonomy has and why it is something we value, and not just how much value autonomy has when weighed against competing goods. These questions are frequently conflated. In asking what happens when the presumed right to autonomy is tested against competing goods, such as personal contentment, well-being, or political security, we might overlook the fact that we are comparing goods that are valued for different reasons.

The task of this chapter is to pursue some of the issues surrounding questions about the value of autonomy that arose in discussing perfectionism and paternalism. In section one, we will examine various goods of moral and social importance which are often seen as bound up with self-governance. Clarifying the differences among these goods will help bring autonomy's comparative value into sharper focus. Section two continues the discussion with a consideration of two different ways of valuing personal autonomy: as an instrumental good and as a good of intrinsic value.

Having settled that autonomy is of value distinct from other, related goods, we still must confront the fact that the premium we place upon autonomy can be tested by the very independence it secures for us. In Chapter 5 we saw that autonomy is not a good to which all persons have a continuing right and that incursions to liberty in order to protect or to exact a future right to autonomy may be promoted. In section three of this chapter, we consider the question of when the right to autonomy may be abridged for reasons other than forfeit of desert or threat to future self-determination. The events of September 11, 2001, for example, have forced citizens of the United States to question the extent to which they regard the right to autonomy as fundamental and the extent to which they should do so. Citizens of the United States now confront the fact that measures that abrogate full autonomy and diminish the apparent right of self-governance are being undertaken in exchange for promises of heightened security. Relaxed civil liberties protections, intensified scrutiny of transactions previously regarded as confidential, and modified legal standards illustrate the conflict.

Autonomy and Associated Values

Well-being

Well-being refers to what is *good for* a person, with philosophical usage generally focused on what it means for life to go well for the person or what makes a life worthy of choice. Certainly there are competing ideals, dating back at least to Aristotle, about what a life that is good for us or that goes well looks like. The debate about what constitutes well-being and why certain things rather than others make life go well remains a spirited one. Among the things in which well-being is alleged to consist are the achievement of objectively valuable and typically subjectively valued goods such as health and material comfort; the experience of mental states such as happiness (or some subset of these pleasurable states, such as those that are the function of propositional attitudes made true by facts about the world); the satisfaction of informed desires; the development of our human nature, and the exercise of virtues distinctive of human beings. Some identify well-being with human flourishing, but treat the latter as a romantic ideal unrelated to autonomy.[1] Some of the qualities implicated in well-being might vary among cultures, while there may be unanimity in finding a place for certain other goods among the list. It is beyond the scope of our discussion to survey, much less critically evaluate, these myriad candidates for well-being. The interested reader may consult the extant literature.[2]

It seems right that the road to autonomy is not always the road to achieving what is good for a person or what makes a person's life go well for the person. Among the conceptions of well-being cited above, only an account that describes well-being as the development of essential human nature or of human excellence might plausibly claim autonomy as a necessary constituent. Even if autonomy in some guise, including autonomy of a purely procedural variety, might be one of a number of factors individually sufficient for some degree of well-being (just as pleasure, or knowledge, or health and friendship might be sufficient), well-being would not necessarily call for the state of self-directedness as I have described it. Those who worry that well-being takes on an unacceptably perfectionist cast if autonomy is what is good for people might take solace in this fact. Nonetheless, we might believe that social-relational autonomy is a component of well-being. After all, one aspect of the ideal of autonomy is a life that is self-directed because it has been fashioned through freely chosen goals and relations. Perhaps a life wherein a person has the ability to decide for himself what counts as a desirable life and the freedom to pursue that life satisfies a generic ideal of a life that goes well.

---

1   Berofsky, *Liberation from Self*, chapter 2.

2   For instance see Aristotle, *Nicomachean Ethics*, trans. W.D. Ross (Oxford, 1925); James Griffin, *Well-being* (Oxford, 1986); Martha Nussbaum and Amartya Sen (eds), *The Quality of Life* (Oxford, 1993); Thomas Hurka, *Perfectionism* (New York, 1993); Derek Parfit, *Reasons and Persons* (Oxford, 1986); and Roger Crisp, "Well-Being," *The Stanford Encyclopedia of Philosophy* (Summer 2003).

I suspect many of us are tempted to call the Taliban Woman, Harriet the housewife, and the military recruit autonomous because we recognize that some value of importance is realized in their lives and is realized as a product of their own initiative. The Taliban Woman finds her informed desires satisfied. The housewife exemplifies a virtue of generosity to others that might appear on a list of characteristics suggestive of well-being. The military recruit is a paragon of self-discipline and physical health, and these two may be among the qualities sufficient for some level of well-being. In each of these cases we find persons who secure what comports with their respective subjective conceptions of well-being and what contributes to a life that might go well for persons.

But a person's conception of well-being may fail to include an interest in autonomy.[3] Persons may believe that life goes well for them when they engage in extremes of self-sacrificing or other-regarding behavior. Others may genuinely need to and wish to surrender an interest in their self-determination for the sake of achieving what is conducive to their well-being. For example, in an effort to elevate mental and physical well-being, a person might commit herself to the institutionalized care of others for medical purposes; she might even be committed against her will to such care for this reason. It may be in a person's interest that she be manipulated into a state of well-being, or that paternalistic measures be taken to advance her well-being, yet this compromises autonomy.

In addition, not every autonomous life is one rich in things that make life go well for persons. This is especially the case if well-being is judged by what the individual happens to value. The would-be surrendered woman does not live a life that goes well for her—or that she judges is good for her—yet she is self-directed. Still other persons who claim to value self-determination may adapt their ideal of well-being to their circumstances when they suffer reduced autonomy. Altered political conditions, a reversal of health or fortune, or even sour grapes may prompt a person to revise the aspirations and the values. Persons may decide that life goes well for them when they acquiesce to situations of diminished autonomy rather than suffer the frustration of challenging social, physical, political, economic, psychological, and environmental forces that have transformed their lives in ways that make self-government difficult.

On the other hand, well-being might involve elements of precisely the sort a social-relational account of autonomy offers. A perfectionist account of well-being or of its cognate, human flourishing, is built upon some idea of the proper and optimum way for persons to be. So construed, well-being consists in the realization of what are in fact features of a proper life, an optimal life, for humans—in the realization of capacities that define the sort of lives humans are by nature intended to develop. Such a theory might be called an objective account of well-being to distinguish it from subjectivist accounts that locate well-being in the mental states a person reports as conducive to happiness. Absent a solid argument that establishes

---

3   Joseph Raz discusses such cases in *The Morality of Freedom* (Oxford, 1986), pp. 390–91.

mental state accounts of well-being or even accounts of well-being premised on the satisfaction of informed desires the best explanations of what makes life good for humans, it is not obvious that Taliban Woman and the rest secure what makes life go well. Certainly it is not obvious that Taliban Woman and the others secure whatever lends itself to an idealized way for humans to be, given human nature. If the most defensible account of well-being is a perfectionist account, then one cannot claim without argument that life truly goes well for a person (in whichever sense "goes well for" is cashed out) if it is devoid of substantive autonomy.

As welcome as a successful defense of perfectionist well-being might be from the point of view of my favored account of autonomy, it would not show that well-being and personal autonomy are essential for one another. Whether or not it is essential for well-being that a person is autonomous depends on what are said to be the elemental features of well-being. I happen to think autonomy is essential for well-being where the latter is construed as living in a manner optimally suited for human beings and have suggested as much in the previous chapter. One reason, perhaps the primary reason, we value autonomy is that it is central to our nature. We will explore this idea in the section that follows. But perhaps substantive autonomy enhances the value of well-being even if it does not constitute well-being. That is, perhaps one's life goes better (or is best) only if components of well-being such as health, virtue, happiness, and informed preferences are autonomously developed and realized. If my autonomy is something with which I ought to be concerned, this may be because autonomy is part of what makes life go well for me *qua* human being; unless I am autonomous, life will not go as well for me as it could. If this is the case, we must do more than figure out what well-being consists in for us. We must also determine what variety of autonomy is vital for our well-being as humans and as individuals.

Self-realization

It is equally important to distinguish between the ideal of self-realization or personal fulfillment and autonomy. I am not quite sure what it means to realize oneself, but I am fairly certain that it does not stand double-duty for autonomy: To realize is to make real, to bring to fruition, to accomplish, or give life to. To realize oneself is to give life to one's identity—to one's defining traits of character. We can speak meaningfully of the person who realizes herself in this fashion at the same time we acknowledge the person's lack of autonomy.

A number of examples illustrate that a path to self-realization may involve a loss of autonomy. Think about the case of Judith Miller, until recently a journalist with the *New York Times*. Miller was imprisoned for eighty-five days (from July 6, 2005 until September 29, 2005) in the Alexandria Detention Center outside of Washington, D.C. for refusing to provide upon subpoena the name of a confidential source with whom she had held conversations.[4] The subpoena was issued by federal

---

4   Her release came after Miller obtained a waiver from the source that freed her from any pledge of confidentiality. As is now known, that source is I. Lewis Libby, chief of staff of

prosecutor Patrick J. Fitzgerald in the course of grand jury investigations into whether persons within the George W. Bush administration were involved in leaking the name of undercover Central Intelligence Agency [CIA] agent Valerie Plame Wilson to the media. Fitzgerald justified the subpoena by citing national security interests. Miller claims she chose imprisonment rather than compromise what she regards are inviolable journalistic principles. She stated: "I went to jail to preserve the time-honored principle that a journalist must respect a promise not to reveal the identity of a confidential source. I chose to take the consequences—85 days in prison—rather than violate that promise. The principle was more important to uphold than my personal freedom."[5]

One might object that the case I have highlighted involves someone who was globally autonomous at the time of embarking on an act of self-realization, or who has not suffered a grave and irreversible loss of global autonomy. Perhaps we do not regard Miller's case as one that illustrates a serious loss of global autonomy because she freely, albeit grudgingly, opted for the loss in the course of self-realization. Perhaps we do not see Miller's relatively short-lived imprisonment as a palpable loss of autonomy. But we know that a person can give up autonomy freely—that a person can be locally autonomous, if you will, in forsaking her global autonomy. We know, too, that global autonomy can be had by degrees, and that it can be manifest in a wider or narrower range of affairs of consequence to a person's ability to successfully manage her life. In a case such as Miller's, where the security of one's job (or, at least, an essential characteristic of the job—in this case, journalistic principle) is at stake, the loss of autonomy is serious and palpable, even if the loss is restricted to one area of the person's life.

Certainly cases of journalists who choose imprisonment on behalf of their ideals are, at least in the Western hemisphere, infrequent. More commonly we hear reports of persons whose opposition to some political action leads them to choose imprisonment in defense of principle, and to realize aspects of their chosen identity in the process. Recently, for example, in October 2005, we have been witness to the forcible removal and detention of some Jewish settlers who resisted evacuation from the Gaza strip in Israel, citing their natural and their Biblical birthright to occupy the land. Instances of conscientious objection to military service are a further case in point. Confronted with having to choose between fidelity to pacifistic principles and imprisonment (or the loss of some highly prized good), the conscientious objector chooses the latter.[6] If the conscientious objector identifies with his choice as the

---

Vice President Dick Cheney.

5   Miller, *New York Times*, September 30, 2005. Oddly, while several journalists have been subpoenaed in the case, only Miller was imprisoned, and she never actually wrote about the Plame case.

6   Sometimes the conscientious objector suffers both the threat of imprisonment and the loss of a cherished good. In 1967, Muhammad Ali (formerly Cassius Clay) was stripped of his World Heavyweight boxing title after being denied conscientious objector status and refusing induction into the Vietnam War. Ali was barred from boxing while his case was litigated; the

choice most consistent with his values, he might be said to have realized himself while bringing imprisonment upon himself.

Persons such as Miller, the defiant Jewish settlers, and the conscientious objector behave in ways that give expression to the things they care about. They behave in ways that makes vivid their identities and that brings to life their most heartfelt values. Each evaluates himself as living in a manner that befits his ideals. It may count with each that he is able to bear his own survey. Each might feel guilty of "selling out" were he to abandon this commitment. Selling out is a form of betrayal of oneself, of one's values. These persons realize themselves and in doing so they may exhibit self-government of a local or episodic variety. Self-realization, like well-being, may complement local autonomy. Each of these persons is "autonomously self-defining." Each lives an authentic life. These are clearly goods, things we admire and seek for ourselves and desire for those whom we care about. Such local exhibitions of autonomy may be evidence of self-realization. But self-realization, like human flourishing, is a conceptually different value from that of social autonomy and there is no direct transition from the one to the other.

Even if autonomy can contribute to self-realization, "[t]he autonomous person is the one who makes his own life, and he may choose the path of self-realization or reject it. Nor is autonomy a precondition of self-realization, for one may stumble into a life of self-realization or be manipulated into it or reach it in some other way which is inconsistent with autonomy."[7] Persons have reported experiencing an "awakening" or an epiphany of self-realization coming upon them quite unexpectedly, with no expenditure of effort on their part. If Miller and the others are self-governing—if they live as autonomous persons must—this is for reasons other than the fact that their actions bring them to a state of self-realization or personal fulfillment.

Why Social-Relational Autonomy is of Value

We have seen that personal autonomy is the condition of being self-directed within a social-relational context that allows the agent authority over choices and actions that are significant to the direction of her life. Given that autonomy is a phenomenon different from goods such as well-being and self-realization, what value does autonomy supply of its own accord? And why is social-relational autonomy of particular value? Why can't psychological authenticity be sufficient to explain autonomy's value? Rather than address each of these concerns independently, let us seek an answer to both by examining three types of value autonomy has—instrumental value, value in association with choice, and intrinsic value.

---

legal battle culminated in the unanimous U.S. Supreme Court decision in his favor, *Clay, aka Ali v. United States, 403 U.S. 698.*

   7   Raz, *The Morality of Freedom*, pp. 376–7.

The Instrumental Value of Social-Relational Autonomy

Let us begin by noting that social-relational autonomy, and not just procedural autonomy over choices and preferences, is valued as a means to realizing the ideal of a democratic society. This is admittedly a value of narrow scope as it serves only one type of society. But since three in five states in the world have democratically elected governments, the ideal is widely shared. Focusing on autonomy's instrumental value in this context will provide a useful point of departure.

Social-relational autonomy brings us closer to assuring the goals of democratic citizenship than does autonomy as authenticity of choice and preference for the following reason. A democracy is, roughly, a sociopolitical alliance of agents who, through representation or direct participation, engage in the task of political governance. It is through the judgment and activity of self-reliant, self-directed persons that the political principles and policies of a liberal constitutional democracy are generated and garner legitimacy. Indeed, there is reason to count autonomy as paramount among the "civic virtues" essential for a successful democracy. Following Will Kymlicka, we may hold that

> [Among] those virtues which are distinctive to modern pluralistic liberal democratic societies [are] the ability and willingness to question political authority, and to engage in public discourse about matters of public policy. These are perhaps the most distinctive aspects of citizenship in a liberal democracy, since they are precisely what distinguish "citizens" within a democracy from the "subjects" of an authoritarian regime.[8]

A person whose reasons for choice and action have been appropriated by others or have been compromised by other persons or natural circumstance, whether or not this is the result of individual self-expression and freely chosen relations, lacks certain essential qualities of democratic citizenship. One quality is the ability to converse with others about matters of public policy that affect their lives. Conversation does not consist merely in presenting one's position. Rather, it involves all parties to the discussion have a standing that empowers them to be heard, to raise questions, and to persuade one another, and it involves recognition by those party to the discussion that each has this standing. Public conversation is genuinely dialogical and is owned by all those who are partners to the conversation. Discourse (especially public, political discourse) permitted by courtesy or granted as an act of munificence by one party is not owned equally by the discussants. It is discourse wherein one or more persons lack the authority to initiate conversation and the other has complete authority to terminate it. This is discourse that signals an absence of autonomy on the

---

8   Kymlicka, *Contemporary Political Philosophy: An Introduction,* 2nd edition (Oxford, 2002), p. 289. Citing Amy Gutmann, Kymlicka continues: "children at school 'must learn not just to behave in accordance with authority but to think critically about authority if they are to live up to the democratic ideal of sharing political sovereignty as citizens.' People who 'are ruled only by habit and authority ... are incapable of constituting a society of sovereign citizens.'" See Amy Gutmann, *Democratic Education* (Princeton, 1987), p. 51.

part of some of the discussants. Autonomy is absent for the reason that the possibility of having one's reasons for choice and action accorded serious consideration—the possibility of having the power to change or to contest public policy by means of the discussion—has been compromised by other persons. Autonomy is absent and the possibility of genuine exchange regarding matters of public policy is defeated "since the speaker and audience are no longer distinct."[9] The conversation, such as it is, follows the lead of one voice alone.

A person who is not autonomous within social roles and arrangements is less than fully capable of full democratic participation for the further reason that she cannot be an active participant in an important range of civic experiences. The person who lacks autonomy may display a veneer of democratic involvement. She may, if permitted, vote, seek public office, or have legal action taken against her. Because she does not manage her own life-choices, however, she cannot fully assume the responsibility of helping to create a government representative of her interests as the democratic ideal requires. For this person, the democratic ideal is largely illusory.

While such a person may have liberty she lacks autonomy. Liberty is, of course, an important value in its own right. It may be significant, for example, that nonautonomous persons be at liberty to satisfy their desires—even desires that were not formed autonomously.[10] Perhaps it is important that a person is "at liberty" to avail himself of an education, of medical care, and of political participation even if she is not at liberty to do so by her own leave. The interface between liberty in both its negative and positive guises and autonomy bears discussion and we will address some of the relevant concerns in the next chapter. It is enough to note at this juncture that liberty is not autonomy, and that the liberty of persons so essential to democratic society is arguably of less value, and less service, if autonomy is absent.

More generally—and more controversially—social-relational autonomy is essential if any society, democratic or otherwise, is to survive. It is especially difficult to keep a political regime in place once it is known that the principles associated with that regime are disrespectful of human rights, including a right to manage one's life, or are indefensibly inegalitarian in the rights they will uphold. Consider, for example, a society in which a despotic regime is sovereign. Examples might be communist North Korea, Soviet Russia, theocratic Iran, and any number of countries in sub-Saharan Africa. (A recent victory for despotism occurred on 3 August 2005 when a military coup d'etat overthrew the democratically elected regime of President Maaouya Ould Taya in Mauritania.) In these societies safeguarding the despotic regime appears to call for an absence of substantive autonomy on the part of the citizenry, though the regime is consistent with procedural autonomy. We find that in these contexts, autonomy is not broadly valued in practice; it may be granted as

9 Onora O'Neill, "The Public Use of Reason," reprinted in *Constructions of Reason: Explorations of Kant's Practical Philosophy* (New York, 1989), p. 46. On the meaning of and centrality of discursive freedom in democratic republics see Philip Pettit, *A Theory of Freedom: From the Psychology to the Politics of Agency* (New York, 2001).

10 I thank Paul Benson for pressing this point.

a gift to a favored few while the majority of the populace consists of persons who, worthy or not, capable or otherwise, are accorded a status similar to that of children at varying levels of maturity. Those few who are autonomous undertake a parental role, with benevolence or severity, of supervising the activities and lives of others.

A political regime of this character can be sustained only with difficulty, even assuming that the members of the populace are able to and willing to exercise self-restraint and configure their lives to the arrangements determined by the authoritarian regime. There will be a minimum of persons who are qualified to assume the administrative burdens of such a society. At a minimum, the leaders of the society need the power and authority to stand up to challenges from other persons and nations that might seek to dominate them; they need the power and authority to plan seriously for the future, and the power and authority to seek out and implement innovative solutions to the problems the society encounters. These are emblematic of the power and authority associated with personal autonomy and all are essential for leadership.

Not every society in which personal autonomy is devalued is despotic or doomed to failure, of course. Devotion to a collective good, for example, need not yield a collapse of society, even one dedicated to democratic principle. The leaders of the society must embody some of the qualities for personal autonomy even if they are themselves permitted to use these skills only on behalf of national rather than personal self-determination. But all societies, including those that do not prize individuality must allow for a modicum of robust social autonomy for its members if they are to thrive. In Anabaptist religious communities what is good for the individual is a function of what is good for the collective. Sustaining the viability of these collectives requires tremendous commitment on the part of all the adult members to a system of governance that makes the collective unit the focus of concern. The commitment to community requires that persons accept roles that may strike us as unduly confining and hierarchical. But at the same time, the viability of the collective depends upon the ability of these same persons to assume an active, participatory role in social management. Compliance with communal goals is not equated with docility or with servility. By contrast, members of Talibanic societies or women in societies governed by strict interpretation of *Sharia* are expected to assume a more docile, biddable role though they may demonstrate similar levels of commitment and though the contributions (to family, for example) they are called upon to make may be highly valued.

Social-Relational Autonomy and the Significance of Choice

In the fictional utopian society of *Walden*,[11] "although one confronts numerous and fecund options, one totally lacks [the] capacity to exercise them autonomously. One has choices to make, but consistently makes them heteronomously."[12] The same is

---

11 B.F. Skinner, *Walden Two* (New York, 1962).

12 Lawrence Haworth, *Autonomy: An Essay in Philosophical Psychology and Ethics* (New Haven, 1986), p. 143.

true of life for the Taliban Woman, the military recruit, and similarly situated folk. Each makes choices, but these are of little practical import because their choices have no force. In these cases, we might say that due to the absence of social-relational autonomy choice has lost its significance. Autonomy anchors the significance of choice for the reason that having and making a choice symbolizes to oneself and to the world one's competence to act for oneself. Social-relational autonomy promises that outcomes can depend on, and not just conform to, one's choice. On this point T.M. Scanlon states:

> The features of oneself which one may desire to demonstrate or see realized in action are highly varied. They may include the value one attaches to various aims and outcomes, one's knowledge, awareness, or memory, or one's imagination and skill ... I want to choose the furniture for my own apartment, pick out the pictures for the walls, and even write my own lectures despite the fact that these things might be done better by a decorator, art expert, or talented graduate student. For better or worse, I want these things to be produced by and reflect my own taste, imagination, and powers of discrimination and analysis. I feel the same way, even more strongly, about important decisions affecting my life in larger terms: what career to follow, where to work, how to live.[13]

The point is not merely that social autonomy is instrumentally valuable because persons confront choices that autonomy helps them realize; autonomy is not of value simply as a means to advancing states of the chooser's own future enjoyment as opposed to enjoyments selected for her. If truth be told, sometimes autonomy is regarded as undesirable and of dubious value for the very reason that it presents a person with the burden of having to make a choice. (Nor is choice always conducive to autonomy. Autonomy might depend on limitations upon choice set by what Frankfurt describes as volitional necessity. Indeed, considerations of what is "unthinkable" may serve to make autonomous agency possible.[14])

The point is that unless persons are socially self-governing the choices they confront will not have the significance of genuine choices at all. For a choice to be of demonstrative or symbolic value—that is, for a choice to be an act wherein one demonstrates one competence and singularity to the world—the act of choosing must be something over which a person can exercise control. Choice loses its significance—it ceases to represent a person's competence and singularity and power—when it is maintained by the leave of another who happens to favor the person, or when it is made possible only because the person successfully ingratiates herself to those who wield power over her, or because good fortune smiles upon the

13 T.M. Scanlon, Jr., *The Significance of Choice*, 2nd lecture, "The Value of Choice," 1986, pp. 179–80.

14 Frankfurt does not state this point as strongly as I do and he may well quarrel with it. But the evidence is that he shares this view. See "On the Necessity of Ideals," in *Necessity, Volition, and Love* (Cambridge UK, 1999). Most recently, Frankfurt reiterates the point in *The Reasons of Love* (Princeton, 2004), p. 20; p. 50; pp. 64–6.

person. But we think it is important that choices should be significant in this way.[15] For this reason, social autonomy is valuable derivatively as an expression of the primary value of choice.

Choice and autonomy remain different values. In part, "the reasons people have for wanting outcomes to be (or sometimes not to be) dependent on their choices has to do with the significance that choice itself has for them, not merely with its efficacy in promoting outcomes which are desired on other grounds."[16] So not only will individuals value different states of affair, but individuals will assign varying degrees of instrumental and symbolic value to the same choices. This is consistent with the idea that there is more to the varying values of choice than whatever value is assigned to the having of choice by the individual. It is also consistent with the idea that one can realize some of the value of choice, or one of the values of choice, absent autonomy, even if part of what makes a choice desirable or admirable is the autonomy of the chooser. All of this is consistent with the point I am making here, a point that has to do with the value of autonomy. This point is that part of what makes autonomy valuable is that it lends significance to choice.

The Intrinsic Value of Social-Relational Autonomy

Autonomy is desirable insofar as it enriches choice and makes matters of public policy viable. But if choice were of less importance to us, or if societies could thrive just as well without a populous of self-determined actors, would autonomy be of less importance? Autonomy might be of less value to us if we failed to value it. But this does not show that autonomy would be of less value *for* us. The value we assign autonomy does not establish that the value of autonomy is agent-relative. There is ample reason to believe autonomy—and social-relational autonomy in particular—is a good quite independent of the value a person happens to assign it. And there is reason to believe the kind of value social-relational autonomy has is intrinsic—that is, reason to believe autonomy is important quite independent of the effect its presence or absence happens to have upon a person's life. The most general reason to believe this is that a life in which autonomy is absent is one in which the possibility of self-initiated practical change is impossible. But things do change in our lives, and if we are to be self-directing in these lives we must have, in addition to the psychological ability to rethink our choices, the opportunity to remake our choices and the options to pursue our lives accordingly. When a diminution of the range of these abilities occurs, autonomy is compromised and change is foreclosed.

More to the point, we do regard autonomy as indispensable for full moral standing and engagement. We need only reflect on the question of how we should

---

15 This assumes, of course, that choice is of value itself, a point of controversy. Gerald Dworkin pursues this point in "Is More Choice Better Than Less?" reprinted in *The Theory and Practice of Autonomy*, pp. 62–81.

16 Scanlon, *The Significance of Choice*, pp. 180–81.

raise our children to see this point.[17] What troubles us about parents who do not bother to encourage the development of autonomy in their children, even where their failure has no actual effect on the maturing child's autonomy, is just what troubles us about parents who expect autonomy of their children prematurely and without sufficient guidance, even where the children happily, but fortuitously, develop into stable, self-governing beings. In both cases the parent exhibits a lack of respect for a fundamental human good, a precondition for being fully functional.

That we regard autonomy as having intrinsic value and that we view it as central to full moral standing is evident in so many of the mundane aspects of life that perhaps only a philosopher would question the claim. In legal contexts, it is necessary that parties to a binding contract be self-governing. This is not because we value contracts and want them to be sustained but because we value autonomy and do not credit a person with having obligated herself unless she has done so in a self-managed way. In health care, the concept of informed consent garners legitimacy because of the intrinsic value of autonomy. Informed consent is critical not because we value consent for its own sake but because we regard patients as discrete entities in possession of sovereign control of their person. For this reason, consent to procedures that invade that sovereign space must be autonomously given, even when consent taxes the emotional well-being of the patient. In these contexts, of course, autonomy is also of instrumental importance. We care about ensuring the autonomy of the pertinent parties in order to realize other desired goods such as patient well-being, trustworthy business transactions, and (less nobly) indemnity against legal action.[18]

A lack of autonomy results in a truncated person, even if it produces happy people. One may experience contentment as a member of a despotic, endangered society. Absent autonomy, the intensity of pleasure and preference satisfaction may even increase—think of the members of *Walden* who have every one of their desires met, or of a person attached to Robert Nozick's "experience machine."[19] But these people know a different and, I would contend, inferior variety of satisfaction than the contentment that is known by one who is a subject and not just an object, an agent and not a patient.[20] A life absent self-governance is the life of one who is like an object made happy through the activities of others. It is a life that reflects the competences of others, a life marked by projects that bear the imprint of other persons rather than one's self. It is controversial that we should regard such life-choices and the social roles these mandate as valuable. Healthy persons do not, as a rule, wish simply to reside in the world or be moved through it. Whether our actions are for good or for

---

17 I thank Don Hubin for planting this idea in my mind.

18 For an argument to the effect that autonomy is only of instrumental value see James Stacey Taylor, "Autonomy and Informed Consent: A Much Misunderstood Relationship," *Journal of Value Inquiry*, 38/3 (September 2004): 383–91.

19 Robert Nozick, *Anarchy, State, and Utopia* (New York, 1974), pp. 42–5.

20 Haworth concurs, stating that "Pleasure and preference satisfaction lose value in proportion as the pleased or satisfied individual lacks autonomy." Haworth, *Autonomy: An Essay in Philosophical Psychology and Ethics*, p. 183.

evil, we care that these actions are ours and that in executing them we do not simply borrow from others but realize our autonomy.

When Should a Person Enjoy Autonomy?

We have yet to address the circumstances under which the right to autonomy ought to be upheld and a self-determined life ought to be protected for capable and deserving persons. In the previous chapter, paternalistic interferences in order to preserve the future possibility of autonomy where this was at risk were offered as one exception to the injunction against interferences to this right. Self-imposed threats to one's dispositional or future autonomy present one set of less than normal circumstances in which paternalistic intervention may be warranted. Another instance of less than normal circumstances in which encroachments of autonomy may be justified obtains when capable persons fail to show consideration for the harm principle and engage in activity that jeopardizes the self-determination of others.

But what are the legitimate restrictions upon autonomy where the circumstances are less than normal owing to something other than the self-regarding autonomy-defeating behavior of a perfectly deserving agent, or when they are due to phenomena apart from other-directed harm? In certain less than normal political circumstances, threats to the autonomy of deserving individuals who are not in need of paternalistic support can be great. In such circumstances, protecting autonomy may go hand in hand with protecting persons from the infliction of loss, falsehood, duplicity, and threats to civil liberties and constitutionally mandated rights. Among a shameful abundance of cases in point from the history of the United States is what occurred sixty years ago in the aftermath of Pearl Harbor. At that time, native born Japanese-American citizens who had harmed no one and who presented no threat to their own dispositional autonomy were dispossessed of their autonomy as much as they were of their property. This occurred with the overwhelming approval of the United States populace. Such restrictions were, in hindsight, illegitimate because unnecessary, whatever was believed to be the threat to national security from the Japanese-American population at the time.

More recently, residents of the United States have confronted the state of affairs that represents the new normalcy, post-September 11, 2001. Circumstances since that date no longer resemble what we once regarded as normal. For example, a rekindled patriotism of a particularly narrow-minded variety has tempered the willingness of many to openly criticize, or even question, the political and military policies of the United States. Restrictions that fetter individual autonomy have become commonplace and enjoy increasing public approval.[21] There is heightened support for surveillance

---

21 The Associated Press reported (June 12, 2002) that "four in five Americans would give up some freedoms to gain security .... one-third favor making it easier for authorities to access private e-mail and phone conversations [and] more than 70 percent favor requiring U.S. citizens to carry identification cards with fingerprints." Judith Wagner DeCew notes that "in the wake of the terrorist attacks on September 11, 2001, it is likely that the literature on

cameras on select street corners of select urban neighborhoods and select points among our borders with Canada to the north and even more so with Mexico to the south. Personal searches at public transport facilities have increased as has a call for profiling passengers of certain ancestry or country of origin. Investigations of personal computer use and electronic communication have intensified. Persons have been detained, incommunicado, for unspecified crimes. The USA Patriot Act (hereafter, the Act) passed by Congress in 2001 and reaffirmed, at least temporarily, in December 2005 provides the Central Intelligence Agency (and organizations of law enforcement in the main) with access to Justice Department records, including secret testimony developed in grand jury investigations.[22] In the Act, former U.S. Attorney General John Ashcroft issued executive directives allowing the Federal Bureau of Investigation [FBI] to eavesdrop on conversations between lawyers and their imprisoned clients in certain cases and gave the FBI greater freedom to use wiretaps and to investigate the usage of media by private citizens, even when they are not suspected of committing a crime.

Most recently, President George W. Bush, claiming congressional authorization of the Executive for use of military force under a resolution passed in the aftermath of 9/11 as well as constitutional authority as commander in chief, has acknowledged secretly instructing the National Security Agency [NSA], which is typically prohibited from intercepting domestic communications, to conduct domestic spying on citizens of the United States and on foreign nationals. The surveillance has taken the form of electronic eavesdropping and includes monitoring e-mail, telephone calls and further forms of communication. Bush ordered the program without first obtaining warrants under the system instituted by current law, in violation of the 1978 Foreign Intelligence Surveillance Act [FISA] that governs domestic covert surveillance. FISA bars domestic covert surveillance not sanctioned by statute but allows the president to seek undisclosed emergency court-sanctioned warrants for domestic surveillance—something Bush did not do. Bush defended his action as "fully consistent with my constitutional responsibilities and authorities," and vowed to continue the highly classified program because it was "a vital tool in our war against the terrorists."[23] The admission was followed by heated defense of the activity from

---

privacy will increasingly focus on how to balance privacy concerns with the need for public safety in an age of terrorism." De Cew, "Privacy," *The Stanford Encyclopedia of Philosophy* (Summer 2002), Edward N. Zalta (ed.).

22 "Uniting and Strengthening America by Providing Appropriate Tools Required to Intercept and Obstruct Terrorism" Act of 2001 (USA PATRIOT ACT) 107 P.L. 56. The relevant portions of the act are Sec. 213, Authority for delaying notice of the execution of a warrant; Sec. 214, Pen register and trap and trace authority under the Foreign Intelligence Surveillance Act (FISA); Sec. 215, Access to records and other items under FISA; Sec. 216, Modification of authorities relating to use of pen registers and trap and trace devices; Sec. 218, Foreign intelligence information; Sec. 412, Mandatory detention of suspected terrorists; Habeas Corpus; Judicial Review; and Sec. 802, Definition of domestic terrorism.

23 From articles by Dan Eggen, *Washington Post*, Friday, December 16, 2005, and David E. Sanger, *New York Times*, December 18, 2005. An attempt to justify the NSA activities came

Bush administration officials such as Vice President Dick Cheney and produced a maelstrom of subsequent revelations that have addressed the questionable legality of the program, the scope of its targets, its necessity for preventing terrorist activity and, perhaps most significantly for our purpose here, the threat to civil liberty it presents.

Certainly many of these measures amount to incursions of privacy. Privacy is characterized by "the special interest we have in being free from certain kinds of intrusion."[24] In 1890, Samuel Warren and Louis Brandeis defended the existence within law of a right to privacy as "part of a more general right to the immunity of the person the right to one's [inviolate] personality" or "the right to be left alone."[25] Warren and Brandeis argued that informational privacy, understood as the ability of an individual to wield control over the timing, the manner, and the scope in which undocumented personal facts about himself could be disseminated, enjoyed special protection under the Fourth Amendment of the United States Constitution.[26] In 1965, a right to privacy anchored in the Fourteenth Amendment of the Constitution was acknowledged explicitly by the U.S. Supreme Court in *Griswold v. Connecticut*.[27] In *Griswold*, the concept of privacy is broadened to encompass safeguards to the interest individuals are assumed to have in their autonomy with respect to significant personal decisions concerning lifestyle.

Whether privacy is a notion that can be given a coherent and distinctive formulation is a matter of disagreement, an examination of which is beyond the scope of this discussion. Judith Jarvis Thomson denies the existence of a unique right to privacy, charging that any interest protected as private can be justified and defended by other interests or rights such as rights to property and bodily security.[28] So understood, privacy is a "cluster concept" designating a value that is defined in terms of an arrangement of interests. Judith Wagner De Cew has noted that "There is a further

---

in a classified Justice Department legal opinion authored by John C. Yoo, a former deputy in the Office of Legal Counsel who maintained that congressional approval of the war on al Qaeda furnished expansive powers to the president.

24 James Rachels, "Why Privacy is Important," *Philosophy and Public Affairs* 4 (Summer 1975): 323.

25 Samuel Warren and Louis Brandeis, "The Right to Privacy," *Harvard Law Review* 4 (1890): p. 207; p. 198. Alan Westin contends that concern for individual privacy dates back to ancient democratic Athens. See John Schwartz, "What Are You Lookin' At?," *New York Times*, Week in Review, Sunday January 1, 2006, p. 4.

26 "Common law secures to each individual the right of determining, ordinarily, to what extent his thoughts, sentiments, and emotions shall be communicated to others." Warren and Brandeis, "The Right to Privacy:" 198.

27 *Griswold v. Connecticut* (381 U.S. 479), Douglas offering the majority opinion. The Supreme Court now claims that there are two different dimensions to privacy: control over information about oneself and control over one's ability to make certain important types of decisions. See *Whalen v. Roe*, 429 U.S. 589 (1977).

28 Judith Jarvis Thomson, "The Right to Privacy," *Philosophy and Public Affairs* 4 (Summer 1975): 295–314.

issue that has generated disagreement, even among those theorists who believe privacy is a coherent concept and a valuable and significant phenomenon worth defending. The question is whether or not the constitutional right to privacy, and the constitutional privacy cases described involving personal decisions about lifestyle and family including birth control, interracial marriage, viewing pornography at home, abortion, and so on, delineate a genuine category of privacy issues, or merely raise questions about liberty of some sort."[29]

Privacy remains one of the principal interests of personal autonomy, whether or not these controversies can be settled. In the first place, personal autonomy is typically associated with the status of the individual in her private as opposed to public person.[30] I think this association is misguided, of course—as a social phenomenon, constituted and made possible by social circumstances, autonomy is as much a characteristic of the individual in her public capacity as in her private. Moreover, an overly zealous attempt to delineate the private from the public spheres may leave a person adrift socially, thereby hindering the possibility of autonomy. Nonetheless, the distinction between a realm in which free persons are held to possess inviolate control over themselves and their property—a realm of uncontested self-governance—and the realm of the *polis*, the ambit of persons in their public capacity as political participants subject to public authority, has a lengthy history even where the distinction has been criticized. For example, Aristotle criticizes the ideal city-state advanced by Plato in the *Republic* on the grounds that Plato is inattentive to the happiness of individuals in their capacity as private persons.[31] Aristotle also takes issue with Plato's apparent refusal in *Statesman* to take seriously the good of personal autonomy for engaged citizenship.[32] De Cew presses the connection between autonomy and privacy on the basis of the two spheres, noting that

> The public/private distinction is also sometimes taken to refer to the appropriate realm of governmental authority as opposed to the realm reserved for self-regulation, along the lines described by John Stuart Mill in his essay *On Liberty*. Furthermore, the distinction arises again in Locke's discussion of property in his *Second Treatise on Government*. In the state of nature all the world's bounty is held in common and is in that sense public. But

---

29 DeCew, "Privacy." For further discussion see Paul, J., Miller, F., and Paul, E. (eds), *The Right of Privacy* (Cambridge, UK, 2000) and Ruth Gavison, "Privacy and the Limits of Law," *Yale Law Journal* 89 (1980): 421–71.

30 The distinction between the realms of the public and the private, and sub-distinctions of the familial and the political, is not uncontroversial nor is universally viewed as desirable. Certain feminist and communitarian political theories contest the distinction on the grounds that it is empirically flawed and normatively suspect. See Michael Sandel, *Liberalism and the Limits of Justice* (Cambridge, 1982); Carole Pateman, "Feminist Critiques of the Public/Private Dichotomy" in Anne Phillips (ed.), *Feminism and Equality* (Oxford, 1987), pp. 103–26; and Susan Moller Okin, *Justice, Gender, and the Family* (New York, 1989).

31 Aristotle, *Politics* II, 1–6, *The Basic Works of Aristotle*, Richard McKeon (ed.) (New York, 1941).

32 Aristotle, *Politics*; Plato, *Statesman* 291d–303b, trans. J.B. Skemp (1952), in Edith Hamilton and Huntington Cairns (eds), *Plato: The Collected Dialogues* (Princeton: 1961).

one possesses oneself and one's own body, and one can also acquire property by mixing one's labor with it, and in these cases it is one's private property.[33]

A second reason why privacy rights are the interest of personal autonomy is that privacy protections generally are essential for autonomy. Violations of autonomy are not always or principally privacy violations, but incursions to privacy siphon a person's ability to live autonomously.[34] James Rachels notes that

> [T]he value of privacy [is] based on the idea that there is a close connection between our ability to control who has access to us and to information about us, and our ability to create and maintain different sorts of social relationships with different people ... Privacy is necessary if we are to maintain the variety of social relationships with other people that we want to have, and that is why it is important to us.[35]

We want it to be up to us what sort of relationships we have with others, but this depends on having control over the right to be left alone. To the extent that information about a person's life—his familial circumstances, his religious practices, his medical history, his sexual preferences, his educational pursuits, his financial transactions, public media use, and so forth—is distributed, made public without the person's knowledge and consent, the person has less control over his life, whether or not he wishes to utilize this control or has the need to do so. Someone else has gained that control, and has the power to use it if she chooses. Privacy is power conferring: it grants individuals the power to define themselves, without fear of scrutiny and shame, as well as the power to determine the nature and the parameters of their relations with others. Both powers are essential if a person is to be self-governing with respect to a variety of social relations.

Privacy in law offers a benchmark for what count as legitimate restrictions upon autonomy. Many of the post-September 11 measures offend privacy by undermining the control persons have over access to and dissemination of information about themselves, and by subjecting intimate aspects of their lives to undisclosed scrutiny. Given the haste with which the USA Patriot Act was passed and the lack of scrutiny paid to the details of its 217 pages, few of the measures it implements for law enforcement are ones private citizens (and, to some extent, elected officials) have had an opportunity to endorse.[36] They are, moreover, measures that encroach

---

33 De Cew, "Privacy."

34 Not everyone agrees that incursions to privacy reduce an individual's ability to live autonomously. James Stacey Taylor argues to the contrary in "Autonomy and Privacy: A Reappraisal," *Southern Journal of Philosophy*, XL (2002): 587–604.

35 James Rachels, "Why Privacy is Important": 326.

36 The Electronic Privacy Information Center writes that "Legislative proposals in response to the terrorist attacks of September 11, 2001 were introduced less than a week after the attacks. President Bush signed the final bill, the USA PATRIOT Act, into law on October 26, 2001. Though the Act made significant amendments to over 15 important statutes, it was introduced with great haste and passed with little debate, and without a House, Senate, or conference report. As a result, it lacks background legislative history that often retrospectively

upon previously protected spheres of activity. The result is that portions of the Act unambiguously impede a person's ability to act without potential scrutiny, embarrassment, or political and personal liability. The measures I have noted, both overt and covert, yield, at a minimum, a decline in the level of civil liberty most of us cherish and regard as crucial to unimpaired self-governance. (Federal detainment for weeks, months, and even years on end particularly without charges and benefit of legal counsel unambiguously assails the detainee's self-government.)

Social security may, of course, surpass autonomy in value and may justify constraints on the powers and freedoms necessary for autonomy. Autonomy is not the sole and may not be the overarching good. Given the prima facie value of autonomy, however, a case remains to be made that measures such as those implemented post-September 11 are justified in the best interests of the populace. It remains to be seen whether encroachments of autonomy are warranted. Do we currently confront a situation akin to that described by Thomas Hill, Jr.? Hill remarks that:

> If ... the only way to persuade someone to make a decision that will prevent a riot or a series of murders were to make an otherwise impermissible threat or a non-rational appeal to his weaknesses, then surely most would grant that such interference would be justified. Though important, autonomy need not be considered an absolute right.[37]

It is important to emphasize that what is at stake are not just encroachments of personal freedoms or liberties, though certainly these goods are at risk. Autonomy or self-governance is threatened. Autonomy is threatened not because (or not principally because) a person's sphere of activity is lessened, just as autonomy is not preserved if a person cheerfully consents to the loss of certain liberties or to a narrowed sphere of activity. Autonomy is eroded because what are lost are phenomena that guarantee the agent authority over her will, over her person, and over the social circumstances that have a potentially coercive influence upon her personal affairs. In the process,

---

provides necessary statutory interpretation. When the legislative proposals were introduced by the Bush administration in the aftermath of September 11, Attorney General John Ashcroft gave Congress one week in which to pass the bill—without changes. Vermont Democrat Patrick Leahy, chairman of the Senate Judiciary Committee, managed to convince the Justice Department to agree to some changes, and members of the House began to make significant improvements. However, the Attorney General warned that further terrorist acts were imminent, and that Congress could be to blame for such attacks if it failed to pass the bill immediately. Extensive and hurried negotiation in the Senate resulted in a bipartisan bill, stripped of many of the concessions won by Sen. Leahy. Senator Thomas Daschle, the majority leader, sought unanimous consent to pass the proposal without debate or amendment; Senator Russ Feingold was the only member to object. Minor changes were made in the House, which passed the bill 357 to 66. The Senate and House versions were quickly reconciled, and the Act was signed into law on October 26, 2001." http://www.epic.org/privacy/terrorism/usapatriot/. Last Updated: November 1, 2004. EPIC is a public interest research organization in Washington, D.C. It was founded in 1994 to focus public attention on emerging civil liberties issues and to protect privacy, First Amendment, and constitutional ideals.

37 Thomas Hill, "Self-Respect Reconsidered," in *Autonomy and Self-Respect*, p. 259.

the foundation for a fundamental status associated with autonomy—the status of being a bearer of protected legal and moral rights, as well as recognition by others as being entitled to a level of respectful treatment as a result—is pared away. To be autonomous is to enjoy not just the ability and the right to decide or to act in certain ways, but the authority to manage the conditions, including the informational conditions, vital to this status.

Summary

Autonomy is a different good from desired states such as well-being and personal accomplishment and is of different value from these goods. Autonomy is valued for instrumental reasons as well as intrinsic reasons. Remanding oneself to the custody of others or surrendering oneself to the will of another person or to a system of belief are actions incompatible with other more general and fundamental activities to which capable and deserving persons are prima facie entitled, *viz.*, making up their minds about how to live their lives. Such actions are objectionable for a number of reasons. They are objectionable because they undermine the significance of a person's opinions and choices. They are objectionable because they tend to threaten the viability of a state or government. Above all, they are objectionable because they erode an individual's status as a distinct, respected variety of person or as a self.

Autonomy may be overridden where concerns of protection to individual interests, desert, or security weigh in. Perhaps less pressing goods, such as the pleasure great numbers of persons would experience given the sacrifice of a modicum of autonomy, suffice to override the supremacy of self-governance. A case presented by Thomas Hurka is pertinent on this point. Suppose that Mozart's initial forays into music were forced—he was only three years old, after all—and so some measure of his potential autonomy was circumvented. Perhaps (to vary Hurka's case) Mozart was a bit older, old enough to demonstrate a preference for carpentry over musical pursuits. Now consider what the world would have lacked in value had Mozart not been pressured at a tender age away from his desired pursuits. If the fruit of Mozart's creative musical genius surpasses in hedonic value the value of the potential autonomy he was made to sacrifice as a child—after all, thousands, maybe millions of people have, over the centuries, derived pleasure from and have learned from his brilliance—then had Mozart been allowed to delve into carpentry to the neglect of musical training something of great importance to generations of music lovers would have been lost. Hurka contends that "Even if autonomy has some value, it cannot have so much as to outweigh all Mozart's music."[38]

I do not think the matter is so simple. This example is instructive for the following reasons. First, we must keep in mind that while the amount of hedonic value or "pleasure-value" Mozart's autonomy had for him might be negligible when measured against the amount of pleasure or artistic edification the deprivation of

---

38 Thomas Hurka. *Perfectionism*, p. 149.

his autonomy brought to generations, pleasure is not the sole value—it is certainly not the sole value of autonomy. Second, and more importantly, autonomy is not just one value among others. When we weigh autonomy we are weighing a good that occupies a central and an irreplaceable position in human life and in the view humans have of themselves. Its value to its bearer cannot be easily balanced.

Chapter 7

What Kind of Freedom Does Autonomy Require?

Introduction

The condition of control stipulates that autonomous persons have the power to determine how they shall live. What kind of freedom does this call for? Does autonomy demand freedom to do otherwise, an issue of concern to philosophers who regard autonomous agency as central to responsible agency? If the presence of alternate possibilities is crucial to the living of an autonomous life, is autonomy possible if causal determinism is true? This chapter will begin by addressing the question of whether personal autonomy is a phenomenon that depends upon the resolution of our metaphysical status relative to the truth or falsity of determinism. Next, we will investigate the differences between autonomy and liberties of a negative and a positive variety. We will also take up the question of whether autonomy is guaranteed by the satisfaction of positive and negative liberty. In the third section we will look at the concept of self-creation. If autonomy requires the freedom to create oneself, what does this involve?

Causal Determinism and Autonomy

Causal determinism is the thesis that every state of the universe, including intentional expressions of will in action and choice, is causally necessitated by some prior state(s) of the world together with the laws of nature. It is the view that, given the past together with the laws of nature, there is at any instant exactly one possible future. If at any instant there is more than one possible future, then indeterminism is true.

Let us start with the assumption that there are autonomous agents. From this fact, and from the fact that autonomous agents are in control of an important subset of their decisions and actions, is it possible to infer anything about the truth or falsity of causal determinism? On the one hand we know that autonomous persons are, if nothing else, agents, and as such must be empowered to deliberate about action and to author action. It is plausible that one who is so empowered must be free to vary the values that guide her deliberations and free to alter her life-activities if she so chooses. It appears, then, that alternative possibilities are essential for autonomy and that the varieties of freedom relevant to autonomy are freedom of the will and freedom of action. Autonomous agents are in control of what they decide and what they do. On the other hand, autonomous action is, as a rule, intentional, and intentional action is caused in some way. The task, then, is to explain how a model of intentional action can be explained in terms of the causal powers of the agent—how it can, that is, accommodate the freedom autonomous action requires—and what this implies for the thesis of causal determinism.

Narrowly construed, freedom of will can be characterized as the power a person experiences in deciding, intending, attempting, and choosing—states that serve as impetus to action. Narrowly construed, freedom of action is the power to execute one's will. An individual in possession of these powers of will and of action is, at least, free from internally or externally induced physical and psychological restraint. Narrowly construed, both freedom of will and of action are central to autonomy. The concept of autonomy has little force if a person is said to be self-governing and self-controlling at the same time she is incapable of initiating and carrying out action.

So described, neither freedom of will nor freedom of action rests on alternative possibilities. The residents of B.F. Skinner's fictional utopia *Walden Two* have the power to act and to will. In fact, unlike most of us, the objects of their will are rarely if ever unrealized. They are always successful in executing their will. But this just is the case because they lack alternative-possibility control—regulative control—over the content of their wills and over the configuration of social arrangements that make the realization of their wills possible. Whatever ends they have are set for them, and their critical abilities have been obliterated. To borrow from Mele, we may say that the citizens of *Walden* are "informationally cut off" from conducting themselves autonomously.[1] They are epistemically cut off from information that would make the independent formation of ends possible. Additionally, success in achieving their ends is guaranteed but only because of the machinations of others. In a nutshell, they lack governance over their own lives.

But perhaps a broader configuration of these freedoms is also the concern of autonomy. More broadly, both freedom of will and freedom of action are explicated in terms of a power to will or to act given the presence of two or more equally realizable alternatives. To acknowledge freedom of action in this broader sense is to acknowledge that a person faced with a choice between doing X or doing Y can do either X or Y. To say that an individual has freedom of will of this broader sort is to say that when faced with deciding "between two or more mutually incompatible courses of action" the individual has the power to will—to intend or to decide upon—either of these.[2] Since both varieties of freedom require that, given the very

---

1   Mele, *Autonomous Agents: From Self-Control to Autonomy* (New York, 1995), p. 181.

2   Van Inwagen, *An Essay on Free Will*, p. 8. Employing the concept of possible worlds, van Inwagen interprets talk of an agent's ability—in terms of which he explicates the notion of free will—as "access-talk:" A person is able to do something, or has it within his power to "bring about an event satisfying a certain description," if he has access to some world, other

conditions that obtain, a person is able to do or to will otherwise than she actually does, both are varieties of freedom incompatible with determinism, and impossible to realize if determinism should be true. Hereafter, let us understand freedom of will and freedom of action in this broader sense.

Given that autonomy demands the possibility of practical change—the ability to revisit our choices and to live in a manner that manifests this revised outlook—the autonomous agent must have options of a particular sort at her disposal. At the same time, however, alternative possibilities of the sort supplied by freedom of will and freedom of action are not necessary for autonomy. A person may be self-governing even where the person cannot will or do otherwise than she in fact does. What will be relevant for autonomy is why the agent lacks these species of freedom and what this implies for her authority over her life.

We noted this in discussing the bearing on personal autonomy of the availability of options. If Sara is a farmer, it will matter for her self-governance whether or not she has the freedom to do otherwise than plant only certain sustainable crops and the freedom to do otherwise than sell them in tightly restricted markets, just as it will matter whether the land is arable, the weather conditions favorable, and the economy in demand of the food she cultivates. If Sara is an instructor at the local university, these conditions will be meaningless for her ability to govern her life.[3] They will be meaningful or meaningless quite independent of the fact that they may be options Sara wishes for, as options she believes would contribute to and enhance her well-being.

Consider freedom of will. Suppose Sam lacks freedom of will with respect to certain motivational states, such as a desire to put the immediate interests of his children above his own where the former are unusually taxing. Sam is constrained by the will he has, finding that he cannot bring himself to will (intend, decide, choose) otherwise than he actually does. We might even say, following Frankfurt, that insofar as Sam remains himself and the needs of his children persist, it is "volitionally necessitated" that he shall never will in such a way as to shortchange his children. Sam's inability is a reflection of who he is, who he cannot help but be, and who he wants to be. It is an expression of what he supports.[4]

---

than the actual world, in which he performs that action or in which an event satisfying that description occurs.

3 Or they will be meaningful only in a very indirect way, insofar as they impact her ability to feed herself and her family.

4 It is arguable that agent autonomy is impossible without certain volitionally necessary characteristics that provide parameters for choice and action. The concept of volitional necessity is developed by Harry Frankfurt, who argues that a person's essential nature or identity as an agent is constituted by certain ineliminable characteristics of a person's will. These volitionally necessary aspects of agency undergird agential autonomy. See Frankfurt, "On the Necessity of Ideals," in *Necessity, Volition, and Love* (Cambridge, 1999). For a different argument that yields a similar conclusion see Alfred Mele's discussion of autonomy and unsheddable pro-attitudes in *Autonomous Agents*, pp. 147–73. Gary Watson questions the

Sam's lack of free will need not be a problem for his autonomy. Sam's inability to will that the interests of his career take precedence over the complicated interests of his children need not undermine the self-managed quality of his will nor need it curtail the self-managed quality of his life. Sam's inability would point to diminished autonomy if, for example, the intention to devote a substantial portion of his time to his children was prompted by the coercive threat of others, or if his will originated from covert influences inaccessible to review and assessment, as is the case of the residents of Walden. Sam's lack of free will would signal reduced autonomy if it was due to the fact that society exerted such domineering influence as to make it unbearable for persons in the role of parent to consider their own professional welfare before the interests of their exceptionally challenging offspring. In such cases, Sam would not be able to change his values and aims by means of his own power and authority, even if the metaphysical freedom to do so remained.

So the inability to will otherwise is not, by itself, enough to signal a lack of autonomy or a diminution of autonomy just as the ability to will otherwise is not always indicative of self-rule. Thalberg's example of actions performed under coercion is emblematic of the latter sort of situation. With respect to freedom of the will, autonomy stipulates simply that what the agent wills (or cannot help but will) shall not be frustrated by the attempt of other persons to will for or through the agent, or by obstacles originating in one's psychophysiology or one's environment, particularly when the forces confronting the agent are ones the agent fails to welcome or resists.

Similarly, whether freedom of action is needed for autonomy will depend on why the person lacks freedom of action and what this lack signals for the person's authority over herself. Suppose I am not free to run a five minute mile, or move to Paris, or appear for a lecture on time. The first is closed to me because of physical limitations, while the second action is unlikely because of complicated personal and monetary constraints. The last is closed to me by simple bad luck—say I am stuck in a traffic deadlock brought on by an unforeseen accident or a freak snowstorm. In the first case, although I am not free to translate a desire to run a five minute mile into action were I to will myself to do so, it is nonetheless within my authority to do so, and I can attempt to do so as a result of my own initiative. In the second case, my ability to control my actions by means of my own authority remains intact. Nothing and no one prohibits me from moving to Paris. But in the third case, nothing I can attempt to do will alter the bind I find myself in. This is important. It makes a difference for autonomy whether agential power and authority are preempted by phenomena over which a person lacks control: If my inability to run a five minute mile or to move to Paris was due to phenomena such as crippling disability, compulsive neurosis, calamitous natural events, grave external threats, social and cultural constraints, serendipity, or the existence of a counterfactual intervener behind the scenes ready

---

concept in "Volitional Necessity" in Sarah Buss and Lee Overton (eds), *Contours of Agency: Essays on Themes from Harry Frankfurt* (Cambridge, MA, 2002), pp. 129–59.

to step in and usurp control should I exhibit signs of successfully executing these actions, no effort on my part would salvage my lack of authority.

It is also relevant for autonomy what effect a lack of freedom of action has upon a person's ability to live in a self-managed way. It is not as if I must run a five minute mile or reside in Paris if I am to live a self-governed life, although either might have been necessary had my occupation been that of professional athlete or avant-garde French film critic. On the other hand, when I am at the mercy of traffic the result is that the control needed in order to carry out a task central to the administration of my life is abridged. At this point one could question whether the freedom of action required for autonomy is unacceptably linked to the contingencies of personal choice. Taliban Woman, for example, wants very little freedom of action and needs very little in order to live as she chooses. If a truncated sphere of free action does not circumscribe her chosen way of life then its loss has negligible impact on her actual condition.

This objection misconstrues the point. It is true that freedom to realize one's will depends on one's personal and environmental circumstances, and these vary. Again, it is relevant for the purpose of assessing autonomy whether what a person is free to do is up to her—whether a person's freedom is vulnerable to the behavior of other persons or forces over which she lacks authority. A loss of freedom of action is a loss for autonomy where what is lacking is not a token ability to get what one wants but a type of power. As we saw in Chapter 4, a certain type of power is imperative for the ability of anyone, farmer or professor, film scholar or athlete, parent or religious devotee, to live a self-directed life and this power is needed whether or not the individual wishes to have it. This is the power to control the configuration of phenomena that make the realization of our wills possible. Among these phenomena are primary social roles and arrangements that bear on the elemental affairs of human life. Hence, the type of power at the heart of autonomous agency is power that transpires within the social framework of which people are active members. The existence or nonexistence of this power is not decided by an individual's need for it or desire for it. Persons in circumstances such as that of the Taliban Woman are denied power of this type even if they have no wish for it and even if they possess certain token abilities to act.

That autonomy calls for alternative possibilities of the sort causal determinism would deny may remain a concern. In the case of my inability to arrive at a lecture on time, one could charge that the phrase "I am at the mercy" of traffic is just shorthand for saying that I cannot do otherwise because my path is causally determined. If I could do otherwise, I would not be at the mercy of anything, and I could get to my lecture on time. So it remains an open question whether the freedom needed for being an autonomous person can obtain independently of the truth or falsity of determinism. I think it can. To borrow from Mele, autonomy may well be "agnostic" between compatibilism and incompatibilism.[5] The autonomous agent might act as

---

5 For a discussion of "agnostic autonomism" see Mele, *Autonomous Agents*, pp. 250–53. In a similar vein Berofsky notes that "We are all limited and, perhaps, our lives are completely

a result of a causal sequence that makes her action inevitable. At the same time, if determinism is true, it will be the case that the autonomous agent is generally disposed to treat herself as authorized to act and to position herself accordingly in her dealings with others. And it will be true that what she wills and what she does is not due to persons and phenomena (psychological, relational, or environmental) at whose bidding or favor she acts.

To see that the conditions for personal autonomy can be satisfied even where there are good reasons for believing that determinism is true, remember that autonomy requires that certain properties (including counterfactual conditions) hold of the actual situation in which a person finds himself. Among these is the ability to decide between motives or courses of action. Now suppose that determinism is true. If determinism is true, then it is established—it is entailed by the past together with the laws of nature—that the personally autonomous individual will make a particular "choice," or will pursue a certain life, or will act in a certain way. Lacking metaphysical freedom, the determined individual can control neither the past nor the laws of nature.

So let us conceive of two individuals, Arthur and Barbara, whose lives are equally determined but who nonetheless differ in the following way. Arthur is autonomous (or at least will be capable of autonomy) because the past, in conjunction with the laws of nature, entail that he will meet the conditions for autonomy including that of interacting with other individuals in a certain way. Barbara, by contrast, is not autonomous (or will lack the capacity for autonomy) since she will be determined not to meet these conditions. Autonomy would then just require that social and psychological conditions of a particular variety were present and that autonomy-undermining phenomena, including social roles, institutions, and relations of a given variety were absent. Causal possibility is still necessary for autonomy—autonomy is, after all, a power of sorts, and power calls for possibility. If a person is to be globally or dispositionally autonomous, it must be causally possible for the person to give consideration to her principles and goals, to modify and live by these, to effect action on the basis of her will, and to interact with other persons in particular ways. If it is causally impossible for Barbara to meet the requisite social and psychological conditions then it cannot be reasonable to regard her as autonomous. In Arthur's case, by contrast, the proposition "Arthur is determined to choose" is consistent with the proposition "Choices relevant to autonomy are available to Arthur in the determined state of affairs."[6] It is causally possible for Arthur to be self-governing

---

determined. But there are crucial differences in the manner in which our earlier life bears on our later life. The possibly deterministic process that has brought us to our current state may have independence and authenticity depending on the character of our current interactions." *Liberation from Self: A Theory of Personal Autonomy* (Cambridge, 1995), p. 3.

6   Harry Frankfurt makes a similar point. He states: "My conception of freedom of the will appears to be neutral with regard to the problem of determinism. It seems conceivable that it should be causally determined that a person is free to want what he wants to want. If this is conceivable, then it might be causally determined that a person enjoys a free will. There is no more than an innocuous appearance of paradox in the proposition that it is determined,

because Arthur's life, unlike Barbara's, is one in which the requisite social and psychological conditions for autonomy are present and autonomy-undermining phenomena are absent.

Mele suggests that the problem determinism raises for autonomy and intentional action can be resolved by adopting the following compatibilist strategy.[7] Determinism is compatible with psychological autonomy even if it is incompatible with autonomy over physical circumstances and the natural environment. Psychological autonomy, Mele charges, is a function of exercising proximal control over doxastic states. Doxastic states "come to mind" in a causally undetermined fashion or perhaps they are determined to come to mind by antecedent states over which we lack proximal control. Either way, we lack ultimate control over their appearance and so over reasons for choice. Nonetheless, we exert considerable proximal control over the influence these beliefs exert on us and thus over the link between reasons, choice, and action. Such beliefs causally determine ensuing mental events such as intentions, but we are not helpless bystanders with respect to these. The result is that "determinists are in a position to distinguish among different causal routes to the collection of values (and "characters") agents have at a time."[8]

From the perspective of one who construes autonomy as a psychological phenomenon, agnosticism about causal determinism can be supported by the idea that evidence of autonomous agency can be found in the dispositional nature of the mechanism from which the agent acts rather than in the presence of alternative courses of action available to the actor. Instead of searching for evidence of the power to do otherwise than what a person actually does, autonomy can make do with 'actual causal control' of a sort that is associated with the source of an agent's reasons for action and that is satisfied when the agent rather than some foreign force guides or directs her actions. Taking pains to restrict his discussion to the phenomenon of actual psychological autonomy, Mele would explain the difference in Arthur's and Barbara's psychological self-governance by appealing to a "modest agent-internal indeterminism" that allows agents "ample control" over their decisions and choices. Even if determinism is true, it is also the case that our decisions and actions are influenced by considerations—beliefs, desires, and the like—that simply "come to mind" without our being in control of their doing so. These become relevant to the agent's deliberations, "opening up alternative deliberative outcomes."[9]

---

ineluctably and by forces beyond their control, that certain people have free wills and that others do not." Frankfurt, "Freedom of the Will and the Concept of a Person," in Frankfurt, *The Importance of What We Care About* (Cambridge, 1988), p. 25.

7   Mele, *Autonomous Agents*, chapters 10 and 12.

8   Mele, "Autonomy, Self-Control, and Weakness of Will," in Robert Kane (ed.), *The Oxford Handbook of Free Will* (New York, 2002), p. 542.

9   Mele, "Autonomy, Self-Control, and Weakness of Will," pp. 544–5. Absent elaboration, the distinct situations of Arthur and Barbara cannot be characterized to the satisfaction of the libertarian who requires "both indeterminism and significant control at the moment of choice." Robert Kane offers a meticulous libertarian tactic for explaining this difference in control in *The Significance of Free Will*.

An account of autonomy that speaks to our ordinary intuitions about those persons whom we regard as in charge of their lives does not preclude fixity of the laws of nature and the past any more than it necessitates such fixity. Once the truth of causal determinism is assumed, it becomes less relevant to the considerations on the basis of which personal autonomy is assessed. At the same time, autonomy calls for more than deliberative power—it calls for practical power as well. Social-relational autonomy demands the truth of certain counterfactuals that a modest agent-internal indeterminism fails to provide. Social-relational autonomy demands agent-external indeterminism of a sort made possible by the fact that a counterfactual state of affairs is available to the agent. For example, autonomy is inconsistent with the presence of slavemasters, even slavemasters that only exert their authority counterfactually. The very existence of the slavemaster, with his powers and intentions, is a bar to the slave's autonomy. The range of options required for self-determination might not include metaphysical freedom to do otherwise. But the social situation in which the individual finds himself coupled with facts about the state of the agent's psychology must be autonomy-friendly.

In sum, autonomy-friendly freedom is the freedom to direct the actions central to the administration of one's life. Again, these are not coextensive with actions a person happens to endorse or with whatever range of freedom a person requires in order to live the life she has settled upon. Where either freedom of action or freedom of the will is absent, it is not their absence *simpliciter* that becomes decisive in determining a person's autonomy but the reasons why the person cannot will or do otherwise—what the lack is owing to—and what this implies. That persons are or are not autonomous is not founded on metaphysical facts about persons but rather is based on a confluence of social and psychological skills, the exercise of these skills, and the social-relational position which persons occupy and in which persons function.

Negative Liberty, Positive Liberty, and Autonomy

Traditionally, theorists have approached the topic of personal liberty or freedom by offering either a negative or a positive analysis of the term.[10] Negative freedom is the libertarian ideal. A person is said to be free in a negative sense when his choices and activities are minimally impeded by other persons, institutions, or natural obstacles to will and action. Advocates of negative freedom include John Locke, Jeremy Bentham, John Stuart Mill, Alexis de Tocqueville, and Robert Nozick, all of whom agree

> that there ought to exist a certain minimum area of personal freedom which must on no account be violated; for if it is overstepped, the individual will find himself in an area too narrow for even that minimum development of his natural faculties which alone make it possible to pursue, and even to conceive, the various ends which men hold good or right

---

10 I use the terms "liberty" and "freedom" interchangeably.

or sacred. It follows that a frontier must be drawn between the area of private life and that of public authority.[11]

By contrast, the central issues for positive freedom are who or what directs the individual to live a certain way and the means by which the individual is so directed. Positive freedom is often understood as liberty of the sort associated with the psychological resources for self-direction. It typically is thought to consist of an assortment of cognitive and emotional traits, conjoined with traits of characters, which a person must possess if he is to function well within the space carved out for personal development by negative freedom. Among the traits in which positive freedom consists are intellectual acumen, physical agility, and emotional health. More narrowly, Isaiah Berlin defines positive freedom as self-mastery, particularly mastery of the individual by the rational self. According to Berlin, positive freedom

> derives from the wish to be self-directed and not acted upon by an external nature or by other men as if I were a thing, or an animal, or a slave incapable of playing a human role, that is, of conceiving goals and policies of my own and realizing them.[12]

Berlin's comment suggests that positive freedom derives from the wish to be autonomous. (That a positive analysis of freedom is believed to depend on some interpretation of personal autonomy is evident from Berlin's suggestion that positive freedom can be achieved by retreating into the inner citadel, the realm of psychological autonomy. In this manner, the individual overcomes obstacles such as "the resistance of nature, [the] ungoverned passions ... irrational institutions, [and] ... the opposing wills or behaviour of others.")[13] Certainly an account of personal autonomy requires that we answer the questions prompted by both a negative and a positive theory of freedom. These are, respectively, "What am I free to do?" and "By what or by whom am I ruled?"

Negative freedom ensures the absence of certain kinds of internal and external impediments (such as psychological infirmities, physical barriers, coercion, and manipulation) from the life of the would-be autonomous agent. The person who is legally free to vote, but whose attempts to do so are confounded by obstacles such as physical barriers to the voting station, misinformation, intimidation, or confusing ballots finds his negative freedom impaired. As a consequence the person is incapable of participating in a political activity of great consequence for his autonomy.

By itself, of course, negative freedom is inadequate to capture many of our deepest intuitions about autonomy. While negative freedom indicates that a person's "actions are not *blocked* or *compelled* by other's domineering wills,"[14] it says nothing about the specific state of affairs that exists once obstacles of an obvious sort are removed. Negative freedom from interference stipulates nothing about

---

11 Berlin, "Two Concepts of Liberty," p. 124.
12 Berlin, "Two Concepts of Liberty," p. 131.
13 Berlin, "Two Concepts of Liberty," p. 146.
14 Berlin, "Two Concepts of Liberty," p. 146.

the management of a person's actions or even about the condition of a person's psychology and entails nothing about what might actually control an individual's actions and choices. As Berlin reminds us, it is possible that a "liberal-minded despot," even one who "encouraged the wildest inequalities," "would allow his subjects a large measure of personal [negative] freedom."[15] Subjects might be availed of protection from interferences with their liberties. They might move about freely and express themselves openly or have legal action taken against them and return the favor against others. But these persons can be described as self-governing only in an attenuated sense. They manage their lives only by the magnanimity of the despot who is their lord. Berlin concludes that "Freedom in this [negative] sense is not, at any rate logically, connected with ... self-government."[16]

Positive freedom fills part of the gap left open by negative freedom by capturing two aspects of personal autonomy. These are the "outer-directed" capacity of the individual to affect his environment and the "inner-directed" capacity for critical reflection on one's values, preferences, and belief. A person's ability to realize her positive freedom is, of course, affected by the scope of negative freedom the person enjoys. Because negative freedom can be limited by environmental circumstances, expressions of positive freedom can be limited as well.

But it is not always straightforward where negative freedom ends and positive freedom begins, and any explanation of autonomy in terms of these would have to contend with the fact that the line between the two is not always clear; what will count as an impediment to liberty in one case might be treated as a resource of self-mastery in another. Berofsky pursues the idea, stating that "The same environmental condition can be regarded as a grand opportunity for one person, shrugged off by another as a minor annoyance, and treated by the third as an absolute barrier ... one and the same internal factor can be called either positive or negative ... There may be no way to provide a general characterization of the distinction between positive internal states required for an action and internal states which would count as barriers to some action were they present."[17] Intelligence, he notes, may be regarded as a feature of positive freedom, but since "stupidity [is] a barrier to action" and

---

15 Berlin, "Two Concepts of Liberty," p. 129.

16 Berlin, "Two Concepts of Liberty," p. 130. Berofsky reminds us that in the United States and like-minded democratic societies, "[t]he removal of social and legal barriers ... to achieve racial equality may be regarded as inconsequential so long as the skills for taking advantage of new opportunities are absent." But as is true of its negative counterpart, positive freedom is not sufficient for autonomy: "the attainment of parity of ability may be regarded as inconsequential if a pervasive pattern of discrimination persists." Berofsky, *Liberation from Self*, p. 42.

17 Berofsky, *Liberation from Self*, pp. 42–3. Phenomena such as racism and sexism, of wealth and celebrity, privilege and power, and of genius and disability can be similarly double-edged. Any of these can test a person's strength of character. Depending on how a person responds to their presence in his life, each may fortify a person's character or debilitate it. For someone lacking in healthy self-esteem, guidance, and a network of support, any of these can present an obstacle to self-management. On the other hand, a person who is endowed

intelligence is the privation of stupidity, intelligence might be a feature of freedom in its negative guise. As a consequence, it may be hard to specify an amalgam of positive and negative freedom that would provide the sort of freedom autonomy requires.

Further, in spite of the fact that the notion of liberty or freedom is often conflated with the idea of personal autonomy, liberty and autonomy are different concepts. To be free or at liberty is to be able to decide or will, or to be able to act, maybe even entitled to do so if the ability is ensconced in law or in natural rights. We have seen that both freedom of will and freedom of action in a basic sense are necessary for autonomy. But, absent further explanation, it is not obvious that negative liberty and positive liberty supply a person with the wherewithal to manage his life and to do so counterfactually, as autonomy requires.

Autonomy is a thicker concept than freedom or liberty, descriptive of a condition persons enjoy in virtue of certain liberties but not guaranteed by the latter. By way of illustration, consider a variation on the case of the monk from Chapter 3. As in the original case, this man is architect of his will and possesses the intellectual, physical, and emotional resources for self-government. He may be amply equipped with the psychological means to assume authority, thus enjoying positive freedom. In this case, let is suppose he is a novitiate—a probationary monk, if you like—whose try-it-and-see-if-it-suits status means that he is not blocked from assuming authority over his activities by superiors in the monastery. He thus enjoys a modicum of negative freedom. Nonetheless, he has given the administration of his life over to the judgments and recommendations of others. He has abdicated himself to a system of belief and to a powerful institution with the result that he faces a situation inimical to autonomy.

Perhaps we can avoid such cases by requiring for autonomy a third variety of freedom over and above freedom of the positive and negative sorts. As we noted in Chapter 4, autonomy requires a variety of what Pettit has called "republican freedom" or "freedom as non-domination" in the political realm. Freedom from non-domination provides assurance of what I have called "counterfactual power" or authority of a sort that is resilient against attempts by other, more powerful, persons in the agent's social-relational environment to wrest *de facto* power and authority from her where choices and actions significant to the direction of her life are at stake. The powerful include familiar figures in our lives—our spouses, our employers, those who oversee our medical care, our teachers, our legislators, and so forth. There is no assurance that a person who is free from interference and who is endowed with the psychological resources of positive liberty would be empowered to challenge potential encroachments on the part of those who have such power over her. In contrast, the person who has the benefit of "freedom as non-domination" is less susceptible to these encroachments because others in the social milieu are

---

with healthy self-esteem, social direction, and a system of support will be better positioned to navigate these challenges with relative ease.

effectively prohibited (by social sanction or by law) from depriving the person of the standing that allows her to contest their power over her management of her affairs.

At the same time, freedom as non-domination does not seem to contribute all we might need for autonomy. For example, it is consistent with positive and negative freedom, even where these are supplemented by freedom as non-domination, that a person goes through life as an entity who echoes the experiences and the endeavors of others. Without doubt an autonomous person's life will expose the influence of others—as social creatures we could hardly expect it to be otherwise. But it is not consistent with self-governance that a person fail to wield authority and power within the space negative freedom and freedom as non-domination have provided, nor that she fail to put the inner-directed and outer-directed capacities of positive freedom to good use, yet this is precisely what the person whose life echoes that of others fails to do.

We have seen, too, that social and political freedom as non-domination of the sort Pettit describes cannot be undermined by impersonal factors or by the natural effects of chance, but only by the intentional and arbitrary efforts of other persons. An individual's autonomy, however—not simply the exercise of her autonomy, not simply the intensity of her autonomy, not even the range of states over which she is autonomous but the condition of being autonomous itself—can be impaired by factors other than the intentional and arbitrary efforts of others. If an individual is dispossessed of a range of resources—those of a cultural sort as well as those stemming from biological and geographic circumstances and so forth—and if the lack of these resources means that a person cannot meet the threshold for *de facto* power and authority and counterfactual power and authority over the management of affairs of fundamental importance to her life; if their lack means she cannot control her life by means of her own authority—her autonomy will be insignificant, perhaps nonexistent. Autonomy, more than negative and positive freedom, and more than freedom as non-domination, calls for a certain dispositional state of persons in conjunction with specific social, political, economic, and environmental arrangements, personal as well as impersonal, that ensure the counterfactual power to alter, adapt, and refashion one's life within the ambit of these freedoms.

I want to close this section with a caveat. Positive freedom, negative freedom, and freedom as non-domination enrich autonomy since their presence or absence can augment or diminish autonomy. But this is not to say they do no more than facilitate or hamper the *exercise* of autonomy. We might claim that the residents of Walden cannot exercise their autonomy due to a shortfall of positive freedom and perhaps to impediments to negative liberty and freedom as non-domination as well. But we would do better to say that the residents of Walden *are not autonomous*, in part because of the constraints on freedom they face. Freedom does not just facilitate autonomy but goes some distance to its materialization. There is, of course, more than a lack of freedom in the lives of the denizens of Walden that renders them nonautonomous. Absent in their lives are not just personal liberties. Even where their personal liberties are intact, the residents of Walden lack access to phenomena, such as informational media, that guarantee them authority over their lives. That is part of the incontrovertible status of global autonomy.

The Freedom to Make Oneself

Autonomous agents are sometimes spoken of as atomistic, self-created individuals, ultimately dependent on none but themselves and, at root, insulated from the influence and guidance of others. Let us refer to this as the idea of autonomy as self-creation or the idea of "metaphysical autonomy." The metaphysically autonomous agent is directed entirely by her own lights, bound by no constraints other than those she imposes on herself. She does not defer to the directives of other persons, and she is free to reject traditions, values, and normative principles not of her own making. To the extent self-definition is regarded as a virtue, these characteristics may be embraced as ones worth cultivating.

But this conception of autonomy is problematic, and not because of the idea that an autonomous individual is self-defining and sovereign over her decisions and actions. Autonomous individuals *are*, loosely speaking, self-defining and sovereign over their decisions and actions. Rather, the story is problematic because it reserves the term "autonomous agent" for entities that bear little resemblance to human beings. They are at best a caricature of human beings.

This is also a picture of persons that has been soundly criticized as undesirable and as implausible.[18] Metaphysical autonomy is undesirable because it demands that the agent be free of all varieties of external control and influence even when such controls are beneficial to the integrity, the well-being, or the self-realization of the agent. The radically self-created autonomous individual is regarded as impervious to constraints of love and kinship, or constraints that cement friendships; she may be characterized as someone who does not settle for tradition or as someone who is not the progeny of her culture. Insofar as the autonomous agent so described may be unresponsive to shared values and objective standards of good judgment, autonomy is a condition likely to disrupt various cooperative enterprises and relations premised on values such as caring and commitment. A depiction of the radical individual unmoved by the merits of social cooperation and unburdened by the obligations that accompany social participation is not a picture towards which persons should aspire. In short, this depiction of persons is flawed on normative grounds.

But it is also implausible to call for the possibility of radical self-creation and ultimate control on the part of the agent. Marilyn Friedman argues that the fact of our interrelatedness makes even the less extreme ideas of self-definition and self-ownership far-fetched. Friedman bluntly states that the "major obstacle facing

---

18 The view that autonomy involves minimal commitment closely approximates Gerald Dworkin's interpretation of substantive independence, as discussed in Chapter 2. Dworkin rejects substantive independence for this reason. For a recent critique of the idea of self-creation see Robert Noggle, "Autonomy and the Paradox of Self-Creation," in James Stacey Taylor (ed.), *Personal Autonomy* (New York, 2005).

those theorists who would develop an account of autonomy" as self-creation is that "[T]here are no apparent limits to the extent to which the self can be thought of as biologically, psychologically, and sociologically determined. If *all* of the standards and values, all of the 'rules' which inform the self's reflections and deliberations, are ultimately the manifestation of conditions other than the self, then it is not clear [on such accounts] how a person might ever come to have rules of her 'own' or to think 'for herself'."[19]

I think it is a mistake to believe self-determination calls for radical self-creation and that it should be rejected on this account. This picture ignores the social nature of persons and discounts the importance of interpersonal relationships in making autonomy possible. Who persons are, how they define themselves, and the content of their motivations, values, and commitments are essentially fashioned by connections to other people, to cultural norms, rituals, and tradition, and enterprises. The autonomous individual must be free to step back from, to question and to judge these phenomena and, if she decides, to opt out of them. But this does not mean the individual is socially unsituated, or is free in the sense that she is self-constituted, where the self is defined prior to and independent of social roles and relations. We cannot reconfigure these phenomena at will. We must have the ability to partition ourselves from them, but given their enormous centrality to our lives, they are phenomena that might elude our scrutiny or our attempts to refashion them at will. Gerald Dworkin presses the point:

> We all know that persons have a history. They develop socially and psychologically in a given environment with a given set of biological endowments. They mature slowly and are heavily influenced by their parents, siblings, peers, and culture. What sense does it make to speak of their convictions, motivations, principles, and so forth as "self-selected"? This presupposes a notion of the self as isolated from the influences just enumerated, and, what is almost as foolish, *that the self which chooses does so arbitrarily.* For to the extent that the self uses canons of reason, principles of induction, judgments of probability, etc., these also have either been acquired from others or ... are innate. We can no more choose *ab initio* than we can jump out of our skins. To insist on this position is to make autonomy impossible.[20]

Joel Feinberg agrees. He notes that though it is natural to think of the autonomous person as self-made, the idea of self-creation cannot and should not be taken literally so as to make a person's character the product solely of the person's doing, *ex nihilo* into something. A conception of autonomy need not demand either metaphysical or cultural independence as a requisite for authentic self-ownership. Instead, Feinberg contends that "[a] common-sense account of self-creation ... can be given, provided

19 Friedman, "Autonomy and the Split-Level Self," *Southern Journal of Philosophy*, 24/1, 1986: 21.

20 Dworkin, "Autonomy and Behavior Control," *Hastings Center Report* 6 (1976): 24.

we avoid the mistake of thinking that there can be no self-determination unless the self that does the determining is already formed."[21]

Briefly, the commonsense account holds that people progress from infancy to adulthood in a continuous fashion. As the individual matures, his contributions to and responsibility for his personality and personal circumstances increase, and do so in increasingly significant ways. But "there is no point before which the child himself has no part in his own shaping and after which he is the sole responsible maker of his own character and life plan. Such a radical discontinuity is simply not part of anyone's personal history."[22] With the exception of persons who have been "severely manipulated, indoctrinated, and coerced throughout childhood," we are all self-created in the sense of having supplied texture and color to the imprint of our characters. This point, Feinberg notes, is frequently overlooked by philosophers "whose conception of autonomy is unrealistically inflated."[23]

Even a person's authentic character cannot be entirely a function of the person's independent design. In order to be authentic with regard to one's motivations and principles, a person must possess an undeveloped but recognizable character, and rudimentary convictions which antedate and inform the activity of critical reflection: "Some principles, and especially the commitment to reasonable self-criticism itself, must be 'implanted' in a child if she is to have a reasonable opportunity of playing a part in the direction of her own growth."[24] What a person identifies with or repudiates is determined by who the person already is. An individual's evaluative commitments are invariably premised on aspects of the self such as race, gender, and sexual orientation. The effect of wholehearted identification or authenticity one experiences relative to one's cognitive and conative states, to one's physicality and to one's social attachments, depends largely on the primitive character brought to the process of reflective appraisal.[25]

The idea that self-creation is essential for autonomy can be further challenged by questioning the idea that authenticity is an essential element of autonomy. I argued in Chapters 3 and 4 that it is not. In order to be autonomous a person must regard himself as someone whose concerns, values, and commitments can be more or less successfully realized. Autonomous choice and action cannot get underway nor persist where a person lacks definite objectives, preferences, or principles that, in conjunction with the person's interests, attachments, partnerships, social roles, and

21 Feinberg, *Harm to Self*, vol. 3 of *The Moral Limits of the Criminal Law* (New York, 1986), p. 34. Also see Berofsky's account of objectivity as a feature of his "liberation view of autonomy" in *Liberation from Self*.

22 Feinberg, *Harm to Self*, p. 33.

23 Ibid.

24 Ibid.

25 The idea is that autonomous choice and action is supported by an antecedent nexus of moral, cognitive, conative, social and cultural factors that enables the person's life-plans to be unequivocally his own. Without this support, we are "vacant of identifiable tendencies and constraint ... unable to deliberate or to make conscientious decisions." Frankfurt, "Rationality and the Unthinkable," in *The Importance of What We Care About*, p. 178.

heritage give the person his own character and enable him to move in a direction that is meaningful to him. A person's self-conception provides some assurance that a person has an active and authoritative voice in the direction of his life.

Accounts of autonomy centered on the ideas of procedural independence and psychological authenticity require that these objectives, preferences, principles, interests, attachments, partnerships, social roles, heritage, and so forth be authenticated, and authenticity, as we have seen, is taken to be a function of the structure and history of a person's will or of the attitude of acceptance a person adopts towards the central components that anchor his self-conception. But, as I have argued, insofar as a person's conception of himself informs his autonomy, the agent need not endorse, be satisfied with, or fail to feel somewhat alienated from the elements constitutive of his identity and his self-conception. Autonomy does not require that an agent's self-conception be self-created even in this sense of being authenticated.

A final point to be made with respect to the question of self-creation is this. Autonomy does not require that a person's desires or values or projects have developed under conditions over which he has complete control, where complete control entails the absence of any variety of factors external to the person that might cause the person to have these desires, values, and projects. In other words, autonomy does not call for self-creation in the guise of ultimate causal freedom. An argument that ultimate causal freedom is needed for autonomous agency might be successfully made, but only if the argument offered a fully naturalistic analysis of ultimate causal freedom. One contender for such a naturalized account would be Robert Kane's theory of free agency. Kane contends that the basis for autonomous action—he speaks of free action—rests in certain indeterminacies occurring at the neural level which are rendered determinate by agential choice and action.[26] Of course, that people have the sort of freedom Kane describes necessitates that the debate about freedom and determinism be resolvable either in favor of freedom or in favor of some form of compatibility. This is not a debate we need to engage in for the purpose of the discussion in this book. What is significant for our purpose is that the sort of ultimacy Kane describes would not suffice for personal autonomy in the lives of persons. To be the ultimate origin of one's choices and actions is not to be in control of the social and relational facets of one's existence where choices and actions come to life.

Summary

Given that our character and our values are, in part, shaped unbidden and that the processes by which these are shaped begins before we are in a position to chart the course of our lives, what are we to say about the variety of freedom autonomy calls for? We can say that autonomy requires the freedom to oversee states of affairs and

---

26 Kane, *The Significance of Free Will*.

events vital to the administration of one's life. To be free is to possess the power to decide or to act. Autonomy requires that power and more. Autonomy requires agential authority over those decisions and actions, but this is more than negative and positive freedom can supply and even more than can be provided by Pettit's "freedom as non-domination." Moreover, the autonomous agent must have the freedom to deliberate about and to change her values and motivations and to alter significant relations in her life if she so chooses. The freedom to do this, I have argued, is agnostic as to the truth or falsity of determinism. Our standard beliefs about those persons whom we regard as in control of their lives neither rule out fixity of the laws of nature and the past nor necessitate such fixity.

Finally, while all competent human beings are self-created in that each imparts a personalized imprint on the rudiments of his character, autonomy does not demand that the individual be remote from the influence of others. A naturalized account of autonomy, whatever its metaphysical commitments, does not entail that the individual be an island of independence. Indeed, the opposite is the case. Insofar as the freedom to make oneself is definitive of agent autonomy, it is a freedom that transpires within the social milieu.

Chapter 8

Loose Ends and Parting Thoughts

Responsible Agency and Agent Autonomy

Throughout this book, I have sidestepped the topic of moral responsibility. This may strike the reader as an oversight. The classic and contemporary literature devoted to the topics of agent autonomy and agent responsibility suggest that there are conceptual connections between the two, although these connections are rarely explored in detail.[1] In the past twenty years alone there has been an abundance of scholarship on the topic of responsibility and, more generally, moral agency, with much of this discussion resting on some theory of autonomous agency.[2] But I have chosen to avoid the topic of responsible agency for the simple reason that this is a book on autonomy. To treat autonomy and responsibility as two sides of a coin is a mistake, despite the fact that this has often been done. The bulk of this final chapter will be devoted to explaining, very briefly, the differences between autonomy and responsibility as I see them.

At first glance, it seems uncontestable that the autonomous agent is a responsible agent in that she is accountable for her behavior where excusing conditions do not obtain. It appears obvious that a person cannot fail to be responsible for behavior she determines. Equally, it appears obvious that when we hold an agent responsible for her behavior and, more generally, regard her as a responsible agent, we assume she is autonomous. It is commonly held that the acts for which people are morally

---

1 Among the ancients, the connection between autonomy and responsibility is found (implicitly) in the views of Chrysippus, a Stoic, as reported by Cicero in *On Fate*, trans. R. Sharples (Warminster, England: Aris and Phillips, 1991), fragments 40–43; in the Aristotelian views of Alexander of Aphrodisias (2nd century AD) in *On Fate*, fragments 11–14; and in Plato, *Republic* 10, "The Myth of Er." All are reprinted in Julia Annas, *Voices of Ancient Philosophy* (New York, 2001), at pp. 18–19; 22–8; 36–41 respectively. The general theme throughout is that it is up to us how to live our lives, even where we are constrained by factors over which we have no control.

2 Harry Frankfurt touches on the relationship between autonomy and responsibility in "Coercion and Moral Responsibility," reprinted in *The Importance of What We Care About*, pp. 80–94, esp. 43–4. John Martin Fischer raises the question of the relationship between the two concepts in "Recent Work on Moral Responsibility," *Ethics* 110/1 (October 1999): 93–139. Also see John Martin Fischer and Mark Ravizza, *Responsibility and Control: A Theory of Moral Responsibility*; Ishtiyaque Haji, *Moral Appraisability* (New York, 1998), Bernard Berofsky, *Liberation From Self: A Theory of Personal Autonomy*; and Susan Wolf, *Freedom Within Reason*.

responsible are those they perform as self-governed agents. Indeed, it is not reasonable to hold a person responsible for particular acts, or to regard a person as a responsible agent, unless the person is in charge of her behavior in the manner of an autonomous being. We do not hold small children and animals responsible just because we cannot credit them with self-government as we can credit adults. We can train them to control their impulses through incentives that reward or punish certain behavior, but at best this signals self-government of a crude variety because the locus of control does not rest with the actor but is contained in the promise of reward or punishment from without.

In the main, then, autonomous agency seems to be both sufficient and necessary for responsible agency. But while beliefs of this sort are routine, I believe they are erroneous. It seems to me that they rest on ignoring the distinction between the global state of being autonomous and the local condition of exhibiting autonomy with respect to some act or decision. Because local autonomy with respect to an act seems closely tied to the condition of being responsible for that act, we tend to think of global autonomy as bound up with responsibility as well. However, global autonomy is not necessary for responsible agency. Moreover, neither global nor local autonomy is sufficient to supply a person with all the elements of responsible agency.

Let us look at what is involved in ascribing moral responsibility. There are at least two accounts we could give of what it means to judge a person to be morally responsible. On the first account—the accountability analysis—we are expressing the belief that the person is accountable for her behavior or character, in the sense that we think it appropriate that the person offer an explanation of her intentions in acting if asked to do so. That is, we may be saying that the person behaved in such a way that it is reasonable for others to expect an account from the person of her behavior. Of course, a person may be responsible even if the person is not morally required to give an account or even if would be appropriate for the person to refuse to give an account beyond saying that the act was her business alone. What we might call "private" moral failures may be the concern of no one but the actor.[3] On a second account—the reactive attitudes analysis—in judging a person

---

3   For example, suppose you are a spiteful person. You resent the fact that your arguably more deserving colleague has been awarded a promotion. As a result, you refuse to include her in social gatherings at which she might meet persons who would be instrumental in furthering her career. Surely it is correct that you are morally responsible for your action. But, it is not obvious that anyone may appropriately ask for an account of that action. Since some moral failures may be nobody's business, an account that goes beyond noting this needn't be appropriately expected in order for ascriptions of responsibility to be warranted. Nonetheless the appropriateness of your providing an account explains the fact that we ascribe responsibility to you, although in this case no right to demand or exact an account exists. To ascribe responsibility is not to insist that a person in fact give an account to someone, nor that there be someone (or some institution) to whom the agent must deliver the account. See Marina A.L. Oshana, "Ascriptions of Responsibility," *American Philosophical Quarterly*, 34/1 (January 1997): 71–83.

responsible we are signaling our belief that the person is liable to a range of attitudes and practices, such as resentment, gratitude, censure, or praise, registered in reaction to the quality of the actor's will.[4] Delineating responsibility from autonomy does not require that we decide which, if either, of these accounts best captures the concept of responsibility.

An attribution of responsibility, if legitimate, rests on the assumption that some of the expectations we have of the person as a moral agent have been satisfied. Most importantly, one who is a morally responsible agent is believed to satisfy an epistemic competency condition as well as certain conditions of control, the conjunction of which provides the agent with some of the power over her actions moral responsibility demands. Satisfaction of the epistemic competency condition grants the agent awareness of herself as a moral agent distinct from others, cognizance of the circumstances in which she acts, and appreciation of established moral directives governing behavior. We assume the epistemically competent actor is able to grasp that doing a particular act (or an act of a given type) or cultivating particular traits of character—say, generosity and humility, or pride, or jealousy, rage, and bigotry—is right or is wrong or morally neutral. The epistemically competent agent has the capacity to recognize a moral community and the ability to evaluate and converse about the plausibility of moral claims. Most importantly, perhaps, the epistemically competent agent has adopted what H.L.A. Hart describes as the "internal point of view"; she regards morality as consisting of norms to which she is subject in part because she regards them as legitimate standards for the governance of behavior.[5] As a consequence, epistemic competence sustains a capacity for moral reasoning and dialogue.

Satisfaction of the control conditions ensures that the agent stands as legislator and executor over the phenomena for which she is held responsible; she controls what to do and is in control when she does it.[6] An agent has legislative control over what to do when her reasons for choice and action do not originate from circumstances of coercion, manipulation, intimidation, and so forth, but rather issue from normal developmental processes of biological, cognitive, and emotional maturation and cultural experience. What to do is up to the agent because it can be traced to her reflectively unimpaired motivational psychology. The agent has executive control—

---

4   Peter Strawson introduced the idea that ascriptions of responsibility are tantamount to holding a person liable to a range of reactive attitudes in his "Freedom and Resentment," *Proceedings of the British Academy*, 48 (1962): 1–25. Although I am not concerned to pursue the disagreement here, I have argued elsewhere that to construe responsibility in this fashion is to change the topic from a discussion of what responsible agency amounts to, to a question of when certain associated practices and attitudes are reasonable. It is one thing to claim the legitimacy of praising and blaming and another to charge that such legitimacy constitutes responsibility. A third alternative is to judge that responsibility for certain states of affair can be attributed to a cause. This is not a sense of responsibility I will consider.

5   H.L.A. Hart, *The Concept of Law* (New York, 1961), chapter 5, section 2.

6   Both types of control are possible by proxy since the actor can authorize another party to act on her behalf as her agent.

she guides her will—when she has the ability to respond to reasons to adjust or amend her behavior in light of moral guidelines or principles. The agent is moved to action by way of a mechanism that is disposed to respond to good reason. The phenomena over which control can be exercised include the agent's dispositional characteristics, values, desires, beliefs, and actions as well as the realization of consequences or states of affairs.

My view is that several of the salient features of responsible agency are not guaranteed by autonomous agency. The epistemic condition I have described as a capacity to recognize a moral community, to evaluate and converse about the normative value of the moral standards to which one is subject, and to regard oneself as subject to these standards mechanisms for the governance of one's behavior is not a condition of autonomous agency. The control condition of responsible agency— the capacity to respond to morally relevant reasons to adjust one's behavior—is not a feature of autonomous agency. In previous work I have characterized the difference between responsibility and autonomy as a difference in type of rationality or the experience of rationality central to each. My thought was that to be a responsible agent is to be receptive and responsive to reasons of a particular variety and in a special way. Alternately, we might describe the difference between responsible agency and autonomous agency in terms of the variety and extent of ability each entails. We might say, that is, that responsible agency requires ability of a different sort than either global or local autonomy can guarantee, and that this is just the ability to participate in moral conversation. In the course of the discussion to follow I will refer to the difference in both of these ways, so as to highlight the manner in which the difference might come into view. But how the difference is characterized is not essential. It is only essential to recognize the fact of the difference and to pinpoint its source.

Let us again consider what is involved in judging a person responsible. In cases where evidence of responsibility is sought, we seek confirmation that the agent is able to regulate her own behavior. We do this as well where evidence of autonomy is required. In the case of responsibility, however, we seek evidence that regulation occurs "through critical reflection on one's conduct under the pressure provided by the desire to be able to justify one's actions to others on grounds they could not reasonably reject."[7] This is because being responsible means being aware of oneself

---

7   Scanlon, *The Significance of Choice*, 1986, *The Tanner Lectures* (Salt Lake City: 1989), p. 173. Scanlon remarks: "Moral criticism and moral argument ... concern features of the agent for which questions about reasons, raised by the agent him or herself, are appropriate. Insofar as I think of a past intention, decision, or action as *mine*, I think of it as something which was sensitive to my assessment, at the time, of relevant reasons. This makes it appropriate for me to ask myself, Why did I think or do that? And Do I still take those reasons to be sufficient? .... [A] person who is concerned to be able to justify him or herself to others will be moved to respond to the kind of demand I have mentioned, will want to be able to respond positively (i.e., with a justification) and will want to carry out the kind of first-person reflection just described in a way that makes such a response possible." *The Significance of Choice*, pp. 171–2.

as subject to certain interpersonal norms. This means the control over their actions that morally responsible agents exhibit stems from a kind of normative rationality or competence. Morally responsible agents have a capacity for moral reasoning that rests on the triple aspects of recognition of reasons that have moral weight, conversational ability, and motivational responsiveness to reasons for action that track certain evaluative norms governing what is permissible, what is obligatory, and what is prohibited. A person is responsible to the degree that she can participate in a social practice of ascribing and of taking on responsibility. This basic idea appears to underlie T.M. Scanlon's contractualist analysis of accountability, according to which "the basic moral motivation is a desire to regulate one's behavior according to standards that others could not reasonably reject insofar as they, too, were looking for a common set of practical principles."[8]

But now consider the case of a sociopath, a person who may be globally autonomous but who, I believe, would fail nonetheless to be a responsible agent. Let us call this individual Ripley, after Patricia Highsmith's fictional character.[9] As I imagine him, Ripley is not ignorant of the circumstances in which he acts and he is cognizant of established moral directives governing behavior in these circumstances. But Ripley's cognizance is that of the observer. Ripley does not and cannot adopt the internal point of view. Ripley does not and cannot recognize himself as a sincere and equal participant with others in moral discourse aimed at deciding what is right—as a potential moral interlocutor—and this is to say he does not recognize himself as belonging to a moral community. A number of things count toward his inability to do this. For one thing, Ripley is a "practical solipsist"[10]—he fails to appreciate that the world consists of a diversity of independent agents deserving of respect in virtue of their distinct identities, values, and goals. Ripley may also be a moral egomaniac, someone who makes normative judgments that reflect only his own private interests: he fails to see such judgments as universalizable.

Ripley does not experience connections with other persons that could generate self-directed emotions such as disgrace, penitence, or guilt in response to his own reduced levels of attachment and regard for the rights of others. He is impervious to any variety of interpersonal attitudes in a wholesale way, though he may be acutely sensitive to self-regarding slights and injury. Ripley suffers from what might be regarded as a deficit of emotional imagination, or an inability to imagine the world as experienced by someone else emotionally.[11] Ripley cannot be motivated simply by the fact that his actions are unjust, unvirtuous, or would adversely affect people, even if he recognizes these facts. What motivates him is the idea that a particular course of action will indispose him or inconvenience him or benefit him in some way. He cannot appreciate the fact that other people (or other sentient beings generally)

---

8 *The Significance of Choice*, pp. 166–7.
9 Patricia Highsmith, *The Talented Mr. Ripley* (New York, 1955).
10 Thomas Nagel, *The Possibility of Altruism* (Princeton, 1978).
11 See J. David Velleman "Identification and Identity" in *Contours of Agency: Essays on Themes of Harry Frankfurt*, pp. 91–123.

are entitled to moral consideration in their own right and cannot accept the fact that, because of this, there are restrictions upon how we may behave toward them, and appropriate penalties for failing to do so. Perhaps he completely discounts the interests or the perspective of others, with the result that he assesses the impact others have upon him as of far greater consequence than any impact his actions might have on others. Ripley may recognize that a person or some set of persons is of value to him, but this will not suffice to make him see these persons as valuable in their own right.

In spite of all this, Ripley satisfies all the criteria for autonomous agency. He conceives of himself, rightly, as a person with a distinctive history and with commitments, values, desires, and goals that he has not merely appropriated from others. He is equipped with knowledge of his circumstances and of the effective forces operative in these circumstances (although he is blind to the moral dimensions of these circumstances). The social situation in which he finds himself is not affected by other persons, by social institutions, or by natural circumstances in ways that render him incapable of living a self-directed life. He is provided with the resources which make possible the activities most essential to self-governance including access to an assortment of options for choice and action adequate to grant him control over weighty aspects of his life. Ripley's behavior can certainly be attributed to him; he is not possessed by some alien force when he acts in morally reprehensible ways. Moreover, Ripley knows that what he is doing is regarded as unacceptable. He just does not regard this consideration as indicating a mark against his character or as a reason not to act as he does. He willfully repudiates moral conventions, regarding himself as insulated from their demands.

Personalities such as Ripley meet the criteria for agential autonomy. But the qualities that signify his autonomy are qualities that can be had in the absence of morally responsible agency. Ripley might reflectively endorse his reasons for action. He does not suffer from psychological dissonance among motives for action, nor duress, weakness of will, or any of the myriad phenomena invoked as encumbrances upon responsible agency. Nor is he lacking moral knowledge; he has the facts straight about what morality expects of people. But due to a failure of normative competence—to what I would call an irrationality of a particular sort—Ripley fails to regard himself as properly and consistently subject to the constraints—the duties and expectations—these norms impose. While he may judge that certain acts are called right and that they have a particular moral valence, and while he might comprehend moral language and its subtleties, he does so from the outside—from the external point of view. We would have to imagine a radical alteration of his psychology in order to imagine him capable of responding to moral considerations.

The case of Ripley shows that autonomy is not sufficient for responsibility. Let us now consider the case of someone who is plainly responsible for her action but who has a low degree of autonomy. Aspects of the life of Harriet Tubman are known to most of us, so let us take her as our example. Tubman's social and legal status as a slave meant that she could not without grave risk and struggle control the forces that shaped her life. But Tubman's lack of autonomy neither excused her nor exempted her from being a responsible agent. Each of the features so glaringly absent in Ripley were qualities Tubman possessed in abundance. She had a profound sense of the universal scope of moral principle. Having examined slavery—from the heart as much as from the intellect—Tubman found it to be an institution in violation of universal moral norms governing what is permissible, what is obligatory, and what is prohibited.

Tubman appreciated the fact that slaves were entitled to moral consideration in their own right. Her recognition of the standing which enslaved persons ought to have signaled an ability on her part to take into account the value of persons other than herself, and for reasons other than any value they might happen to have to her. Her recognition of the slaves she assisted as distinct agents—not as patients or as instruments—compelled her to acknowledge the effects, the benefits as well as the costs, her actions would have upon them. Said Tubman: "I had reasoned this out in my mind, there was one of two things I had a *right* to, liberty or death; if I could not have one, I would have the other."

The point to be made here is not that Tubman was responsible because she was motivated by something akin to natural and direct concern. The point is that Tubman was willing and able to consider herself as a moral partner with the slaves. More importantly, perhaps, Tubman considered herself an equal moral partner with the slave owners with whose property she had absconded. She did not assess the moral valence of the norms of slavery from the point of view of an external observer, but from the intimate perspective of a participant—someone entrenched within the culture and the manners these norms imposed.

Tubman was responsible for her behavior because she had the capacity to heed moral counsel and the general disposition to do so; she recognized reasons for action that were granted moral weight and recognized the duties and expectations morality imposed upon her. But while Tubman took seriously the moral considerations and behavioral expectations of this community she refused to comply with these considerations. The principles of the community were morally corrupt—arbitrarily discriminatory and inegalitarian in the demands they placed on persons, black and white. In order to be responsible it is not necessary that a person take the views of her community, or of any existing community, to be right. What is necessary for responsible agency is that a person satisfies the epistemic and control conditions and that the person is disposed to regard a society's view about right and wrong as relevant considerations for her own conduct, whether the person abides by these views or not. The agent must regard the norms as response-worthy, though she may respond to the norms in a variety of ways, including opposing their legitimacy. Indeed, opposition to the moral expectations of a community can be a form of conversational engagement.

Moreover, Tubman was willing to face the music. She realized her actions would be considered evil by some and was acutely aware of the penalties her violation of conventional morality invited. But she accepted the risk of brutal retaliation for her own escape from slavery and the assistance she provided countless other slaves. In accepting the risk, Tubman engaged in action that she believed others could not reasonably reject were they to desire to be able to justify their actions to all other moral agents—not just those of a narrow, morally suspect group. She weighed the moral arguments for desisting from her mission against moral reasons that urged her on, and was capable of appreciating, no less than explaining, her reasons for action in a way that made the decision to carry through morally intelligible.

Responsible agency demands a capacity for social participation and involvement, and insofar as an enslaved person is not socially and epistemically incapacitated we can continue to consider him a competent subject of moral address, even though he is not autonomous on my account. The slave can recognize that he is bound by moral considerations that encompass the interests of others even if he rejects the idea that he is bound by the rein of a master. The slave, that is, can be morally responsible even if he lacks autonomy. In general, enslaved persons have the ability to account for their acts, so they meet the conditions for responsibility as accountability discussed above. For example, a slave might be responsible for the affection and nurturance he provides his children. While it is tempting to infer that no person bound by slavery can possess the epistemic competence, the authoritative voice, and the normative sensitivity to bear the burden of responsibility, this temptation must be resisted. Surely, we believe that slaves such as Harriet Tubman were responsible for their character and for their courageous efforts to free their brethren. Indeed, we applaud their efforts and praise them for their courage.

Tubman is responsible for her behavior despite the fact that she is not, on the account of autonomy developed in this book, autonomous. By virtue of her enslavement, Tubman is denied the power to live in a self-managed way. Others manage her life for her. But, one might object, Tubman is in charge of her behavior, and isn't this why she is responsible? Similarly, isn't Ripley responsible for his behavior just because he is in charge of it? That is, aren't both persons responsible agents because both are autonomous—locally autonomous, at any rate? Ripley lacks the ability to be an engaged moral interlocutor who takes up the internal point of view but this seems unimportant to his responsibility. Is it not true that both Tubman and Ripley control what they decide to do with their lives—with what is of fundamental interest to their lives—even if, admittedly, the range of activity over which they exercise control is narrow for Tubman, wide for Ripley? Certainly both exercise ample self-control in executing their plans.

A number of points must be made in response to these objections. First, Tubman's action is forced upon her by the prospect of being subjugated for as long as her masters see fit. Because of coercive social-relational circumstances, the only options available to Tubman are escape or abject servility. She therefore lacks global autonomy. Second, the difference between local and global autonomy is relevant here. Local autonomy pertains to self-governance over decisions and actions considered individually, and here, arguably, Tubman had a high degree of autonomy. The decision she made to resist slavery was without a doubt one that expressed her will—her considered, resolute will—rather than the will of the master. I would hesitate to claim full local autonomy for her choices and actions, given they were pressed upon her by the lack of social autonomy she enjoyed and the desperate environmental circumstances she had to cope with. Tubman's circumstances conditioned—colored, influenced, prompted—her decisions and diminished her local autonomy, though they did not remove all measure of local autonomy over the decisions.

Third, both autonomy and responsibility presuppose rationality sufficient to filter out the intentions, goals, and actions that thwart self-control from those that do not. Tubman and Ripley each possess this variety of rationality. They are each rational in the sense of being socially agile, adept at comprehending the vulnerabilities of others, and shrewd enough to effect their plans. They can read others; they know what others take to be good reasons for action. They are each, in short, paradigms of instrumental rationality, and this is just what autonomy demands.

But, fourth, this variety of rationality will not suffice for the moral sensitivity responsible agency requires. Nor will socially savvy, instrumental rationality suffice for global autonomy. This variety of rationality might leave a person indifferent to moral considerations, as it has left Ripley. But if the rationality we require of responsible agents amounts to a kind of normative competence, then rationality cannot be limited to instrumental reason. Ripley can comprehend what people in the community of moral agents consider good and evil and so has a handle on what moral violations involve. Ripley grasps the social employment of characteristically moral dialogue; he is "capable of reasoning, weighing evidence, estimating future consequences, understanding the norms of ... society, anticipating the blame and condemnation that result from violations of those norms, and [is able to use] these cognitive skills to make and carry out [his] plans."[12] Ripley can even offer reasons for actions that mimic moral beliefs. But the fact that Ripley can do this does not by itself mean he can be motivated to act from such beliefs, any more than it shows ability on his part to accept that what he does is noninstrumentally morally right or wrong. A thought of this sort is needed for full moral engagement. The preparedness to justify one's behavior or to account for it—as is required for responsibility on the accountability analysis—entails some motivation to act for those reasons, and here Ripley falls short. He is therefore not a responsible agent.

Autonomous people, then, can be "beyond the pale" in the sense that they lack the ability to be responsive to the expectations any moral community has of its members. The fact that such people are not responsible or accountable does not mean their behavior cannot rightly be attributed to them, nor that they lack extensive control over their lives, including self-control, of the sort that makes the behavior in question intentional and their own. But this sort of "autonomy-salient" control over one's behavior is not adequate for the sort of control a responsible agent needs. Even if Ripley's behavior can be attributed to him, it is doubtful that sociopaths such as he have a sufficient degree of the types of control—legislative and executive— necessary for responsibility. Ripley lacks sufficient legislative control over what to do because the reasons he acts from are the product of an abnormal, morally impaired motivational psychology. Ripley lacks sufficient executive control in guiding his

---

12 John Deigh, "Universalizability and Empathy" in *The Sources of Moral Agency* (Cambridge, 1996), p. 160.

will because he is not able to adjust his behavior in light of shared moral guidelines or principles; he is not capable of doing otherwise where that would involve sincere moral engagement.

Of course, we may care less about whether such persons as Ripley are accountable participants in the moral community and care more about the fact that they act in ways, and display a quality of will toward us, that invites blame and punishment. We may not particularly care whether or not there is evidence of attunement to moral principles or evidence of morally salient interlocutionary powers. We might consider Ripley responsible because he is "in possession of concepts like those that bear on what ought to be done, what is justifiable or unjustifiable, what is worthy of blame or praise, and [is] in a position to understand reactions like resentment and gratitude...."[13] Perhaps the possession of competence in moral conversation is just icing on the cake.

Certainly this is implied by much of the standard literature on responsibility, which treats a liability to blame (or praise) as the whole of responsibility. This is the reactive attitudes analysis I mentioned above. According to a popular Strawsonian line of thought, we call a person responsible simply to express our views that their behavior reveals a particular quality of will towards others and that an attitude such as praise or blame is deserved and appropriate.[14] But while someone might want to regard the Ripleys of the world as responsible on this approach, it would be a mistake to do so. Attitudes and practices such as praising and blaming are legitimate only where they are deserved, and if Ripley cannot engage in moral interlocution and cannot take up the internal point of view—if he is morally incompetent—it is hard to see how he deserves such reactions to his behavior.

That sociopaths such as Ripley have access to the concepts and attitudes that typically inform some of our familiar normative practices is suggested by the fact that he may hold others accountable for what they do to him. But this seems too little to require for moral responsibility. What he cannot do is return the favor; he cannot apply these concepts and attitudes to himself as an actor. Lacking genuine moral interlocutionary ability, persons such as Ripley cannot make judgments about their own behavior that are consistent with the judgments others make of them and that they make of others. But this is exactly what moral responsibility calls for. To judge someone a morally responsible agent is to credit them with an appreciation of the reflexive and the dialogical qualities of moral assessment.

We might wish to deny that Ripley is responsible for a more fundamental reason. Perhaps such persons fail as responsible agents for the elementary reason that they lack freedom of a particular variety. It is true of Ripley that while he can detect what we call moral reasons for action, the reasons which in fact motivate him do not emanate from a mechanism of deliberation that is responsive to moral reasons. The inability to appreciate, no less than to explain, one's reasons for action in a way that

---

13 Pettit, *A Theory of Freedom: From the Psychology to the Politics of Agency*, p. 29.

14 After the line of argument developed by Peter Strawson in his influential paper "Freedom and Resentment," *Proceedings of the British Academy*, 48 (1962): 1–25.

makes one's action morally intelligible, and that makes one someone who can be a partner in sincere moral conversation, is a want of freedom or ability as much as it is a kind of irrationality. It is the unfreedom of one who is handicapped in an activity.

But is this a deficiency of the kind of freedom required for responsibility? I stated in Chapter 1 that the responsible agent must be a free agent, that is, a person who is in control of his actions in some sense and who has a capacity for psychological self-governance. There is reason to believe Ripley is not a free agent in the relevant sense, despite the fact that he meets the criteria, including some of the control conditions, for global autonomy. Ripley lacks legislative and executive control over his behavior where morality is concerned. And, of course, if Ripley were incapable of engaging in sincere moral conversation but he genuinely wished for just such a capability—if he regarded the character he has and the behavior he engages in as alien to him, as if he were moved by a will he repudiates—some might describe him as suffering from an inability to act freely. We would then have further cause to claim that he is not a responsible agent. Ripley might then be considered not to be even locally autonomous or self-governing with respect to some of his choices and actions considered individually. Ripley's actions would be "inauthentic," to return to the language of procedural and psychological accounts surveyed previously. But of itself, the mere inability to grasp and to explain the moral measure of one's reasons for action does not yield or imply inauthenticity in any standard sense, nor does it strike me as unfreedom sufficient to compromise local autonomy. Many of Ripley's actions may have transpired as the foreseeable result of past choices which he endorsed.

Overview

My aim in this book has been to work out a theory of personal autonomy that explains the key idea expressed by the term. Autonomy is a standing that is critical to anyone who lives amid other persons in a cultural and political setting where coercive influence upon the person is possible. In addition, it has been my aim to explain autonomy as a thoroughly naturalized phenomenon that can actually be instantiated in our world. On a thoroughly naturalized conception, personal autonomy is an empirical phenomenon; the conditions for autonomy are conditions a person can be known *a posteriori* to satisfy. A Kantian account is not naturalistic in this sense. As I use the term, there is a second aspect to a naturalized conception of autonomy, an aspect that takes account of the conditions of human life in a realistic way, a way that is faithful to familiar empirical facts. Among these are the facts that most persons live in societies or in groups with other persons, and that they are shaped by these groups. I therefore view as nonnaturalistic accounts that treat autonomy as depending on such things as the existence of true selves liberated from the encumbrances of socialization, for example. In addition, persons differ in the resources available to them—"resources of physical strength, technical advantage, financial clout, informational access, ideological position, cultural legitimation, and the like"[15]—or in the relative advantages granted by their different positions, such as the advantage of being one of a limited number of persons in possession of highly valued and much needed skill. People who are relatively advantaged in such resources have power of a sort that can be wielded over others who are comparatively disadvantaged, and in ways that truncate the ability of others to successfully manage their lives. A naturalized theory of autonomy must take such facts into account.

Accordingly, I have argued that individuals are not self-governing unless they have a status that guarantees them the power they need to be "an independent source of activity in the world." Individuals who are autonomous have a status that secures them authority over themselves and over the management of choices and actions that are central to the direction of their lives, as well as the power to act on that authority should others arbitrarily attempt to deny them this authority. It is an obvious fact that a person's power and authority to manage such activities can be undermined by factors that are extrinsic to the individual. But it is also true that these factors do not consist just of other persons who could arbitrarily subvert this power and authority, but can be impersonal and environmental in nature. Although the account I have developed focuses on the relevance of interpersonal relations within the social arena for personal autonomy, the account also calls attention to the wider range of factors in the social-relational arena, including impersonal, natural factors, which can generate autonomy or can destroy it.

In Chapter 1, we raised a number of pretheoretical claims about autonomy. We noted that autonomous persons own their choices, actions, and goals. An autonomous person is someone who can shape the world on the basis of standpoint that is of her own making, and she is mindful of herself as having this ability. The self-directed person is disposed to set goals for her life that are of personal significance, and will make a distinction between goals that are her own from those that are fashioned by others. Autonomous people are by and large motivated to control themselves in the face of incentives to behave in ways hostile to their interests, and they able to do control themselves.

Personal autonomy is a phenomenon distinct from its cousins, moral autonomy and political autonomy. Moral autonomy is a matter of being self-determined with regard to the moral principles one accepts and upon which one acts. Personal autonomy involves much more than this. Of course, personal autonomy must be analyzed in terms that are useful for moral theory and an understanding of autonomy should be of assistance in resolving practical problems of morality. It is clear that violations of personal autonomy are frequently moral violations and that some violations of personal autonomy contravene a person's moral commitments. When we treat persons merely as means rather than as ends in themselves we commit a moral violation of their autonomy. When we forbid certain freedoms—typically, of thought, of movement, and of speech—we violate personal autonomy, and at the same time we threaten moral autonomy. An entire book could have addressed this

---

15 Pettit, *Republicanism*, p. 59.

topic; I have noted the connections between these varieties of autonomy in only a cursory fashion.

Political autonomy is a matter of the political and legal status of individuals who are members of societies, subject to the coercive arm of the state. The core idea is that individuals have the right of final authority over themselves where matters of state and political interest are concerned. This idea is based on a principle of self-ownership, that is, on the belief that no person can be the literal possession of any other and on the idea that individuals are by birthright entitled to a certain degree of respect for their personhood. This being the case, whatever legitimacy political establishments garner is at the behest of those subject to its force. There is a divergence of opinion about the institutional structures that best realize political autonomy, and about the relation between political autonomy and personal self-governance. A theory of personal autonomy need not address the special concerns of political autonomy. A person who counts as politically autonomous might lack personal autonomy and persons can live in a manner consonant with having a high degree personal autonomy even though subject to law, and to other non-arbitrary directives of the state.

Chapter 2 examined the popular account of autonomy as psychological authenticity. The common thread of authenticity accounts is that self-rule is a phenomenon that depends on the procedures a person employs in decision making and in acting. All such accounts maintain a person is autonomous when her actions agree with and transpire as a result of her having of a point of view that she has reflectively sanctioned. But authenticity accounts do not succeed in meeting the pretheoretical views about autonomy laid out in the first chapter. Any account that makes autonomy depend merely upon hierarchical congruity among a person's different desires, for example, faces technical difficulties, including the "authority" problem—that is, the fact that a desire occupies a higher level of a person's psychology is no reason in itself to take that desire to be authoritative of a person's preferences, and no reason to regard the desire itself as authentic. A person's highest-level operative motives might result from causal chains that are inauthentic, and because of this it is implausible for hierarchical models to declare higher-order preferences authentic simply in virtue of the position they occupy in the agent's motivational economy. Authenticity accounts that are sensitive to the history of a person's psychology and to the role the person played in its development fare better against the pretheoretical intuitions, as do approaches that highlight the procedural skills of the candidate for autonomy. But they remain content-neutral explanations of self-determination, meaning they reject substantive conditions—particularly conditions that guarantee material independence—as constitutive of autonomy,

Supporters of content-neutrality boast of its superiority over substantive accounts, especially in making sense of how we think of autonomy in applied contexts. In the medical field, for example, the resolution of questions about patient autonomy is tremendously important. In deciding whether a patient's autonomy is to be respected, we ask whether the patient has the capacity to grant informed consent to the medical treatment of which she is in need. Informed consent is demonstrated, at least in part, by the patient's ability to critically evaluate her preferences and values, and to decide which option for action is best for her in light of such evaluation. Consent does not require that the patient express preferences or values that are uninformed by, say, her religious beliefs or familial commitments, nor that they be preferences and values that those responsible for her medical care share.

But the substantive account that I favor does not demand this, either. My social-relational analysis does not demand that the autonomous person be dedicated to a particular way of life nor that she subscribe to a specific range of value commitments such as a trust in her own moral importance, although the nature of her beliefs about such matters certainly can affect the likelihood that the person will be autonomous. The social-relational account does not claim that the person who is autonomous must be uncommitted to others or uninfluenced by other persons. In general, content-neutral explanations of self-determination that reject the inclusion of conditions that require substantive independence are no better equipped to uphold the principle of informed consent than are accounts of autonomy that demand substantive independence and that place certain constraints upon the social status of the autonomous agent.

Moreover, the requirements of authenticity and procedural independence at the heart of psychological explanations of self-determination are themselves content-specific. Both depend on facts about the circumstances of the agent and facts about the character of the agent's desires, for some circumstances and some desires will give rise to a procedurally independent psychology, while others will not do so. If content-neutral proceduralist accounts of autonomy are less compelling intuitively than rival substantive analyses of autonomy, the latter are to be preferred.

In the third chapter I developed the social-relational account of autonomy by presenting a series of case studies that documented the inadequacies of psychological authenticity accounts. The social-relational account of autonomy is content-specific since it declares certain values and practices inconsonant with self-governance. Autonomy calls for a measure of substantive independence from certain social roles and expectations. At the same time, the social-relational account harmonizes with other ideals a self-governing person might adopt. Substantive independence does not force a person into social isolation, for example. The social-relational analysis remains faithful to empirical fact in the manner of a properly naturalized approach. The account explains autonomy as depending on the social standing of the agent along with facts about her mental state and dispositional temperament. In addition, the social-relational analysis vindicates our intuition that self-governing persons possess the *de jure* right and the *de facto* ability to avail themselves of alternatives for ways of life; they have "counterfactual power" over the course of their lives.

The case studies prompted us to ask why we would think the people in the examples are not autonomous, despite the contrary verdicts supplied by psychological accounts. Why, that is, aren't people like the Taliban Woman self-governing? What is missing in her life that leads us to call her self-governance into question? These questions led to the formulation of a fairly precise set of conditions for an adequately naturalized account of autonomy, the topic of Chapter 4. I argued that there are seven broad conditions for autonomy: *epistemic competence, rationality, procedural independence, self respect, control, access to a range of relevant options,* and *substantive independence*. Rather than require authenticity or the absence of estrangement, I argued that the self-governing person must acknowledge the factors central to her self-conception, as it is these that supply the foundation upon which autonomous choice and action hinge.

Not surprisingly, the formulation of these conditions generates its own set of questions. Is everyone who confronts grave risk to social and psychological security lacking autonomy? Is a person's autonomy compromised every time she faces a challenge in executing her will or when executing her will costs her great effort? (Was Rosa Parks's autonomy diminished when she stood up to Jim Crow?) Does the social-relational account mandate that a person never confront obstacles such as imprisonment if the person is to be autonomous? Is this not too much to require of autonomy?

In response, I contended that in certain circumstances autonomy can be so difficult to achieve that the effort to live in a self-managed way will cost a person dearly. What effect does the fact that tremendous effort must be expended in order to execute one's will have on the life of an individual, in particular on her ability to control the social procedures that make the realization of her will possible? What is in the balance for socially positioned individuals whose interpersonal status is crucial to their self-governance? In deciding whether autonomy has been compromised in a given case it is important to examine what has led a person to confront conditions of social and psychological insecurity, or to find the execution of her will an ordeal. It would be a mistake to suggest that autonomy depends on a person's successful navigation of various obstacles such as those mentioned above. Rosa Parks's autonomy was not diminished when she rose up to—or more accurately, sat down on—Jim Crow. Parks took charge of her life on this occasion. Nonetheless, Park's global autonomy was impaired just because impediments to self-government were ever present in her life; the threats she faced at that historical moment in 1954 Montgomery, Alabama persisted even though a furor of support arose in its wake. Any person who lives in an environment she cannot challenge, change, or contribute to without the say-so of others lives in a place where impediments to self-government are present. This person lives in the shadow of others, insecure of what her steps toward self-government might incur from others. These might be mighty steps, as in Park's case, or they might be tentative. But we can hardly call the person who takes these steps autonomous even if we can call her act an expression of autonomy, a defiance of subjugation.

In Chapter 5 we examined the complaint that the social-relational analysis of autonomy is objectionably perfectionist and illiberal since it implies that many persons, including the most marginalized members of a society, are not included in the class of autonomous agents. The charge that the social-relational account is paternalistic and thus antithetical to political liberalism was examined and found unwarranted. Here, as elsewhere, lies room for further discussion.[16] With respect to the charge of perfectionism, I claim that a realistic study of autonomy must acknowledge that autonomous persons may have very different goals for their lives, but I maintain that the social-relational account is compatible with this. People differ in the lives they genuinely yearn for, and political liberalism will defend the right of people to experience the diversity life offers. But from this it does not follow that political liberalism is incompatible with the social-relational account of autonomy. Indeed, if one goal of liberalism is to assure that all adult citizens have a right to be heard in the political process, the liberal should understand autonomy in the way the social-relational account explains it. Unlike its thin, content-neutral, comprehensive counterpart, a social-relational "perfectionist" notion of autonomy demands a right to political participation as a requirement of autonomy. Political self-governance fares best where social-relational autonomy flourishes. If the goals of democratic citizenship in particular are to be realized the liberal has reason to adopt a social-relational perfectionist account of autonomy.

Some will continue to see paternalism as a specter looming over the social account, and prompted by the account itself. There will no doubt be disagreement about whether attempts to promote the autonomy of a person would itself involve interferences with the individual's choices and actions severe enough to assail her self-government. Recall that the perspective of the person whose autonomy is at stake may decide whether we regard a kind of interference as objectionable, but not whether it is interference. I argued, however, that the social-relational account does not require the promotion of autonomy. Even if we agree global autonomy is good for all persons, and that its goodness is objective in that it does not depend on the value perspective of the individual, autonomy may not be paramount among a person's set of goods, and it may be better that autonomy is given short shrift in that person's preferred life-plan. The goal of promoting autonomy must be tempered by what is gained for it in exchange. Values such as liberty are possibly more important than autonomy, and may supply us with reason to limit state interference designed to enhance global autonomy. Moreover, there will be times when an individual's renunciation of particular liberties does not entail a renunciation of global autonomy. Paternalistic efforts to restore autonomy, particularly when this entails interfering with affairs that are of great significance to another person, must be sparing and judicious, an avenue of last resort. As a rule, global autonomy is the bedrock of local autonomy and personal freedom, and ought not to be sacrificed for their benefit. Again, here lies fertile ground for subsequent discussion.

Chapter 6 broadened the discussion of autonomy's value. The social-relational account was defended as best positioned to account for the instrumental value of autonomy as well as autonomy's intrinsic value and its value in regard to the good

---

16 For exploration of related concerns, see Marilyn Friedman, *Autonomy, Gender, Politics* (New York: 2003), and Paul Benson, "Taking Ownership: Authority and Voice in Autonomous Agency" in John Christman and Joel Anderson (eds), *Autonomy and the Challenges to Liberalism* (New York: 2005).

of choice. We explored what might happen when the value we place upon autonomy clashes with the value we place upon a right to individual self-expression and a right to subjective well-being. We examined the legitimate restrictions that might be placed upon autonomy when socio-political circumstances depart abruptly from the norm. Personal contentment, well-being, self-respect, privacy, and political security are goods that might be in accord with autonomy but might compete with it as well; there would be occasions when the one but not the other would be preferred by a person. As the political climate becomes increasingly globalized, nuanced, and even treacherous, we will no doubt continue to wrestle with the question of when a person's right to autonomy may be overridden for the benefit of other socially desirable goods.

In Chapter 6, particular attention was paid to the idea of self-respect and respect for others. Respect for the individual is often cited as the major casualty of the perfectionism in social-relational accounts. Marilyn Friedman no doubt echoes the views of others who favor a proceduralist approach to autonomy when she charges that, unlike a content-neutral account, "An account of autonomy that is too demanding will prompt persons to regard a greater number of others as failures at personhood and thereby reduce the number of others they regard as respectworthy."[17] But there is no need for this to be so. The moral worth of a person upon which respect rests is not solely—perhaps not even primarily—a function of her degree of autonomy, even if personal success is bound up with success at autonomous living. We often respect persons for reasons that do not involve respecting their autonomy. (Equally, a life of autonomy need not be a life that deserves our respect; recall Feinberg's Robespierre from Chapter 5.) We can respect persons by not interfering in their choices, by encouraging them to take control and ownership of their lives and by refraining from treating them paternalistically even if the lives they ultimately select are not lives rich in autonomy. Self-respect and respectful treatment from others may increase the likelihood that a person will be autonomous. But neither guarantees that a person will become autonomous. We can respect cloistered monks for their principled commitment to God, the conscientious objector for his willingness to test the resources of his inner firmament, and the concentration camp internee for her triumph of spirit while we wonder about, even bemoan, their lack of self-governance. Similarly, while the person who respects himself may find it easier than most to transcend (or better, conquer) conditions unfavorable to his autonomy, self-respect will not suffice for autonomy.

In Chapter 7 we questioned whether causal determinism threatens autonomy. I argued that it need not do so; autonomy is agnostic with respect to the truth or falsity of this metaphysical thesis. Autonomous persons must be free to change their values and to alter certain life-activities if they choose to do so, and this implies a capacity for control connected to freedom of will and freedom of action. But this does not mean that alternative possibilities incompatible with determinism, or metaphysically robust freedom of will and of action, are needed for autonomy. Nor does autonomy

---

17 Marilyn Friedman, *Autonomy, Gender, Politics*, p. 23.

require that the agent have the freedom to create herself in any metaphysically or socially robust fashion. Rather, autonomy concerns the manner in which a person comes to plan and to make certain decisions relevant to the direction of her life, opting for one course of action rather than another, and the reasons for which the person decides and acts as she does. Just as we must account for the compatibility of autonomy with causal determinism, so, too, we must defend the compatibility of autonomy with the fact that our lives are profoundly affected by the society around us. So, for example, whether agents who have been subjected to a certain mode of socialization are deprived of autonomy depends on the effects of the socialization. It makes a difference for autonomy whether the agent can successfully counteract the influence of socialization and whether its effects remain in force. On the social-relational account, for example, autonomy is incompatible with various forms of social interaction that are premised on the preeminence of others, even forms that restrict the agent where she has immersed herself in the situation freely and without reservation, and even forms that do not give rise to actual interference with self-expression.

The notion of autonomy is rich, complex, and perplexing. More can be said, and probably ought to be said, about the many questions that remain. More could be said, perhaps, about the differences between local autonomy and global autonomy. Is there a measurable threshold of violations to choice and action a person can sustain, a minimal level of constraint in social relations a person can experience, or a threshold of narrowed options a person can sustain, before a loss to her global autonomy ensues? More attention might be devoted to the question of when autonomy should be preserved over rival values. Had I the luxury of time, and even more the gift of greater insight, perhaps more would have been said. But in fact, I think no one can answer these concerns in a definitive way, and certainly not in a way that will satisfy every reader. Open questions are one of the attractions of philosophy. And at any rate, the discussion in this book is long enough. In the space of these pages, my wish has been to have contributed to the dialogue by bringing the reader's attention to some of the many questions to which the concept of autonomy gives rise, and to have made some headway toward their resolution.

Selected Bibliography

Antony, Louise M. and Witt, Charlotte E. (eds), *A Mind of One's Own: Feminist Essays on Reason and Objectivity*, 2nd ed. (Boulder, Colorado: Westview Press, 2002).

Appiah, K. Anthony, "Identity, Authenticity, Survival: Multicultural Societies and Social Reproduction," in Gutmann, Amy (ed.), *Multiculturalism* (Princeton: Princeton University Press, 1994).

Aristotle, *Nicomachean Ethics*, trans. W.D. Ross (Oxford: Oxford University Press, 1925).

Barclay, Linda, "Autonomy and the Social Self," in Mackenzie, Catriona and Stoljar, Natalie (eds), *Relational Autonomy: Feminist Perspectives on Autonomy, Agency, and the Social Self* (New York: Oxford University Press, 2000), pp. 52–71.

Benn, S.I., "Freedom, Autonomy, and the Concept of a Person," *Proceedings of the Aristotelian Society*, 66 (1976): 109–30.

———,"Privacy, Freedom, and Respect for Persons," in J.R. Pennock and J.W. Chapman (eds), *Privacy*, Nomos 13 (New York: Atherton Press, 1971).

Bennett, Jonathan, "The Conscience of Huckleberry Finn," *Philosophy*, 49 (1974): 123–34.

Benson, Paul, "Taking Ownership: Authority and Voice in Autonomous Agency," in John Christman and Joel Anderson (eds), *Autonomy and the Challenges to Liberalism: New Essays* (Cambridge, MA: Cambridge University Press, 2005), pp. 101–26.

———, "Free Agency and Self-Worth," *Journal of Philosophy*, 91(12) (1994): 650–68.

Berlin, Isaiah, *Four Essays on Liberty* (Oxford: Oxford University Press, 1969).

Berofsky, Bernard, *Liberation from Self: A Theory of Personal Autonomy* (New York: Cambridge University Press, 1995).

Bogen, James and Farrell, Daniel, "Freedom and Happiness in Mill's Defence of Liberty," *Philosophical Quarterly*, 28(113) (1978): 325–38.

Buss, Sarah and Overton, Lee (eds), *Contours of Agency: Essays on the Themes of Harry Frankfurt* (Cambridge: MIT Press, 2002).

Christman, John, "Procedural Autonomy and Liberal Legitimacy," in James Stacey Taylor (ed.), *Personal Autonomy:New Essays on Personal Autonomy and Its Role in Contemporary Moral Philosophy* (Cambridge U.K.: Cambridge University Press, 2005), pp. 277–98.

———, "Relational Autonomy, Liberal Individualism, and the Social Constitution of Selves," *Philosophical Studies*, 117 (2004): 143–64.

———, "Liberty, Autonomy, and Self-Transformation," *Social Theory and Practice*, 27(2) (April, 2001): 185–206.

————, "Defending Historical Autonomy: A Reply to Professor Mele," *Canadian Journal of Philosophy*, 23 (1993): 281–90.

————, "Autonomy and Personal History," *Canadian Journal of Philosophy*, 20(1) (March, 1991): 1–24.

————, (ed.), *The Inner Citadel* (New York: Oxford University Press, 1989).

————, "Constructing the Inner Citadel: Recent Work on Autonomy," *Ethics* 99(1) (October, 1988): 109–24.

————, "Autonomy: A Defense of the Split-Level Self," *Southern Journal of Philosophy*, 25(3) (1987): 281–93.

Christman, John and Anderson, Joel (eds), *Autonomy and the Challenges of Liberalism* (New York: Cambridge University Press, 2005).

Cockburn, Alexander and St. Clair, Jeffrey, "Driving While Black," http://www. counterpunch.org/drivingblack.html.

Crisp, Roger, "Well-Being," *The Stanford Encyclopedia of Philosophy* (Summer 2003), http://plato.stanford.edu/archives/sum2003/entries/well-being/.

Darwall, Stephen, *Impartial Reason* (Ithaca: Cornell University Press, 1983).

————, "Two Kinds of Respect," *Ethics*, 88 (1977): 36–49.

De Cew, Judith, "Privacy," *The Stanford Encyclopedia of Philosophy* (Summer 2002), http://plato.stanford.edu/archives/sum2002/entries/privacy/.

————, *In Pursuit of Privacy: Law, Ethics, and the Rise of Technology* (Ithaca: Cornell University Press, 1997).

Defoe, Daniel, *Robinson Crusoe* (New York: Modern Library, 2001).

Deigh, John, "Universalizability and Empathy" in Deigh, *The Sources of Moral Agency* (Cambridge, U.K.: Cambridge University Press, 1996).

Dillon, Robin S. "Respect," *Stanford Encyclopedia of Philosophy (Fall 2003)* http://plato.stanford.edu/archives/fall2003/entries/respect/.

————, (ed.), *Dignity, Character, and Self-Respect*   (New York: Routledge, 1995).

Dennett, Daniel D., *Elbow Room: Varieties of Free Will Worth Wanting* (Cambridge: MIT Press, 1984).

————, "I Could Not Have Done Otherwise—So What?," *Journal of Philosophy*, 81 (October 1984): 553–65.

Dworkin, Gerald, *The Theory and Practice of Autonomy* (Cambridge: Cambridge University Press, 1988).

————, "Paternalism: Some Second Thoughts," in *Sartorius* (1983), pp. 105–11.

————, "Autonomy and Informed Consent," in *Making Health Care Decisions*, 3 (Washington, D.C.: U.S. Government Printing Office, 1982): 63–82. Reprinted in Dworkin (1988), pp. 100–120.

————, "Is More Choice Better Than Less?," in *Midwest Studies in Philosophy* 7 (Minneapolis: University of Minnesota Press, 1982): 47–61. Reprinted in Dworkin (1988), pp. 62–81.

————, "The Concept of Autonomy," in *Science and Ethics*, R. Haller (ed.) (Rodopi Press, 1981). Reprinted in Christman (1989), pp. 54–62.

———, "Autonomy and Behavior Control," *Hastings Center Report*, 6 (February 1976): 23–8.

———, "Paternalism," *Monist*, 56 (January 1972): 64–84.

———, "Acting Freely," *Nous*, 6 (November 1970): 367–83.

Dworkin, Ronald, *A Matter of Principle* (Cambridge, MA: Harvard University Press, 1985).

Elster, Jon, "Sour Grapes—Utilitarianism and the Genesis of Wants," in A. Sen and B. Williams (eds), *Utilitarianism and Beyond* (Cambridge: Cambridge University Press, 1982).

Feinberg, Joel, *Harm to Self*, vol. 3 of *The Moral Limits of Criminal Law* (New York. Oxford University Press, 1986).

———, "The Nature and Value of Rights," *Journal of Value Inquiry*, 4 (1970): 243–60.

Fischer, John Martin, "Frankfurt-Style Compatibilism," in Buss and Overton (eds), *Contours of Agency: Essays on the Themes of Harry Frankfurt* (Cambridge: MIT Press, 2002), pp. 1–26.

———, *The Metaphysics of Free Will: An Essay on Control* (Oxford: Blackwell, 1994).

———, "Responsiveness and Moral Responsibility," in Ferdinand Schoeman (ed.), *Responsibility, Character, and the Emotions: New Essays in Moral Psychology* (New York: Cambridge University Press, 1987), pp. 81–106.

———, (ed.), *Moral Responsibility* (Ithaca: Cornell University Press, 1986).

———, "Responsibility and Control," *Journal of Philosophy*, 89 (January 1982): 24–40.

Fischer, John Martin, and Mark Ravizza (eds), *Perspectives on Moral Responsibility* (Ithaca: Cornell University Press, 1993).

———, *Responsibility and Control* (Cambridge, U.K.: Cambridge University Press, 1998).

Frankfurt, Harry, *The Reasons of Love* (Cambridge, MA: Cambridge University Press, 2004).

———, "Reply to Fischer," in Buss and Overton (eds), *Contours of Agency: Essays on the Themes of Harry Frankfurt* (Cambridge: MIT Press, 2002), pp. 27–31.

———, *Necessity, Volition, and Love* (Cambridge, U.K.: Cambridge University Press, 1999).

———, *The Importance of What We Care About* (Cambridge, U.K.: Cambridge University Press, 1988).

Friedman, Marilyn, *Autonomy, Gender, Politics* (New York: Oxford University Press, 2002).

———, "Autonomy and the Split-Level Self, *Southern Journal of Philosophy*, 24(1) (1986): 19–35.

———, "Moral Integrity and the Deferential Wife," *Philosophical Studies*, 47 (1985): 141–50.

Gavison, Ruth, "Privacy and the Limits of Law," *Yale Law Journal* 89 (1980): 421–71.

Goodin, Robert and Pettit, Philip (eds), *A Companion to Contemporary Political Philosophy* (Oxford: Blackwell, 1993).

Griffin, James, *Well-being* (Oxford: Clarendon Press, 1986).

Gutmann, Amy (ed.), *Multiculturalism* (Princeton: Princeton University Press, 1994).

Hart, H.L.A., *The Concept of Law* (New York: Oxford University Press, 1961).

Haworth, Lawrence, *Autonomy: An Essay in Philosophical Psychology and Ethics* (New Haven: Yale University Press, 1986).

Highsmith, Patricia, *The Talented Mr. Ripley* (New York: Random House, 1955).

Hill, Jr., Thomas E., "The Autonomy of Moral Agents," in Becker and Becker (eds), *The Encyclopedia of Ethics* (New York: Garland Publishing, 1992).

———, *Autonomy and Self-Respect* (Cambridge: Cambridge University Press, 1991).

———, "The Kantian Conception of Autonomy," in Christman (ed.), *The Inner Citadel* (New York: Oxford University Press, 1989), pp. 91–105.

———, "Autonomy and Benevolent Lies," *The Journal of Value Inquiry*, 18 (1984): 251–67.

Hobbes, Thomas, *On the Citizen*, Richard Tuck and Michael Silverthorne (eds) (Cambridge UK: Cambridge University Press, 1998).

Honderich, Ted (ed.), *Essays on Freedom of Action* (London: Routledge & Kegan Paul, 1973).

Hurka, Thomas, *Perfectionism* (New York: Oxford University Press, 1993).

Kane, Robert (ed.), *The Oxford Handbook of Free Will* (New York: Oxford University Press, 2002).

———, *The Significance of Free Will* (New York: Oxford University Press, 1998).

Kant, Immanuel (1793), *Religion Within the Limits of Reason Alone*, trans. T.M. Greene and H.H. Hudson (New York: Harper & Row, 1960).

——— (1785), *Groundwork of the Metaphysic of Morals*, trans. H.J. Paton (New York: Harper & Row, 1964).

——— (1775–80), *Lectures On Ethics*, trans. Louis Infield (Indianapolis: Hackett, 1963).

King, Jr., Martin Luther, "Letter from Birmingham Jail" (16 April 1963), *Liberation* (June 1963): 10–16. Reprinted in King, *Why We Can't Wait* (Signet Classics reissue edition, January 2000): 64–84.

Kittay, Eva Feder and Meyers, Diana Tietjens (eds), *Women and Moral Theory* (Totowa, N.J.: Rowman and Littlefield, 1987).

Kymlicka, Will, *Contemporary Political Philosophy: An Introduction*, 2nd edition, (Oxford: Oxford University Press, 2002).

———, *Multicultural Citizenship* (Oxford: Oxford University Press, 1995).

Locke, John, *Two Treatises on Government*, Peter Laslett (ed.) (Cambridge UK: Cambridge University Press, 1988).

Mackenzie, Catriona and Stoljar, Natalie (eds), *Relational Autonomy: Feminist Perspectives on Autonomy, Agency, and the Social Self* (New York: Oxford University Press, 2000).

Mansbridge, Jane and Okin, Susan Moller, "Feminism," in Goodin and Pettit (eds), *A Companion to Contemporary Political Philosophy* (Oxford: Blackwell, 1993), pp. 269–90.

May, Thomas, "The Concept of Autonomy in Bioethics," in James Stacey Taylor (ed.), *Personal Autonomy: New Essays on Personal Autonomy and Its Role in Contemporary Moral Philosophy* (Cambridge UK: Cambridge University Press, 2005), pp. 299–309.

Mele, Alfred, "Autonomy, Self-Control, and Weakness of Will," in Robert Kane (ed.), *The Oxford Handbook of Free Will* (New York: Oxford University Press, 2002), pp. 529–48.

———, *Autonomous Agents: From Self-Control to Autonomy* (New York: Oxford University Press, 1995).

———, "History and Personal Autonomy," *Canadian Journal of Philosophy*, 23(2) (June 1993): 271–80.

Meyers, Diana, *Self, Society, and Personal Choice* (New York: Columbia University Press, 1989).

———, "Decentralizing Autonomy: Five Face of Selfhood" in Christman and Anderson (2005), pp. 27–55.

Mill, John Stuart (1859), *On Liberty*, Currin V. Shields (ed.) (New York: Macmillan, 1956).

———, *Principles of Political Economy*, 2 vols. (1848; reprint, New York: P.F. Collier & Sons, 1900).

Nagel, Thomas, *The Possibility of Altruism* (Princeton: Princeton University Press, 1978).

Narayan, Uma, "Minds of Their Own: Choices, Autonomy, Cultural Practices, and Other Women," in Antony, L.M. and Witt, C.E. (eds), *A Mind of One's Own: Feminist Essays on Reason and Objectivity*, 2nd ed. (Boulder, Colorado: Westview Press, 2002), pp. 418–32.

Nedelsky, Jennifer, "Reconceiving Autonomy," *Yale Journal of Law and Feminism*, 1(1) (Spring 1989): 7–36.

Nichols, Shaun, "How Psychopaths Threaten Moral Rationalism, or Is It Irrational To Be Amoral?," *The Monist*, 85 (2002): 285–304.

Noggle, Robert, "Autonomy and the Paradox of Self-Creation," in J.S. Taylor (ed.), *Personal Autonomy: New Essays on Personal Autonomy and Its Role in Contemporary Moral Philosophy* (Cambridge U.K.: Cambridge University Press, 2005), pp. 87–108.

Nozick, Robert, *Philosophical Explanations* (Cambridge: Harvard University Press, 1981).

———, *Anarchy, State, and Utopia* (New York: Basic Books, 1974).

Nussbaum, Martha and Sen, Amartya (eds), *The Quality of Life* (Oxford: Clarendon Press, 1993).

Okin, Susan Moller, *Justice, Gender, and the Family* (New York: Basic Books, 1989).

O'Neill, Onora, "The Public Use of Reason." Reprinted in O'Neill, *Constructions of Reason: Explorations of Kant's Practical Philosophy* (New York: Cambridge University Press, 1989), pp. 28–50.

Oshana, Marina A.L., "Autonomy and Self-Identity," in John Christman and Joel Anderson (eds), *Autonomy and the Challenges to Liberalism: New Essays* (Cambridge University Press, 2005), pp. 77–97.

———, "Autonomy and Free Agency," in *Personal Autonomy*, J.S. Taylor (ed.), *Personal Autonomy: New Essays on Personal Autonomy and Its Role in Contemporary Moral Philosophy* (Cambridge U.K.: Cambridge University Press, 2005), pp. 183–204.

———, "How Much Should We Value Autonomy?," *Social Philosophy and Policy*, 20(2) (2003): 99–126.

———, "Personal Autonomy and Society," *Journal of Social Philosophy*, 29(1) (Spring 1998): 81–102.

———, "Ascriptions of Responsibility," *American Philosophical Quarterly*, 34(1) (January 1997): 71–83.

———, "Autonomy Naturalized," *Midwest Studies in Philosophy*, 9 (Minneapolis: University of Minnesota, Winter 1994): 76–94.

Pateman, Carole, "Feminist Critiques of the Public/Private Dichotomy," in Anne Phillips (ed.), *Feminism and Equality* (Oxford: Blackwell, 1987), pp. 103–26.

Paul, Jeffrey, Miller, Jr. Fred D., and Paul, Ellen Frankel (eds), *The Right of Privacy* (Cambridge: Cambridge University Press, 2000).

Pettit, Philip, "Freedom and Probability" presented at the 4th Conference on Moral Theory and Practice, Granada, Spain, June 2005.

———, *A Theory of Freedom: From the Psychology to the Politics of Agency* (New York: Oxford University Press, 2001).

———, *Republicanism: A Theory of Freedom and Government* (Oxford: Oxford University Press, 1997).

Pettit, Philip and Smith, Michael, "Freedom in Belief and Desire," *The Journal of Philosophy*, 93(9) (September 1996): 422–49.

Phillips, Anne (ed.), *Feminism and Politics* (Oxford: Oxford University Press, 1998).

Plato, *Statesman* 291d–303b, trans. J.B. Skemp (1952), in Edith Hamilton and Huntington Cairns (eds), *Plato: The Collected Dialogues* (Princeton: Princeton University Press, 1961).

Rachels, James, "Why Privacy is Important," *Philosophy and Public Affairs* 4 (Summer 1975): 323–33.

Raz, Joseph, *The Morality of Freedom* (Oxford: Clarendon Press, 1986).

Rorty, Amelie O. (ed.), *The Identities of Persons* (Berkeley: University of California Press, 1976).

Ryan, Alan, "Liberalism," in Goodin and Pettit (eds), *A Companion to Contemporary Political Philosophy* (Oxford: Blackwell, 1993), pp. 291–311.

Sandel, Michael, *Liberalism and the Limits of Justice* (Cambridge: Cambridge University Press, 1982).

Sartorius, Rolf (ed.), *Paternalism* (Minneapolis: University of Minnesota Press, 1983).

Scanlon, T.M., Jr., "The Significance of Choice," *The Tanner Lectures on Human Values* 8 (University of Utah Press, 1986).

Schoeman, Ferdinand David (ed.), *Responsibility, Character, and the Emotions: New Essays in Moral Psychology* (New York: Cambridge University Press, 1987).

———, (ed.), *Philosophical Dimensions of Privacy: An Anthology* (Cambridge: Cambridge University Press, 1984).

Self, Peter, "Socialism," in Goodin and Pettit (eds), *A Companion to Contemporary Political Philosophy* (Oxford: Blackwell Publishers, 1993), pp. 335–55.

Sen, Amartya, *Inequality Reexamined* (Oxford: Oxford University Press, 1992).

Sidgwick, Henry, "The Kantian Conception of Free Will," *Mind*, 13(51) (1888). Reprinted in *The Method of Ethics* (New York: Dover, 1966).

Silber, John R., "Introduction," Kant's *Religion Within The Limits of Reason Alone*, trans. T.M. Greene and H.H. Hudson (New York: Harper & Row, 1960).

Skinner, B.F., *Walden Two* (New York: Macmillan Press, 1962).

Strawson, P.F., "Freedom and Resentment," *Proceedings of the British Academy*, 48 (1962): 1–25.

Styron, William, *Sophie's Choice* (New York: Random House, 1976).

Taylor, Charles, *Sources of the Self* (Cambridge, MA: Harvard University Press, 1989).

———, "Responsibility for Self," in Rorty, Amelie O. (ed.), *The Identities of Persons* (Berkeley: University of California Press, 1976).

Taylor, James Stacey (ed.), *Personal Autonomy: New Essays on Personal Autonomy and Its Role in Contemporary Moral Philosophy* (Cambridge: Cambridge University Press, 2005).

———, "Autonomy and Informed Consent: A Much Misunderstood Relationship," *Journal of Value Inquiry*, 38(3) (September 2004): 383–91.

———, "Autonomy and Privacy: A Reappraisal," *Southern Journal of Philosophy*, 40 (2002): 587–604.

Thalberg, Irving, "Hierarchical Analyses of Unfree Action," *Canadian Journal of Philosophy*, 8(2) (June 1978): 211–26. Reprinted in Christman (1989), pp. 123–36.

Thomson, Judith Jarvis, "The Right to Privacy," *Philosophy and Public Affairs*, 4 (Summer, 1975): 295–314.

Tomasi, John, "Should Good Liberals be Compassionate Conservatives? Philosophical Foundations of the Faith-Based Initiative," *Social Philosophy and Policy*, 21(1) (Winter 2004): 322–45.

Van Inwagen, Peter, *An Essay on Free Will* (Oxford: Clarendon Press, 1983).

Velleman, J. David, "Identification and Identity," in Buss and Overton (eds), *Contours of Agency: Essays on Themes of Harry Frankfurt* (Cambridge: MIT Press, 2002), pp. 91–123.

Waldron, Jeremy, "Moral Autonomy and Personal Autonomy," in Christman and Anderson (eds), *Autonomy and the Challenges to Liberalism: New Essays* (Cambridge, MA: Cambridge University Press, 2005), pp. 307–29.

———, *The Right to Private Property* (Oxford: Clarendon Press, 1988).

Wall, Steven, *Liberalism, Perfectionism, and Restraint* (Cambridge, U.K.: Cambridge University Press, 1998).

Walman, Ruth and Stahl, Susie, *Hutterite History: Past and present* (Saskatoon Inn, Saskatoon, SK, Oct. 5, 1985). http://sesd.sk.ca/grassroots/Riverview/page17.html.

Warren, Samuel and Louis Brandeis, "The Right to Privacy," *Harvard Law Review*, 4 (1890): 193–220.

Watson, Gary (ed.), *Free Will*, 2nd edn (Oxford: Oxford University Press, 2003).

———, "Volitional Necessity" in Buss and Overton (eds), *Contours of Agency: Essays on the Themes of Harry Frankfurt* (Cambridge: MIT Press, 2002), pp. 129–59.

———, "Two Faces of Responsibility," *Philosophical Topics*, 24(2) (Fall 1996): 227–48.

———, "Responsibility and the Limits of Evil: Variations on a Strawsonian Theme," in Schoeman (ed.), *Responsibility, Character, and the Emotions: New Essays in Moral Psychology* (New York: Cambridge University Press, 1987), pp. 256–86. Reprinted in Fischer and Ravizza (eds), *Perspectives on Moral Responsibility* (Ithaca: Cornell University Press, 1993), pp. 119–48.

———, "Free Agency," *Journal of Philosophy*, 72(8) (April 1975): 205–20.

Witmer, Joe, *The Gentle People: Personal Reflections of Amish Life* (Washington, Indiana 2001). http://www.blackbuggy.com.

Wolf, Susan, *Freedom Within Reason* (New York: Oxford University Press, 1990).

———, "Sanity and the Metaphysics of Responsibility," in Schoeman (ed.), *Responsibility, Character, and the Emotions: New Essays in Moral Psychology* (New York: Cambridge University Press, 1987), pp. 46–62.

Wolff, Robert Paul, *In Defense of Anarchism* (New York: Harper & Row, 1970).

Woolf, Virginia, *The Virginia Woolf Reader*, Mitchell A. Leaska (ed.) (New York: Harcourt, 1984).

Young, Robert, *Personal Autonomy: Beyond Negative and Positive Liberty* (New York: St. Martin's Press, 1986).

"Zalta, Edward N. (ed.), *The Stanford Encyclopedia of Philosophy*, http://plato.stanford.edu/archives/.

Zimmerman, Michael J., "Moral Responsibility, Freedom, and Alternate Possibilities," *Pacific Philosophical Quarterly*, 63 (1982): 243–54.

Index